Explor

NELLES

BALI
LOMBOK

Authors:
Bernd F. Gruschwitz, Dorothee Krause,
Barbara Müller, Berthold Schwarz

An Up-to-date travel guide with 147 color photos
and 17 maps

Second Revised Edition
1997

Dear Reader,

Being up-to-date is the main goal of the Nelles series. To achieve it, we have a network of far-flung correspondents who keep us abreast of the latest developments in the travel scene, and our cartographers always make sure that maps and texts are adjusted to each other.

Each travel chapter ends with its own list of useful tips, accommodations, restaurants, tourist offices, sights. At the end of the book you will find practical information from A to Z. But the travel world is fast moving, and we cannot guarantee that all the contents are always valid. Should you come across a discrepancy, please write us at: Nelles Verlag GmbH, Schleissheimer Str. 371 b, D-80935 München, Germany, Tel: (089) 3571940, Fax: (089) 35719430.

LEGEND

BALI - LOMBOK
© Nelles Verlag GmbH, 80935 München
All rights reserved

Second Revised Edition 1997
ISBN 3-88618-114-6
Printed in Slovenia

Publisher:	Günter Nelles	**Translation:**	Jane Baunebridge
Editor-in-Chief:	Berthold Schwarz		Angus McGeoch
Project Editor:	Bernd F. Gruschwitz	**Cartography:**	Nelles Verlag GmbH
Editorial:	Eva Ambros	**Color**	
English Editor:	Anne Midgette	**Separation:**	Reproline, Munich
	Angus McGeoch	**Printer:**	Gorenjski Tisk

TABLE OF CONTENTS

GUIDELINES

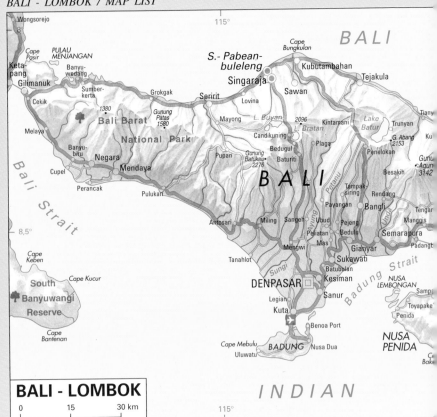

BALI - LOMBOK

0   15   30 km

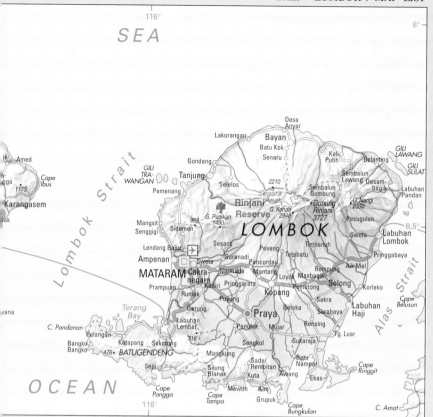

INTRODUCTION TO BALI

Hardly another island in the world exerts the same fascination on Western travelers as does Bali. And small wonder. For nowhere else can you find the same combination of beaches of both white and black sand, lined with palm trees; a lush wealth of tropical vegetation; and terraced rice paddies,where the hand of man has picturesquely enhanced the contours of nature. Inhabiting this paradise is a wonderful local population, deeply allied to nature and their gods, and faithful to traditional religious ceremonies centuries old, which they continue to stage in memorable, colorful pageants against the stunning backdrop of this unforgettable landscape.

True, the advent of a modern infrastructure, coupled with mass tourism, have confined this idyll to more prosaic dimensions; yet much of the old Bali has been preserved to entrance the visitor. And as long as you're in the area, take a side trip to Lombok, Bali's nearest and most dissimilar neighbor. There, too, you'll find stunning landscapes as well as that indescribable, ineffable tropical air.

Geography

Both Bali and Lombok belong to the Republic of Indonesia, which, with some 13,700 islands, encompasses the world's largest archipelago. Stretching north and south of the equator, these tropical islands mark the boundary between the Indian and Pacific Oceans. Indonesia extends from Sumatra in the west to Irian

Preceding pages: "Die to live": a Hindu cremation ceremony in Ubud, Bali is anything but a sad occasion. Sunrise in the mountains around Lake Batur. The mythical bird-god Garuda. Left: Once the rice is harvested, ducks keep down insects and keep the fields fertilized.

Jaya (part of New Guinea) in the east, and from northerly Kalimantan, which occupies 70% of the island of Borneo, to the island of Roti, off Timor, in the south. If placed over a map of Europe, the archipelago would stretch from Gibraltar to the Urals, and from southern Sweden to Sicily. Indonesia's land area alone amounts to some 770,000 square miles (2 million sq. km), or four times the size of France, and the total coastline of all the islands is about 25,000 miles (40,000 km) – which is almost as great as the circumference of the earth.

Bali and Lombok are the most westerly of the Little Sunda Islands, which stretch eastward from Java as far as Timor. Bali lies roughly at a latitude of 8°S and longitude 115°E; measuring 2,147 square miles (5,561 sq. km) in area, it is more than twice the size of Luxembourg. From east to west it measures about 90 miles (145 km), and the maximum distance from north to south is around 53 miles (85 km). All that separates Bali from Java is a narrow stretch of water, only a little more than a mile (2 km) wide, which was dry land until the end of the last Ice Age. The province of Bali includes three other islands to the southeast, the largest of which is Nusa Penida. Bali's highest peak, 10,308 feet (3142 m) in altitude, is the active volcano of Gunung Agung. To the west of it is a chain of volcanoes, five of which are more than 6,500 feet (2,000 m) high. North of this chain, the land falls steeply down to the sea, leaving room for only a narrow coastal strip. To the south lies a broad plateau, etched with deep ravines by southward-flowing rivers: this region is the fertile rice-bowl of the island.

Separating Lombok from Bali are the Lombok Straits, which are nearly 1,000 feet (300 m) deep in the middle. The island lies exactly midway between latitudes 8° and 9°S and at a longitude of 116°E. Measuring 1,829 square miles (4,739 sq. km) in ara, it's about half the

size of Cyprus. It and Sumbawa comprise the province of Nusa Tenggara Barat. The northern part of Lombok is a mountain chain from which the active volcano of Gunung Rinjani rises to 12,225 feet (3,726 m).

Volcanic Activity

Like the rest of Indonesia, Bali and Lombok owe their existence to the collision of two tectonic plates on the earth's crust, and the volcanic activity that resulted from this. The formation of these islands began some 70 million years ago, when the relatively light Australo-Indian plate (the Sahul plate) drifted into the heavier southeast Asiatic plate (the Sunda plate), and gradually worked its way underneath it. This process, which continues today, has caused the edge of the Sahul plate to melt at a depth of about 30 miles (50 km). The molten magma

Above: Extinct volcanoes. Right: Good outlook for an abundant rice harvest.

rises through cracks and fissures in the brittle fringe of the Sunda plate, and forms the chain of volcanoes which dominate the landscape of both islands. At the same time, the Sunda plate has ground off part of the sedimentary rock of the Sahul plate, so that in the south the landscape is dominated by limestone hills dotted with individual rocks broken off from the Sunda plate. Because of this tectonic turmoil, earth tremors, earthquakes and volcanic eruptions are part of everyday life in Indonesia; the archipelago can boast some 200 active volcanoes. In this century, two of Bali's 10 active volcanoes have given the island a grim reminder of their presence with several devastating eruptions, while one on Lombok has reared its head in a more subdued manner.

Flora

After their volcanic genesis, the islands gradually acquired their cloak of tropical rain-forest over a period of sev-

eral million years. This unique ecosystem, still not yet fully explored, boasts a truly astonishing wealth of plant and animal species; sadly, the march of human settlement is forcing it back into more inaccessible regions. Today there are only a few areas in the foothills of the central volcanic chain, and in the national park in the west of Bali, which still have a dense cover of evergreen jungle. The true rainforest now accounts for only about 10% of the island's land area. It has been replaced, in fertile areas, by extensive rice fields and other types of plantation. At lower altitudes, where the climate is hot and dry, the land has often turned to steppe-like plains, where nothing will grow but elephant-grass (*alang-alang*) and *lontar* palms.

In all the profusion of flora, there are one or two species of tree which are so widespread as to be easily noticeable. Many villages center around an ancient banyan tree (*waringin*), recognizable by the roots extending from the trunk several feet *above* ground; this tree is sacred

to the Balinese, and may not be cut down. According to legend, it was under just such a tree that the Buddha received enlightenment. Around temples you will frequently find the shrub-like frangipani, whose propellor-shaped white or pink flowers are sometimes the only adornment left on the bare, silver-gray branches. Like the frangipani, the brilliant red or orange hibiscus flower is used to adorn temple figures and their worshippers. Another beautiful shrub is the datura, with white or pink, bell-shaped flowers. The poinsettia, which Europeans generally encounter in foil-wrapped pots at Christmastime, grows to the size of a tree in these parts, as do rubber plants, ferns and bamboos. The air is often filled with the scent of jasmine, and bougainvillea washes the eye with a sea of color. Lakes and ponds are carpeted with water-lilies and the incomparable Indian lotus. Particularly striking, yet a common sight at flower markets, is the profusion of orchids. Make sure you bring along an identification guide to tropical plants.

Fauna

British zoologist Sir Alfred Russel Wallace (1823-1913) held that the deep and fast-flowing current of the Straits of Lombok formed the natural boundary between the fauna of Asia and that of Australia. Later scientists have modified this notion, so that both islands have now been identified as forming part of a transitional zone known as *Wallacea.* It is nevertheless a remarkable fact that east of Bali none of the larger land mammals, such as tiger or rhinoceros, are to be found, while on the islands to the west of Lombok there are none of the marsupials so typical of Australian wildlife.

Today, however, you will look in vain for the Balinese tiger, a smaller cousin of the Indian and Asian carnivore. The last reported sighting of this creature was in 1937. Also long gone is the orignal local rhinoceros population.

Above: The only orangutans left on Bali are in the zoo. Right: Banteng at work.

A few of the shapely, doe-eyed, wild red cattle called *banteng* are still said to be roaming the West Bali National Park; their smaller domesticated relative is a common sight throughout the countryside. Around many temples and sacred groves you will run into gray Javanese monkeys, but you should approach them with caution: they can easily snatch glasses or earrings from the unwary tourist. On Lombok, in the Rinjani region around Tetebatu, you can also still encounter black long-tailed monkeys.

Among the larger animals which add color to village life on both islands are the pot-bellied pig, and two species of water buffalo, which are used to pull ploughs and carts. The menfolk of the village are very proud of their fighting-cocks, often with brightly dyed feathers, which crow at passers-by from their wicker cages. Every morning and evening you will see crowds of ducks waddling along, driven by a duck-herder with a feather broom, through the meadows to or from the rice fields. Indoors there are two species of gecko to keep down the swarms of mosquitoes. These shy creatures, though often as much as a foot (30 cm) long, stay hidden during the day, behind pictures or mirrors, and only appear at dusk. On Bali, hearing a gecko's sharp *to-keh* sound nine times in a row is supposed to bring happiness and prosperity.

A particularly remarkable species of bird is the Balinese white starling. It can be seen on Nusa Penida, in the West Bali National Park and often, sad to say, in cages. There are only somewhere between 60 and 200 surviving members of the species in the wild, and extinction stares them in the face. In Petulu, in central Bali, a sight not to be missed is that of flocks of white herons returning from the rice fields every evening to roost.

Another worthwhile natural spectacle is the view of the clouds of bats issuing from the Goa Lawah caves, on the southeast coast.

Economy

In spite of the boom created by the influx of tourists, now in excess of 1 million a year, the backbone of Bali's economy remains its highly developed but traditional agriculture. About one-fifth of the arable land is given over to rice-cultivation in flooded rice paddies. These are usually built in terraces up the sides of valleys, and yield two harvests a year. An even larger proportion of the land, about one-quarter, is given over to dry rice cultivation; forced to depend on natural rainfall, this method only yields one crop each year. In the highlands there are plantations of coffee, tobacco, fruit, vegetables and cloves. By the sea the main sources of income are fishing, salt-panning and the harvesting of seaweed.

About 10% of the population are employed in the tourist sector. Tourism has also spawned small businesses, mainly in textile manufacturing and retailing. As of yet, the island has not developed any industries of any great size or significance.

Very sensibly, the Balinese authorities are carefully monitoring tourist growth and restricting development to certain defined areas, such as Nusa Dua.

Lombok has remained, apart from a cluster of tourist hotels near Senggigi, a purely agricultural community, and one which is subject – even more than Bali – to periodic famines, particularly in the dry belt of the southeast. The main farm products are similar to those of Bali. Remarkably, though, tobacco is the second largest agricultural export after rice. The most important of Lombok's exports, by value, is volcanic pumice-stone. Since 1985 it has been shipped to Hong Kong where it is used, among other things, in the manufacture of fashionable stone-washed jeans.

From humble beginnings, tourism has created a veritable gold rush in the west of the island. In Senggigi, buildings are going up wherever you look. The figure of 100,000 visitors a year, which once seemed like a distant dream, was reached as early as 1991.

HISTORY AND CULTURE
OF BALI

Prehistory and Early History

, Before researchers in East Africa un-earthed human remains of an even earlier date, the Indonesian archipelago was considered to be the cradle of mankind. In 1891, near Trinil on the river Solo in Java, a skeleton was discovered which was identified as that of an ape-like man who walked upright – *pithecanthropus erectus*, to put it in scientific terms. How-ever, later, more precise classification has shown it to be a *homo erectus*, whose relatives evolved, as we now know, more than two million years ago. The age of the biped known as Java Man is put at 1.8 million years. From this we can assume that in the early Palaeolothic period an-cestors of *homo sapiens* walked upright through the Indonesian rain-forest look-ing for food. Their territory would have included Bali, which was at that time still linked to Java by a land isthmus. In the late Palaeolithic age, around 30,000 years ago, negrito and Melanesian peoples began to settle on the island. At this point, they were probably still only hunter-gatherers and fishermen. Palaeoli-thic axe-heads and other stones, sharp-ened on one side, have been found near Sembiran in northern Bali.

From about the third millennium B.C., proto-Malay and early-Malay peoples, related to the Mongols, arrived from the Asian mainland and either intermingled with the aboriginal inhabitants or drove them into the mountains, the jungle, or onto islands to the east. Some 100 grave-stones and the remains of a Neolithic set-tlement from this period were discovered after World War II near Cekik in the west of Bali; some stone axes and pottery shards had been found earlier in this area.

The next wave of migration started around 300 B.C., when Austronesian Malays came from south China and the area that is now North Vietnam. They brought metal-working skills with them to Bali; too, they introduced new agricul-tural methods, notably that of cultivating rice in flooded paddies. There are mega-liths in some temples dating from this pre-Hindu period. The most impressive relic of the time is the Moon Drum, said to be the world's largest bronze gong to be cast in a single piece, which you can see (with a little effort and the help of bi-noculars) in the temple of Penataran Sasih at Pejeng. The decoration of the gong and the way it was made relate it to the Bronze Age Dongson culture of North Vietnam; it is not clear whether it was actually brought from there, or made in Bali. Once again, the new arrivals drove the native population into the mountain regions; known today as the Bali-Aga, they have been able to live relatively autonomously to the present day, adhering to their traditional cults, which bear scarcely a trace of Hindu in-fluence.

The Indianization of Bali

More than 2,000 years ago, Indian traders reached the archipelago, attracted by its wealth of minerals and spices, and Bali became part of a trading network which reached as far west as the Mediter-ranean and the Roman Empire. From China came both merchants and Buddhist pilgrims seeking the holy places of their religion in western Indonesia. As early as the 2nd century A.D., Chinese docu-ments attest to the existence of states es-tablished in Java and Sumatra; a little later, this is backed up by Indian texts and the works of the Greek geographer

Left: Gilded statue of a god, in the house of the artist Blanco in Ubud.

21

Ptolemy. But earlier still, the Indian epic *Ramayana* (around 300 B.C.) talks of a "Golden Isle" *(Suvarnadvipa)*, which can be identified as Sumatra. The name is indicative of the kind of goods that were exported from Indonesia at that time: predominantly valuables, including gold and other precious metals; tortoise-shell; medicinal herbs; aromatic woods and spices. Contemporary reports of China frequently mention Indonesian emissaries at the Imperial court; they were presumably there to secure the emperor's continued support and good will against possible negative influences from the Indian subcontinent.

Following the Indian traders came Hindu priests, scholars and artists who established themselves at the courts of the Indonesian rulers and were soon setting the tone for religious and cultural life. This is why the earliest inscriptions to be found in Indonesia are written in

Above: The bronze gong of Pejeng is the largest in the world made in a single casting.

Sanskrit, the priestly language of the Brahmans. Even the writing they used, called the *Pallava* alphabet, after a Tamil dynasty, was an Indian import.

After around the 7th century, a steady stream of pilgrims reaching as far as India fostered the spread of Buddhism. At the same time that Charlemagne, in Europe, was commissioning the building of his relatively modest Palatine Chapel in Aachen, the Borobudur, a Buddhist temple on a vast scale, was being completed in Java. But, as if Buddhism's strength had been sapped by this great achievement, it began to decline soon afterwards, while Hinduism experienced a new flowering. Probably no more than 50 years later, a major Hindu temple complex, a kind of counterpart to Borobudur, was built as at Prambanan, also in central Java.

Until well into the 10th century, there is little written documentation of the course of events in Bali. Early Chinese sources mention a kingdom called *P'o-Li*, which presumably refers to Bali. Not until around the year 930, when the Javanese king Sindok shifted the center of government power to the east of that island, does Bali step onto the world stage. By this period the ruling house of King Sindok, who governed the Javanese kingdom of Mataram, already had extensive family connections between the princely families of Bali. But conflict between the expanding kingdom on eastern Java and the powerful Srivijaya empire on Sumatra culminated in the crushing defeat of the former, Mataram: its capital, on Brantas, was destroyed and its king put to death. Concerned for the future survival of the Mataram empire, the high priests implored the 28-year-old Balinese prince Airlangga (sometimes spelled Erlangga) to leave the monastery where he was living in seclusion and take up the reins of government in eastern Java and Bali. Airlangga, who ruled from 1019 to 1042, was the son of the Balinese ruler Udayana II and the Javanese princess Mahendradatta, a great-granddaughter of the same King Sindok who had made eastern Java the new center of power in Indonesia in 930.

Airlangga's reign is considered to be the first cultural flowering in the region in which Bali was involved. Inscriptions in the ancient Balinese language, which began to appear in the 9th century, rank, from the 11th century onwards, alongside those in ancient Javanese. From this era, too, date the most impressive of Bali's archaeological monuments: Goa Gajah, a monastery complex in Bali's "Holy Land" around Pejeng, and Gunung Kawi, a temple built in a style reminiscent of Indian sacred architecture.

Balinese legends have devoted particular attention to the mother of Airlangga, casting her in a scarcely flattering light. An outbreak of plague which overshadowed the final years of Airlangga's reign was supposedly brought about by the evil machinations of this embittered widow, archetype of the witch-figure Rangda. She has represented the embodiment of everything that threatens the life of the village community ever since, and she must regularly be fought off by the good animal spirit of the village, the Barong, in a spectacular ritual. Legend has it that she is buried in the temple of Bukit Dharma, near Kutri.

Before Airlangga stepped down from power, he divided the kingdom between his two sons. One of the resulting empires, named for the city Kediri, was able to achieve the upper hand through force of arms. Bali became independent; its political power was centered between the rivers Petanu and Pakerisan, in Bedulu and Pejeng. Not until a regent of the rival Singhasari line, King Kertanagara, had broken the power of the Kediri empire and usurped its throne was Bali reconquered; the new king sent in an expeditionary force in 1284. Only eight years later, Kertanagara was himself ousted by political rivals, and Bali once again became independent. From the dynastic wranglings in east Java, Kertanagara's son-in-law, Raden Vijaya, emerged as the new king. He went on to found the Majapahit empire, whose influence extended throughout southeast Asia until the arrival of the Europeans.

As his power expanded, in 1343 Bali once again fell under the sovereignty of Java. Leading the invasion was Gajah Mada, who as a chief minister at times exercised the power of a king. As part of the Majapahit empire, Bali, in line with Java's adoption of Indian customs and religion, became "Indianized" once again. The year 1343 marked the beginning of the development of a civilization which, at first only slowly and reluctantly accepted by the islanders, still exists in Bali today. Artistic traditions, both indigenous and appropriated from abroad, were refined in the courts of the vassal kings of Bali and brought to new heights of perfection. Hinduism, once adopted, was permeated with local beliefs and

traditions; its rituals and festivities became such a part of life on Bali that it would be hard to imagine the island and its people without them. In the ancient Javanese epic *Nagarakertagama,* Bali is described as "that other island, which in all its customs and traditions concurs with Java" – pre-Islamic Java, of course.

In the 15th century, while the Islamic colony of Malacca, on the mainland Malay peninsula opposite Sumatra, was establishing itself as the main trading center of the region, the death-knell was already sounding for the Majapahit empire. At the same time, the Islamic faith was spreading rapidly through southeast Asia, not least because it challenged the Hindu caste system and thus won many converts among the non-aristocratic merchant class. When the Majapahit empire finally collapsed in 1520, and most of the bastions of Hinduism fell to Islam, the

Above: A terra-cotta figure from Majapahit.
Right: Dutch sailing ships at anchor in Batavia harbor, 1657.

elite of the Hindu priests and artists sought refuge on Bali. In 1550, under the leadership of Batu Renggong, the island became, for the first time in its history, a united, independent kingdom, and began in its turn to expand its power: Lombok, Sumbawa and parts of eastern Java (Balambangan) were obliged to submit to Bali's rule. For two centuries, Bali's political and cultural capital was Gelgel, near Klungkung; Klungkung itself replaced it in the 17th century, and maintained its claim to be Bali's intellectual center, at least nominally, until the 1950s.

From the First Europeans to Complete Colonization

For a long time Bali didn't hold much interest for Europeans. No one knew of the existence of any particular wealth of natural resources; furthermore, Bali was surrounded by reefs, and thus difficult for ships to get to. And in addition, Bali was densely populated, and therefore less easy to convert into large-scale plantations than, for example, Sumatra.

The first European seafarers to sight Bali were Portuguese, and the island appears as *Java Minor* on charts from the beginning of the 16th century. One of the first to land there looking for treasure was the English privateer Sir Francis Drake. Five years after Drake, in 1585, some Portuguese attempted to set up a trading-station there, but their ship ran aground off Bukit Badung, and only five of the crew survived. Then, in 1597, the little Dutch fleet of Cornelis de Houtman dropped anchor; he and his exhausted crew were charmed by the island paradise, which they christened *Young Holland.* Two of the Dutchmen stayed ashore, married Balinese girls and learned the language; one of them later looked after Dutch interests, acting as a middle-man. For the time being, however, the Netherlands did not set up a permanent colony. Even when the Dutch

East India Company was created in 1602, it was content with maintaining official trade relations, in which the Rajas of Bali distinguished themselves by selling their subjects as slaves in exchange for opium for their courtiers and nobles. This trade, in which Chinese merchants also tried to challenge the monopoly for which the Dutch were striving, lasted more than 200 years. During this time the Dutch limited themselves to driving off Balinese incursions into east Java and keeping foreign competitors off the island.

When the Netherlands were briefly annexed into the French empire during the Napoleonic Wars, Britain, in the person of Sir Stamford Raffles (who later founded Singapore), expressed an interest in establishing a base in the Far East. In 1814, in his capacity as Governor of Java, Raffles thus paid a visit to Bali. The Congress of Vienna restored to the Netherlands their former colonial possessions, but suspicion of Britain's ambitions drove the Dutch colonial administration to take a firmer grip on Bali.

After long negotiations, which the Balinese rulers cleverly managed time and again to prolong, the Dutch finally used military force in northern Bali for the first time in 1846. The excuse which they offered, on this and later occasions, was that islanders were picking up cargo which had come ashore from wrecked ships and treating it as their legal property – something the Balinese in fact regarded as their legal right. The Dutch arrived with 58 ships; their force of 3,000 men, including 1,700 infantrymen (only 400 of whom were Europeans), equipped with rifles and mortars, came ashore at Buleleng. Overcoming the opposition of some 15,000 Balinese, armed mainly with spears and *kris* (large Malay daggers), the Dutch captured Singaraja and destroyed the royal palace. When they were preparing to advance on the secret hiding-place of the Raja's brother, Prince Gusti Ketut Jilantik, in Jagaraga, in order to take over all of northern Bali, a Danish merchant named Mads Lange, who had his own little business empire based in

25

Kuta in the south of the island, stepped in and offered to act as mediator. With his help, the Dutch managed to get the Raja of Buleleng to sign a treaty acknowledging the supreme authority of the Dutch government in Batavia (now Jakarta). In order to enforce this treaty and to extract a fine of 400,000 guilders, the Dutch established a military garrison on Bali. However, the resistance of the Balinese was by no means broken, and found a charismatic leader in Prince Gusti Ketuk Jilantik, who, as soon as the main Dutch force had left the island, made it his job to see that the treaty was not observed. A result of the alleged treaty violations was that the Dutch determined, in 1848, to force the Raja of Buleleng into submission by military means, and there was another battle. This time they marched on Jagaraga with

2,400 men, 775 of them Europeans, but they were caught in an ambush which Jilantik and his 16,000 warriors had prepared for them. The Balinese now had 1,500 rifles and 25 cannon, and killed 264 of the invaders, losing 2,000 of their own men in the process. The Dutch fled back to their ships. The Raja of Buleleng had won a battle, but not the war.

Only a year later another, even larger Dutch force appeared on the north coast, and this time they succeeded in capturing Jagaraga. The Raja of Buleleng and his brother Jilantik withdrew to the south. The Dutch crowned their victory by turning their attention to other kingdoms. With the help of 4,000 soldiers provided by the Raja of Lombok, a vassal of the Netherlands, they subdued the kingdom of Karangasem in 1850. Confronted with a hopeless situation, the Raja of Karangasem led his entire entourage in an act of mass suicide *(puputan)*. Prince Jilantik's wife had already led all the women of the royal court of Bululeng in a similar tragic *puputan* in Jagaraga.

Above: The ritual mass suicide of Prince of Badung and his retinue. Right: The family of a Dutch colonial official.

26

The highest-ranking kingdom in Bali, Klungkung, was initially spared from conquest by the Dutch. Some 30,000 warriors, led by the Raja of Buleleng and Prince Jilantik, had assembled there. The Dutch soldiers, already weakened by an epidemic of dysentery, suffered heavy losses in a night battle, and were preparing to retreat when some of the Raja of Lombok's guerillas managed to get into Klungkung, where they ambushed and killed the Raja of Buleleng and poisoned Jilantik.

Now, of course, the Dutch regrouped and prepared to reattack. Enter Mads Lange once again; the Danish merchant saw that Dutch conquest of the island could pose a threat to his own business interests. He persuaded the Raja of Tabanan to step in with his troops and tip the scales against the invaders. The Dutch, faced with the prospect of having to fight on two fronts, negotiated a truce with the Dewa Agung (ruler) of Klungkung and his ally Gianyar. This was Mads Lange's finest hour.

The Dutch now briskly set about consolidating their power in the territories which they had been able to occupy. In "their" principalities, they installed Balinese regents, generally members of old princely families well-disposed towards the Dutch, and supervised by local colonial administrators or governors. Dutch troops continued to step in whenever the struggle for power between different Balinese states threatened to undermine colonial security and authority. In 1882, the Dutch established their capital in the port of Buleleng, also known as Singaraja. In their sphere of influence they banned the Hindu ritual of burning widows on their dead husbands' pyres; and they decreed that Balinese women should always keep their breasts covered in public – something which hitherto had only been required of prostitutes. Despite these regulations, people continued to burn widows and plunder wrecked ships, which had also been forbidden by the Dutch.

In 1906, an episode of this kind of plundering gave the Dutch an excuse fi-

nally to bring the southern part of the island under their control, as well. They dispatched a disproportionately large force against the Prince of Badung, who had refused to make any reparations for goods stolen from a Chinese merchant ship. The prince had no alternative but to save face through honorable death; in a ritual *puputan*, he and 600 members of his court died either by their own hands or by walking into a hail of Dutch bullets. The Raja of Tabanan, who had cherished the hope of being appointed regent, received the devastating news that his palace had been burned down and that he was to be exiled to Lombok, whereupon he also took his own life.

Two years later, in 1908, Klungkung fell to the colonial troops. Again there was scarcely any resistance, and the Dewa Agung entreated his gods in vain to open the earth and swallow up the

Left: Gusti Bagus, Raja of Karangasem (in about 1920). Right: The German painter and musician Walter Spies.

enemy "long-noses" and their native lackeys. Helpless, he and 200 of his courtiers were forced (albeit reluctantly) to choose ceremonial suicide. Bali now belonged indisputably to the Netherlands.

Independence and Beyond

In the decades that followed, the Dutch extended their administration over the whole of Bali. It was this period which saw the birth of the myth of Bali. In 1920, a German doctor, Gregor Krause, who had been working in Bali in the years up to World War I, published an illustrated book about the island, which gave many Europeans their first glimpse of one of the last paradises on earth. This sparked off a motley procession of artists, anthropologists, drop-outs, jet-setters, and anyone else trying to get a piece of a living legend, all streaming to the island. Foremost among them was the German painter and musician Walter Spies whose home at Campuan (Ubud) became a place of pilgrimage for both well- and unknown visitors. Enlightened citizens of the western world enthusiastically embraced the notion that every Balinese person was a peasant-artist living in perfect harmony with the cosmos. In fact, these years saw the beginning of a new wave of Balinese artistic activity which showed clear European influences without denying its ancient cultural heritage.

The outbreak of World War II brought all this to an end. In February, 1942, Japanese troops invaded the island without encountering any resistance. The Dutch forces, together with most of the civilian European population, had already been evacuated to Australia.

In 1945, following the capitulation of Japan, an Indonesian independence movement was launched under Ahmed Sukarno and Mohammed Hatta, who later became Sukarno's vice-president. During the war years, these two men had, in collaboration with the Japanese, set up an armed militia to take the place of the Dutch authorities.

The Dutch now tried to reclaim their former colony, but found themselves up against determined resistance both from an motley but decided liberation movement, including everyone from right-wing nationalists to Communists, and from the anti-colonial nation which had defeated Japan in the Pacific war: the United States.

In Bali, at least, the Dutch overcame this resistance without much difficulty. In November, 1946, a detachment of less than 100 Indonesian soldiers were cornered near Marga and fought to the very last man under their commander, Ngurah Rai. However, in Java, it was the nationalists who finally prevailed, not without the help of the U.S.A. In 1949, Indonesia was declared independent, though the republic continued to owe formal allegiance to the Queen of the Netherlands until 1954.

Even after independence, right- and left-wing factions continued to wage a bitter civil war, from which Sukarno eventually emerged victorious. This charismatic leader, whose mother was Balinese, contrived to stay in power by playing off conservatives against Communists in a series of cleverly-managed coalitions. On the international stage, Sukarno stood alongside Tito, Nasser and Nehru at the head of the group of non-aligned nations; at an important conference at Bandung in 1955, they proclaimed a "third way" between the two dominant power-blocks of East and West.

At home, after a brief honeymoon with democratic elections, Sukarno ushered in a dictatorship under the name of "Guided Democracy." However, political tensions remained acute between the still rather feudal local rulers and the Communists, who had won many supporters in the impoverished and overpopulated islands, Bali among them. Nevertheless, Sukarno enjoyed visiting Bali with his large retinue. These visits were much resented, since the local population were expected to provide free food, gifts and even, it was rumored, their daughters. To make matters worse, a plague of unusually large rats ravaged the crops in 1962; then, in March 1963, the sacred Mount Agung erupted with tremendous force, blanketing eastern Bali with ash and lava.

An attempted military coup in Jakarta in 1965 provoked massive retaliation against suspected Communists throughout Indonesia. Bali, being a Hindu society in a predominantly Moslem nation, and known to have separatist ambitions, was singled out for particularly vicious retribution; tens of thousands of civilians lost their lives. At the end of it all, Sukarno's position was permanently weakened, and power was transfered to the army strong-man, General Suharto. With his policy of a "New Order," which still prevails today, he assumed dictatorial powers, at the same time opening up Indonesia to foreign investment.

BALINESE SOCIETY

Despite Bali's increasing orientation toward the world market, despite the advent of the modern international entertainment media, and despite the relentless advancement of foreign tourism, Balinese society has managed to retain much of its original character. It is still based on a virtually self-sufficient agricultural village community, which is the cornerstone of a highly developed traditional culture with sophisticated artistic and aesthetic standards.

Underlying everything, now as ever, is the rice-growing season. Organizing rice cultivation, particularly irrigating the fields, requires strong social structures extending beyond the boundaries of the immediate family. A majority of Balinese, therefore, are not only involved in the rhythm of agrarian cycles and the rituals which have grown out of them, but have a responsibility to do their share toward the community effort of a village's food production. It's taken for granted that contributing one's share of work and participating in the community administration are as essential to a successful harvest as observing traditional ceremonies.

The Balinese Universe

Generally speaking, the horizons of the traditional country villages are limited. Their world is centered around village life and contacts with surrounding villages, extending as far as the nearest market town and any temple precincts of significance in the area, which are the goals of occasional pilgrimages. Before the advent of radio and TV, the Balinese knew virtually nothing of the world beyond the island. Though brought up on the Indian epics, like the *Ramayana*, enacted by

Left: Important religious festivals are always attended by a pedanda, or high priest.

shadow-puppets or dancers, they believed these to be ancient Indonesian, or even Balinese legends.

The sea which surrounds the island is strange and rather frightening to the Balinese, and so one often finds other races, such as the Bugis, settling on the coast and making a living from seafaring and fishing. Although water in general is sacred to the Balinese, the sea, in their tripartite conception of the world, is the home of demons and spirits unfriendly to man.

At the opposite pole are the soaring volcanic mountains, above all Gunung Agung, which is to Bali what Fujiyama is to Japan. This is the dwelling-place of gods, divine spirits of nature, and ancestral spirits. Between the mountains and the sea lies the world of man, the bone of contention over which the forces of Good and Evil continuously struggle.

This cosmology determines the whole attitude of the Balinese, down to the details of everyday life. People don't orient themselves according to the abstract concepts of north, south, east and west, but rather the axes of sunrise and sunset, mountains and sea. Particularly important is the mountain-sea relationship: anything between an individual and the mountains is considered to be closer to the gods than he is and therefore holy; while anything that lies in the direction of the sea is thought to be closer to the underworld and hence impure. Not only is every village laid out according to these coordinates, but the same principles apply to individuals. Thus the holiest part of the body is the highest part, the head (and for this reason it is generally thought bad manners to touch a Balinese person on the head); but the feet are the most impure part of the body, since they touch the earth, which in turn is close to the underworld. For this reason new-born babies are for several weeks kept away from the ground, or are only allowed to touch it lightly.

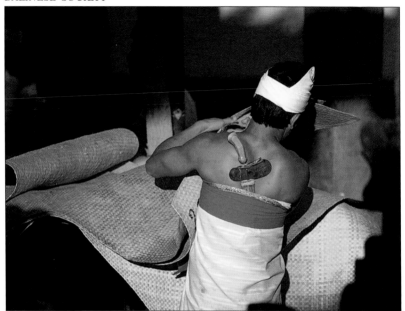

The Caste System

One decisive element in the development of Balinese society was the adoption of a social structure which Aryan peoples had already rigidly imposed on the Indian subcontinent. When the Hindu aristocracy of the Majapahit Empire fled to Bali in the 16th century, they brought with them Indian customs and traditions, and their influence spread across the island. The most notable effect this had was a division of society into two classes. The great majority of the population, probably more than 90%, belongs to the lowest caste, the *Sudra* or *Jaba*, which consists in the main of peasants and manual laborers. Above this is an upper class, itself divided into three castes, collectively known as the *Triwangsa*. In theory, the supreme caste is the *Brahmana*, made up of the priests and learned

Above: The kris is an embodiment of masculine authority. Right: Women of the lowest caste often have to do the hardest work.

scribes, whose names always include the title *Ida Bagus* for men and *Ida Ayu* or *Ida Dayu* for women. Their knowledge of hallowed religious rituals, and the exclusive right which they have to bless the holy water, ensures their privileged position in society. The highest caste in political terms, however – and therefore a caste which has often in fact been equal or superior to the Brahmanas in the course of history – is the *Ksatriya* or *Satriya*. This is made up of the senior members of the royal families of Klungkung, Gianyar, Bangli, Badung and Tabanan. Male members of this caste bear the titles *Anak Agung, Cokorda, Cokorda Gede, Dewa, Dewa Agung* or *Ratu,* while the women are called *Anak Agung Istri* or *Dewa Ayu.* The lowest of the three noble castes is the *Wesya,* to which high-ranking warriors and rich merchants once belonged. *Wesya* men's names include the title *I Gusti*; women are *I Gusti Ayu.* Membership in all three *Triwangsa* castes is determined solely by hereditary factors.

Bali differs from India in that this hereditary class division has never been regarded as absolutely immutable; today, political and economic changes, especially in the towns, are contributing to its gradual dissolution. Nevertheless, one encounters traces of its influence again and again. For example, at ceremonies a Sudra will always avoid sitting in a higher position than a member of a noble caste. But the relationship between the castes is shown most noticeably in the highly complicated modes of address used in conversation.

Each caste has its own special language, but a caste member abandons this as soon as he starts talking to a member of another caste. This results in the odd, but apparently accepted phenomenon of an aristocrat addressing a Sudra in the latter's idiom, while the Sudra in turn has to speak to the noble in *his* own eductated form of language, of which the Sudra, lacking the requisite education, has only limited mastery. Gradually, however, the official state language *Bahasa Indonesia*, which all Indonesians speak, is becoming an instrument of social equality, serving as a means of communication that transcends caste boundaries.

Alongside the caste divisions, certain professions have achieved a special status. Particularly notable in this connection are the blacksmiths, once venerated for their quasi-mysterious ability to control fire and molten metal. The *Pande*, as they are called, have their own temples and graveyards. Another sign of their special social standing is that members of the noble Triwangsa talk to them in the High Balinese language.

The Village

Village planning and organization follows the same principles all over the island and is based on the east-west (sunrise-sunset) and mountain-sea axes. The main street always runs from the seaward side (*kelod*) towards the mountains (*kaja*) and is crossed by side streets running east (*kangin*) to west (*kauh*). Along the main

cock-fights. Housed in a tower is the *kulkul* drum, whose deep. muted beats can, depending on their rhythm, announce village assemblies or temple festivals, warn of an accident or disaster, summon help or mourn the death of a villager. Sometimes the *kulkul* hangs over a platform in the spreading branches of the *waringin* or banyan tree that towers over the village square. This relative of the fig tree also shades the village market, held here every three days. This is the province of the village women. Whatever money they earn at the market is their own personal property.

Towards the sea, at a little distance from the village, stands the temple of the dead, the *pura dalem*, which is dedicated to the underworld, with the village burial-ground and cremation area, usually unfenced. Worshipped here is Durga, the goddess of death.

The Banjar

The inhabitants of a village belong to various functional associations, the largest of which is called the *banjar*. Larger villages are made up of several banjars, each of which includes about 70 families. The banjar is a kind of self-governing committee, to which any villager who has attained majority can belong, regardless of trade or occupation. In this context, "majority" means that a person is married and, in some cases, also has a first child. When a man joins a banjar, his wife automatically becomes a member as well. Interestingly, the younger generation forms the bulk of the banjar, and parents step down when their son becomes a member. The group meets about once a month to discuss and make decisions about village affairs. Decisions can only be reached by a unanimous vote; therefore, the meetings are often protracted, and characterized by continual searching for compromises that everyone can live with. This of course means that making major

street, one rectangular farmstead follows another. Each is surrounded by a wall delineating the boundary between the private, or family, sphere and that of the village community as a whole.

The village is divided into three zones, corresponding to the Balinese cosmos, and each equipped with its own appropriate temple. From the mountains to the sea, these zones symbolize the three abstract common stages of human existence: birth, life and death. Nearest the mountains, usually to the east of the village, is the temple of birth or beginning, *pura puseh*, dedicated to the god Brahma, creator of the world. In the middle of the village, where the daily life of mankind is embodied, not only symbolically but also in a very practical sense, stands the village temple of *pura desa*; beside it, a large meeting-hall or *bale agung*; and, as often as not, a *wantilan*, or arena for

Above: The banyan tree in the middle of a village is sacred to the Balinese. Right: Tidying up the village before a festival.

changes in village life is a very gradual process.

The principal task of the banjar is to see to the building and maintenace of the village infrastructure. Every member is obliged to help out with the physical labor when it comes to, for example, repairing the meeting-hall, constructing a new bathing-place, holding a religious festival, or cleaning and tidying up the village. Special family celebrations, such as the tooth-filing ceremony, weddings, the first birthday of a new member of the family, or a cremation, are communal festivities for the whole banjar. On such occasions, the proceedings are accompanied by the village *gamelan* orchestra playing the banjar's own instruments. For certain religious ceremonies, old weathered shrines are opened to yield the banjar's masks and costumes, which are shaken out, dusted off, and used in the dramatic reenactment of, for example, the conflict between Barong and Rangda, the opposing spirits between whom the world is held in equilibrium. Such cere-

monies serve to restore, at least for a time, a village's inner harmony.

The Subak

There is an association specific to rice-growers, called the *subak*. Each one includes all the farmers whose fields belong to a common irrigation system. An average subak has about 200 members, making it larger than a banjar. Subaks convene every 35 days under the leadership of an honorary chairman and discuss all matters relevant to rice cultivation. In the subak, as in the banjar, the principle of unanimity prevails. Decisions relate to problems of irrigation, fertilization, the use of insecticides, and the labor required for the harvest, as well as questions relating to the observation of traditional ceremonies is also on the agenda. The most time and effort are devoted to the building and regular repair of the irrigation canals and retaining-dykes.

Every subak traditionally maintains its own temple consecrated to the rice-god-

dess Dewi Sri. Believing that she reigns over the rice itself, the people of Bali reverently make offerings to her so that the harvest may prosper. Being so imbued with divinity, rice is sacred to the Balinese, and is therefore considered a most suitable food to be used as an offering to the gods.

The Family and the Farmstead

Balinese villagers live in extended families in their own farmsteads, shielded by walls from demons and from the rest of the village. The extended family includes the paternal grandparents, parents, children and daughters-in-law, since adult sons remain at home until they have acquired farmsteads of their own. In addition, widowed or impoverished relatives are often taken in, as well. Besides assuring the basic livelihood of its members, the principal aim of any family is to produce children. Childless bachelors are regarded as failures. There is a strong tradition of having large families, although recently the state has been trying to bring down the high birth rate with a family-planning campaign which endeavors to restrict couples to two children each.

Although new babies are greatly cherished and protected in the first months of life, the process of naming them seems, by Western standards, to reflect little individuality. Children are generally named according to their position in the family. The first-born, whether boy or girl, is nearly always called *Wayan*; more rarely, *Gede* or *Putu*. The second child is called *Made* or occasionally *Kadek* or *Nengah*, the third is *Nyoman* or *Komang* and the fourth is called *Ketut*. For subsequent children, the naming cycle starts again with Wayan, or else they are all simply called Ketut. To differentiate between boys and girls, an *I* or *Ni* is put in front of the name.

Above: Rural peace away from the main highway. Right: Bali's women have to juggle many different roles.

The more prosperous the family, the more pets and farm animals they will have sharing their homestead. Yapping dogs and loudly crowing fighting-cocks mingle with free-ranging hens and pot-bellied pigs. A well-to-do rice-farmer will usually have a team of water buffalo and a few of the antelope-like *banteng* cattle.

The organization of the farmstead once again reflects the Balinese concept of the universe in miniature. In the *kangin* corner, nearest the mountains, stands the family temple, where the gods and ancestral spirits are worshipped. Beside it, also facing the mountains, but on the *kauh* (west) side, are the closed-off sleeping quarters of the head of the family and his wife, built on stone foundations. The bed is so arranged that the sleeper's head is nearest the mountains, the seat of the gods, or the sunrise, the second most favorable position. Communal family life is played out at the center of the complex. Here are the living or sleeping bungalows, called *bales*, open to varying degrees. Some *bales* are ceremonial pavilions, reserved for such occasions as wedding nights or family meetings. On the side furthest from the mountains are the hen-coops, pigsties, rice-silos, and the kitchen. Even outside the walls, the height and size of the storage-loft are a good indication of a family's wealth. The entrance to the farmstead is usually a narrow passageway, reached by steps, and behind which stands the *Aling-Aling*, a wall intended to keep out evil spirits. It seems that these demons, though dangerous, are not very bright and can only move in straight lines. Thus they invariably bump into this obstacle, and this teaches them that the farmstead is a place to be avoided in future.

In the construction of a farmstead's buildings, the basic dimensions stem from the body measurements of the head of the family. Before building starts, an expert well-versed in the ancient *lontar*

writings takes the head of the family's measurements in the prescribed manner, and then, based on his caste, the size of his fortune, local conditions, and the stipulations of the relevant *lontar* documents, determines how long his outer wall, or how large certain *bales* should be. The length of the enclosing wall, for example, is always a multiple of the length of an armspan (measured from middle finger to middle finger of a man standing with both arms extended from his sides), plus one cubit (arm's length), plus one hand's breadth, with thumb and little finger outstretched. The proportions of the *bales* are similarly calculated on the basis of other smaller units of measurements from the head of the household.

These methods are supposed to ensure the harmony between the owner of the new house and his immediate environment. In fact, a similar notion has also played a role in Western architecture at least since the Renaissance, although it's retreated today from the forefront of our consciousness.

RELIGION ON THE "ISLAND OF GODS AND DEMONS"

Bali is called the "Island of Gods and Demons" or "Island of a Thousand Temples." And with good reason, since the life of the Balinese, right down to the most routine detail, is governed by religious beliefs and accompanied by religious observances. Perhaps one of the most striking examples of this are the innumerable wicker baskets filled with flowers, rice, or other offerings, presented to the gods or demons as a gesture of appeasement or request. You can see them outside a boutique in Kuta or on the edge of the crater of Gunung Agung, at a dangerous intersection or on a stone altar in the middle of the garden of your hotel. If you travel through the countryside, you will often come across women on their way to a temple balancing tower-

Above: Decorations woven from palm-leaves hang in the main street. Right: A religious procession going to a sacred spring.

ing piles of offerings on their heads. And even the most harmless, seemingly secular forms of popular entertainment are based on religion. Although Westerners may find this intertwining of the sacred and the profane unusual, we should remember that the lives of our forefathers, not so very many generations ago, were governed, from the cradle to the grave, by the bells of the parish church – on Bali, it is only the tune that is a little different.

Agama Hindu Dharma

Balinese religion draws upon a number of different sources, and, even within the relatively narrow confines of the island, has always taken a variety of forms. In fact, a resident of one village may be completely at a loss to understand the significance of certain rituals that are observed a few villages farther on. It also seems to be the case that he cannot follow the incantations the priest mutters at his own village ceremonies, and isn't even particularly interested in their meaning. This religion, it seems, is not especially concerned with grappling intellectually with notions of a single, universal road to truth. Evidently, it's more concerned with incorporating a range of religious beliefs and concepts into a common and rather abstract concept of salvation. "Harmony through diversity" could well be its motto. But in spite of the variety of religious forms, there are certain clear and fundamental principles.

In very broad terms, it can be said that the religion of the Balinese is a very distinctive form of Hinduism which exists only on Bali and a few neighboring islands influenced by Bali. This Hinduism, which arrived in Bali from India by way of eastern Java, recognizes the trinity of the gods Brahma, Vishnu and Shiva, focusing on Shiva in particular. Even on Java, this form of Hinduism had already absorbed certain characteristics of Budd-

hism, so that some major ceremonies would be unthinkable without the participation of a Buddhist priest. However, the most striking difference between Balinese Hinduism and other forms of the religion is that it's incorporated many ancient Malayan animistic beliefs, which are a particularly important element of popular religion in Bali. From this peasant source derives the belief that all the elements of nature have their own souls – down to the very rocks. These forces of nature are subordinated to an all-powerful godhead, on whom man can only have a very limited influence. This explains why the Balinese are so anxious to maintain contact with their ancestors, since according to their beliefs, they are dependent on their ancestors for protection against these natural forces. Ancestor-worship is a way of warding off the angry and unpredictable outbursts of the elements.

These animistic foundations support a Hindu pantheon permeated with a number of additional Balinese deities.

Underlying this theology is the belief in a well-ordered cosmos, which is in a constant state of evolution. The force which holds the universe together is called *Dharma*; working against this is the destabilizing force of *Adharma*. The interaction between the two accounts for the continuous creation, existence and dissolution of things. Beyond the reach of human imagination rules the Supreme Being, the bringer of order, Sanghyang Widhi Wasa. He is the Absolute, beyond comprehension, the unification of all divine powers. Therefore he stands above and outside the cosmos, which is characterized by the constant struggle of opposing forces. This embodiment of the divine principle incidentally provides the Balinese with a useful argument to prove that their form of Hinduism is perfectly compatible with the tenets of the Indonesian state ideology. For one of the five basic stipulations of the Indonesian constitution requires that every citizen should be a follower of a monotheistic religion.

39

More familiar to ordinary people than Sanghyang Widhi Wasa is his embodiment in the form of a trinity: the *Trishakti* or *Trimurti*, comprising Brahma, Vishnu and Shiva. Brahma is held to be the Creator of the world, Vishnu its Preserver, and Shiva, its Destroyer. Shiva shows clearly the extent to which Hinduism thinks in terms of mutually compatible opposites. Destruction is not merely seen as something negative, but as a precondition for renewal, for the regeneration of the world. To the Balinese, Shiva is often no more than another name for the ancient sun-god Surya, or the mighty god Mahadewa who inhabits the volcano of Gunung Agung. But in Hinduism such transformations are not uncommon. Each of the three divinities is quite capable of manifesting himself in various different forms, or has, according to sacred texts, already been through many different incarnations. Vishnu, in particular, has had legion incarnations, some of them quite nationalistic in character: for instance, Rama, the hero of the *Ramayana* epic, is also considered to be an earthly representation of Vishnu. Another Vishnu avatar is Krishna, the flute-playing cowherd and seducer of women, who is usually portrayed with a greenish-blue face.

So that the gods should not be alone, and, more importantly, to prevent them from weakening and pining away, they are provided with divine consorts, who embody their *Shakti*, their godly energy and creative power. This also means that it is the female deities who maintain the dynamism and creativity of the gods in this cosmology.

Brahma is paired with Saraswati, the goddess of wisdom. Vishnu has as many female partners as he has earthly incarnations. The most important are Dewi Lakshmi, the goddess of fortune and prosperity; Dewi Sri, the goddess of fertility or of rice; and the especially popular Sita, Rama's steadfast wife.

Shiva's partners represent the most flamboyant and violent aspects of life among the gods. Dewi Uma, the goddess of love and beauty, is one of them, as are Durga, goddess of death, and Kali, the bloodthirsty goddess of destruction.

The world of the gods is rounded off by a whole army of demons and spirits, which are attributed to the night, the underworld and the realm of shadows. Like the gods, they make frequent appearances in the middle world of men, where they do their evil work. Man's endeavors are directed, not simply towards ridding the world of evil, but rather toward neutralizing its effect, so that his middle realm may achieve a harmonious coexistence of opposites.

Man possesses an immortal soul, called *Atman*, which according to its *Karma Pala* is incarnated again and again in an endless series of rebirths (*samsara*). The Karma Pala is a kind of destiny which derives from one's behavior in earlier lives. Unlike the Hindus of India, the Balinese believe that the soul of an ancestor enters the body of a newborn baby and thus returns to his own clan. This cycle is so important that the Balinese consider the fate of being reborn in an alien and unknown body more terrible and painful even than death itself.

The highest goal of human existence is to break out of the cycle of reincarnation so that the soul can be reunited with the Supreme Being, in perfect harmony. This release from *samsara* is called *moksa*; and there are three ways, or *marga*, by which *moksa* can be achieved. The direct way, which is, however, the most difficult and worthy of admiration, is that of complete renunciation. Through mystic contemplation and meditation, a person can free himself of his earthly fetters and prepare the way for his soul to find eternal harmony.

Right: Seated above the masses, the pedanda seeks contact with the gods.

The second path is that of knowledge and exemplary behavior. Anyone who decides to follow this path has teachers instruct him in the holy writings, focuses on expanding his knowledge, and, thus fortified with inner moral strength, strives throughout his life to uphold the Ten Commandments, which are not so very different from those of the Christian tradition.

The third path, the one taken by the majority of Balinese, is that of ritual devotion to the gods. This consists of observing the prescribed rites and sacrifices and thus, step by step, getting ever closer to *moksa*.

Priests: Pedanda and Pemangku

Average Balinese citizens generally derive their ideas of religion and morality from dramatic performances of the Indian epics *Ramayana* and *Mahabharata* in dances, spoken drama, and shadow-puppet plays. Priests, on the other hand, draw their wisdom from the oldest sacred

writings of Hinduism, the ancient Indian *Vedas* and *Upanishads*. These are hermetic texts of great lyrical power, and riddled with mysterious allusions. The priests who devote themselves to these scriptures are known as *pedanda* and belong to the Brahmana caste. Keeping remote from the mundane distractions of secular life, they spend their days meditating in their private temples and seeking union with Surya, the Balinese form of Shiva. Their main link to the common people is in providing them with holy water, since they are generally the only ones who know the required methods of preparation and benedictions. At the same time, the sale of this water is a source of income for them. They are only to be seen at major temple festivals or important ceremonies. On these occasions, they sit enthroned like saints on specially constructed seats, above the heads of the masses, as if they were already existing on some higher plane, and invoke the gods with ritual gestures and murmured mantras. The Shivaitic priests wear their

hair pinned up in a knot on top of their heads, while the Buddhist clergy have hair of shoulder-length.

Closer to the common people are the ordinary temple priests or *pemangku,* who generally belong to the lowest caste. They are charged with carrying out all the daily duties connected with the temple. These include receiving offerings, supervizing temple festivals and organizing processions. While the pedanda, as High Priest, is responsible for the spiritual quality of a ceremony, the pemangku is busy seeing that everything goes according to plan. He may give the signal for the next phase of the ritual, or take the holy water from the pedanda and sprinkle it over the congregation.

Someone who stands in a key position between the people and their gods is the *Dalang*, or shadow-puppet player. He is

Above: Colored rice-cakes are the construction blocks in these beautiful pillars of offering. Right: The mighty gates of the new Pura Ulun Danu temple in Batur.

considered to be a priest, or at least has an elevated social position comparable to that of the priests. His art brings the myths of India and Indonesia alive for the people. The characters which he presents perform on various social, linguistic and dramatic levels. His noble heroes speak a language of which the common people only have a rudimentary understanding. For this reason, and to add to the entertainment value, there is an almost Shakespearian gallery of servants, fools and yokels, who provide a running commentary on the action in a simpler *lingua franca*, thus enabling the audience to appreciate the epic drama and get some laughs into the bargain.

Balinese Temples: Pura

In addition to the hundreds of thousands of family temples, there are a large number – no one has ever counted them, but it must be at least 20,000 – of village, association, tribal, clan and state temples in public places. These *Pura* differ from

family temples only in their size and furnishings. Unlike Hindu temples in India, the ones in Bali generally do not have any closed rooms. Even in the innermost parts of the temple the view to the mountains, held to be the throne of the gods, must remain unrestricted, so that the gods, whose presence is desired at temple festivals, will have an easier time finding their way down.

A temple is comprised of two or three rectangular walled courts, which either lie on the same level, or (in mountainous areas) are built in terraces one above the other. The forecourt (*jaba sisi*) lies nearest the sea, and the innermost court, the Holy of Holies (*jeroan*), is nearest the mountains. Between these two, larger Pura often have another interior court (*jaba tengah*). You enter the temple through a tall, divided gateway (*candi bentar*), representing a mountain of the gods (*meru*), rent asunder exactly down the middle. The outer and central courts contain various buildings which are used in the preparation of temple festivals. A

second gateway (*kori agung* or *padu raksa*), of which the upper part is usually closed, gives access to the Holy of Holies. This entrance is often guarded by the stone face of a terrifying *Kala-Boma*. In addition to this, two figures of demons (*raksasa*) armed with clubs stand to the left and right of the entrance, to keep out others of their kind. An *Aling-Aling* wall behind the Kori-Agung gate makes the interior of the temple definitively demonproof.

In the innermost area of the *jeroan* is a raised chair for the pedanda (*bale pawedaan*); the pagoda-shaped *merus* with as many as eleven roofs (*tumpang*), chiefly dedicated to the triple gods of the Trishakti; several shrines (*pasimpangan*) to other gods; and finally the most important throne for a god, the *Padmasana*, decorated with lotus blossoms to induce the Supreme Being to linger in the temple. In accordance with its importance, this throne is located in the propitious *kaja-kangin* corner of the Holy of Holies.

Festivals and Ceremonies

Apart from modern holidays, such as Indonesian Independence Day on August 17th, all festive occasions in Bali have a religious background and look back on long traditions, often 1,000 years old or more. The first historically documented holy man to have brought Javanese-Hindu philosophy and religion to Bali was named Danghyang Markandeya. In the 8th century, he established himself in an old hermitage on the slopes of Gunung Agung in order to teach the Balinese to believe in the Absolute Being, Sanghyang Widhi Wasa. Today, this holy place is still the site of the most important temple on the island, the mother temple of Besakih.

The son of Markandeya, Empu Sang Kulputih, was responsible for introduc-

ing the colorful offerings ceremonies and regular temple festivals, of which the most important is the festival of *Odalan*. Then, in the 11th century, Empu Kuturan laid down the outlines of the Balinese cosmos, the alignments of which continue to determine Balinese orientation today, and are still reflected even in decorative details and the smallest architectural measurements. The basic framework of Balinese ceremonies can also be traced in these alignments. What followed were simply refinements, usually introduced by one of the rajas or his court. These customs and beliefs were soon firmly rooted in the Balinese mentality, and not even the arrival of the Europeans changed them, especially as the Dutch, for quite a long period, were careful to protect the islanders from foreign influences. This is certainly one of the reasons why the number of native Christians on Bali remained so small, and the only Moslem communities of any size are in the north and west of the island and in the capital.

Odalan and Galungan/Kuningan

Out of the wealth of festivities, two of the most important are the *Odalan* festival and the week of celebrations from *Galungan* to *Kuningan*. *Odalan* takes place once a year, and is the time when every temple is brought out of obscurity, and for one, two, or as many as ten days, depending on its importance, is transformed into a the scene of a religious celebration for gods and men.

Every villager or member of a Subak has a particular responsibility in the preparations. The women's task is to prepare the offerings. They weave little baskets and symbolic figures, bake and color the small rice-cakes, and at the climax of the festival carry these to the temple, piled high on their heads. Later the consecrated gifts are brought home again and eaten by the family.

Above: The gate of the Puri Saren in Ubud. Right: After the festival, the consecrated offerings are brought home again.

In the temple forecourt, the menfolk enthusiastically stage cock-fights, which the authorities expressly allow only during the period of the festival. The blood of the defeated bird flows into the earth and is supposed to propitiate evil spirits. A *gamelan* orchestra plays late into the night in honor of the gods who, drawn by the meditation and ritual incantations of the priests, have come to take their places on the decorated thrones of stone. Shadow-puppet plays and dramatic spectacles are presented for the entertainment both of the gods and of the worshippers, who are dressed in festive sarongs, temple sashes and blouses or shirts. The most elaborate dancing takes place on the last evening of the *Odalan* in the Holy of Holies, as a fitting farewell to the gods. After that the temple and its spirits sink back once again into a holy slumber.

Whereas the *Odalan* festival is dedicated to one specific temple, the purification of the whole village is the chief purpose of the ten-day festival from *Galungan* to *Kuningan* (in the pre-Islamic *Wuku* calendar). Before the festival the men erect tall bamboo poles, from which dangle figures attractively crafted of palm leaves, mostly representing the rice-goddess Dewi Sri. The whole village is swept, public buildings are decorated, little domestic altars are set up in front of each homestead, and here and there faded paintwork is touched up. On the feast-day of *Galungan* itself a rich array of offerings are brought to the Temple of Birth to celebrate the creation of the world and the provisional victory of Good over Evil. After the temple ceremonies everyone gets together for big family parties; even grown-up children make a special trip home from the towns.

On the day of *Kuningan* (the word means "yellow"), yellow-colored rice is brought to the temple. On this, the second most important feast after *Galungan*, the Balinese remember their ancestors and holy men, and go on joyful pilgrimages to the most important temples associated with the holy men. The day after *Kuningan*, the festival ends with games.

RITES OF PASSAGE

The Balinese consider life as no more than a transitional stage for their souls on the way to *moksa*, that redemption which for the Hindu believer represents complete harmony with God. The particular emphasis on transition – in the literal as well as the metaphorical sense – is reflected not only in the way temples are constructed but also in the ceremonies which mark the stages in a person's earthly life. Not surprisingly, no part of the temple is given more attention than the gates, which symbolize the passing from one world into the next. Similar importance is laid on the occasions marking the beginning of a new stage of life.

Birth and First Birthday

Even before a birth takes place, between the third and sixth months of preg-

Above: Participants at a tooth-filing ceremony are sprinkled with holy water.

nancy, a purification ceremony is held in the home. From now on the parents must refrain from swearing. The expectant mother is considered impure in a religious sense, and must therefore stay away from temples and rice-fields.

After the birth, the ceremonies center around the by-products of the birth, known as the "Four Sisters": placenta, umbilical cord, amniotic fluid and blood. These have to be buried in a yellow-painted coconut shell near the entrance to the parents' sleeping quarters. This spot is felt by every Balinese to be his immediate spiritual home, and for the rest of his life he will always lay offerings here on special days.

For a long period the new-born baby may not touch the ground (considered impure), and for 42 days mother and baby are themselves held to be impure, though the father only for three days. On the twelfth day after birth, the infant is given a provisional name and the cradle is watched over by the winged god Rare Kumara, protector of children.

At the end of 42 days, a purification ceremony is held in a special bathing-place, after which the mother may once again enter the temple. The child is now also freed from the impurity of its birth. After 105 days, which is half the period of the Wuku calendar, a festival is held in which the child receives a new name. It is usual on this occasion for a life-size dummy of the child to be made and thrown outside the farmstead, to distract the evil spirits who are lurking there. The next festival takes place 210 days after the birth, when the baby may be put on the ground for the first time. It has now left its divine existence and entered the earthly world. But it is not allowed to crawl – it is not an animal, after all. The baby's head is now shaved, except for one lock over its forehead, and the god of children, Rare Kumara, is presented with a final offering.

Less attention is paid to the child's subsequent birthdays. The next significant ceremonies are held when a child loses its baby teeth, a girl menstruates for the first time, or a boy's voice changes.

Tooth-filing

Another indispensable ceremony for evey Balinese who wants his life-cycle to follow the proper path is the filing of teeth. Normally this should take place in late adolescence, and certainly before marriage. In this ceremony, which is attended by as many family members as possible, six teeth in the upper jaw, in other words the jaw nearest to the realm of the gods, are filed down to an even, straight line. The symbolic value of this is that, by having his animal-like canine teeth filed down, a person is freed from animal desires. Each of the six teeth stands for one of the undesirable vices of lust, anger, greed, insanity, drunkenness and envy. It is to be expected that anyone who has his or her teeth trimmed in this way will behave as a mature adult from

then on. Furthermore, pointed canine teeth are considered not only unseemly, but downright unattractive.

Marriage

Even today, marriages on Bali are still customarily arranged by negotiation between the parents of the couple. Such marriages are a product of both social and economic considerations, and are an occasion for costly celebrations. In addition to this, there's always been a less expensive way of starting a marriage: stealing a bride. This was in fact closer to the Western conception of marrying for love, since the bride-to-be was always warned in advance that she was to be "stolen" and was generally only too happy to co-operate. The bride's parents were expected to pursue the abductor and make an elaborate show of objecting for days before finally coming to terms with their daughter's "fate" and reaching an amicable arrangement over it.

Nowadays, abduction has a more symbolic character and is a joke in which the whole village can share. After the abduction and the obligatory honeymoon, spent away from the village with friends of the bridegroom, the two families get together for a proper wedding ceremony. This varies in form from village to village, but the end result is the same in all cases: the woman leaves her family and moves into her husband's homestead. Through the marriage the couple both become full members of their banjar.

Cremation

Without doubt the most important event in the ceremonial cycle of earthly existence is the one celebrating the cremation of the dead. In this way, those left behind can assure that the soul of the dead relative, freed from its physical trappings, will ascend to heaven. Depending on the wealth of the family, the

47

corpse is either first buried until enough money is available for a ceremonial cremation, or it is placed in a *bale* in the farmstead until the prescribed period of 42 days has elapsed and the body can be consigned to the flames. Often several families, or the whole village, will get together and organize a mass cremation of all the bodies which in recent years have been laid to rest in temporary graves. Sometimes it is possible to join in the celebrations of rich families and thus save some of the costs.

It often takes weeks of work to prepare two gaudily decorated coffins for each body: one to transport the body, the other to be used in the cremation itself. On the day of the cremation, once the domestic ceremonies are ended, the corpse is taken in the first coffin to the place of cremation. Along this route, the coffin is borne tempestuously, repeatedly shaken or

turned in circles; this makes for a lively spectacle, in the course of which the pall-bearers are frequently doused with water. The purpose of this is to confuse the soul of the dead person so that it will not find its way back to the farmstead and haunt the living occupants. Once arrived at the place of cremation, the corpse is transferred to the cremation coffin. What follows is rather anticlimactic. The result of weeks of work, with the corpse in it, is set alight by propane torches. When everything is reduced to ashes, the white ash from the bones is separated from the rest and at a later date is taken in a ceremonial procession to the sea or a river, where it is scattered over the waters. Thus is the soul of the departed finally set free.

When a Brahman or other leading figure is cremated, the ceremony is immensely elaborate and draws visitors from far and wide. Every ten years at Besakih, there is a ceremony of purification, before which all the island's graveyards have to be emptied and the bodies burned.

Above: A cremation in Ubud. Right: Who is dancing, and who is calling the tune?

ETIQUETTE: DOS AND DON'TS

A Western visitor to Bali can make many mistakes. But the Balinese are very forgiving – provided you show a willingness to treat the country and its people with consideration. However, if in your wanderings you carelessly trample down the dyke-like boundary walls between the rice-fields, making hours of work for someone and threatening the very basis of existence, you will make yourself very unpopular. If you're in some kind of conflict situation with a Balinese and do not give him the opportunity to save face, you must be prepared for him to become even more entrenched in his position; his concept of honor leaves him no other choice. Even in Kuta's crowded streets, you should always maintain your own dignity by respecting that of street vendors importuning you to buy their watches. Behavior which may seem simply tiresome to you may be another person's fight for survival; you may not be able to make his or her lot any easier, but you don't need to add to their problems by being unpleasant. If you are not interested, don't raise false hopes. A quiet but firm refusal is more appropriate than nervous dithering.

Incidentally, not everyone will be trying to sell you something. Often, people just want to chat and try out their latest English words on you. You have to learn to tell the difference. In any case, if you can master a few words or phrases in the national language, Bahasa Indonesia, this will make for better understanding and will endear you to your island hosts. Most shopkeepers will be prepared to accept defeat in the face of a firm "*(saya) tidak mau*" – "I don't want it."

At Temple Festivals

Foreigners are usually allowed to enter temples and to take part in temple festivals. However, since the Balinese are

communicating with their gods in these ceremonies, visitors are expected to abide strictly by certain rules.

Great restraint is called for in all behavior. This begins with your clothing, which must be modest and decent. Shorts, T-shirts and the like are completely unacceptable. Men are required to wear a long-sleeved shirt, a sarong and a temple-sash (*selendang*), and sometimes also a cloth tied round the head (called a *destar* or *udeng*). Women should wear a long-sleeved blouse, or a *kebaya* like the Balinese women. You should not arrive at a fetival hot, sweaty, and ungroomed. Walls and other parts of the temple structure are sacred to the Balinese, and it is sacrilege to touch them with your feet, since these are regarded as impure. You should also take care never to place yourself between people praying and the shrine or throne of a god. It is more appropriate to sit than to stand. In this way you avoid insulting the gods or their priests, who should be physically above everyone else, by appearing to stand above them. If you want to leave your seat before the end of a ceremony, show your respect for this Balinese custom by walking with your body slightly bowed.

You should never take photographs without the permission of your potential subject. A friendly glance may be sufficient to secure this permission. However, flash-bulbs should not be used at temple festivals; in fact, it is positively dangerous to use them on occasions when dancers go into a trance.

Even if there is no festival in progress, you should not enter a temple unless you are decently dressed and preferably wearing a temple-sash, tied round your waist like a belt.

People who have recently suffered a bereavement in the family, anyone with open wounds, and women who are menstruating are considered impure (*sebel*) and may not enter a temple. If any human blood were to "defile" the floor of a temple, it would entail an elaborate (and costly) ceremony of purification.

Invitations

If a Balinese family invites you to their home, you should always arrive properly dressed, though you don't have to go to the length of wearing a sarong. Westerners tend, anyway, to look rather less than elegant in these garments. It is quite usual to bring a little house present for your hosts or their children. This will be accepted rather discreetly and put to one side, since the host does not wish you to get the impression that he is acquisitive. Except for business meetings, and sometimes even then, it is customary to arrive about half an hour later than invited. You should leave your shoes at the front door and enter the house in your stocking feet.

Once inside, introductions and greetings proceed with brief handshakes (not

Right: "Wanna take a photo? OK, any time, Mister!"

too firm), rather in the European manner, and always according to the correct order of precedence among those present, based on age and title. Don't sit down until you're invited to do so. If people are sitting in the traditional style on cushions and mats on the floor, be careful not to point the soles of your feet in anyone's direction, since this is considered an insult. Nor should you point with your foot at anyone or anything.

If you are invited to a meal, do not start eating or drinking until your host has indicated in a friendly way that you should do so. It's wise not to take too much on your plate for the first serving, since you will always be served a second helping which you must not refuse, unless you are actually feeling ill. Your host will also deem it an honor if you try at least a small helping from every dish that you are offered.

If bowls or dishes are handed round, be sure always to take them with the right hand and pass them on with the same hand. The left hand is held to be impure, as it's used to clean intimate parts of the body after going to the toilet; at most, you can use it to support your right elbow when passing things round the table. At the end of the meal, you should always leave a little food on your plate. This is meant as food for the gods, and shows both that your host has provided more than enough to eat and that you, the guest, have not indulged in the vice of gluttony.

Dealing with Officials

If you have matters to take are of in a government office or other official institution and want things to proceed quickly, make sure – paradoxical as it may seem – to allow plenty of time, or at least appear to have plenty of time. A calm, friendly approach, showing respect for the person you're dealing with without being obsequious, is the surest way to

success. Impatience seldom does any good; on the contrary, it just means that the official has to control his anger at the disgraceful behavior of his customer, and this can take quite a while.

What does help, however, is to dress your best, despite the tropical temperature. For men this means polished slippers, long trousers, and a long-sleeved shirt; for women, a decent dress, or knee-length skirt and modest blouse, always with a bra underneath. Whatever you wear, you should always try to look clean and well turned-out.

Behavior in Public

Although it is not unusual for Balinese of the same sex to go around hand in hand, it's not customary to make an open show of affection *between* the sexes in public.

Things which seem very uninhibited to Europeans – such as swimming naked or washing in a river – have their own unspoken restrictions: men and women have separate bathing-places, or bathe at different times. It is extremely impolite to stare at someone, still worse to photograph him, while he is washing. A Balinese who is relieving him- or herself is simply "invisible" to others.

When talking to a Balinese person, you should neither fold your arms in front of you nor put your hands on your hips. Both gestures give an impression of arrogance and are therefore very impolite. Although the Balinese may touch you frequently without meaning any disrespect, you as a foreigner should be very reticent about touching other people. The Balinese code of behavior forbids touching someone on the head, even if it's meant in a friendly way; you shouldn't even pat children on the head. For the Balinese, the head is the most sacred part of the body.

As in the west, it is impolite to point at people. If you want to beckon to someone, you do it by stretching out your arm and waving your hand with the palm facing downward.

51

ISLAND PARADISE, TOURIST HUB

DENPASAR

KUTA / LEGIAN

BUKIT BADUNG

NUSA DUA

SANUR

LEMBONGAN

NUSA PENIDA

If you're looking for the "real" Bali, the best place to start is the triangle of luxuriant tropical landscape which fans out from the limestone knob of the Bukit Badung peninsula in the south of the island. Here, proverbially at the feet of the gods who sit in the mountains, is where the heart of Bali beats. The fertile river valleys and plains provide ideal conditions for rice cultivation; and this, with its attendant green rice paddies and terraces ascending the hillsides, is the cornerstone of Balinese civilization. Not surprisingly, this rice-growing center is the most densely populated part of the island, where every aspect of its varied, colorful life unfolds before you.

The main population center is the southern tip, with the rapidly expanding capital, Denpasar, and the tourist centers along the surrounding coasts, with their alluring sand beaches. Since the 1960s, hordes of tourists have been descending in increasing numbers on this part of Bali; the number of foreign visitors expected in 1997 is a staggering 1.5 million.

Gone forever are the days when Denpasar was just a small town, residence of

Previous pages: On the beach. Young Legong dancers take a break. Left: A temple monkey enjoying the view from the Pura Luhur Ulu Watu.

the local raja, and Kuta, the inexpensive tropical paradise on the coast southwest of Denpasar, was no more than a fishing village. In a higher price-range, but equally booked up, are the luxurious beach resorts of Sanur and Nusa Dua, the former once occupied by the old-guard Brahman caste, the latter originally a deserted beach on the bone-dry peninsula of Bukit Badung.

DENPASAR

Honking, three-wheeled taxi-buses (*bemos*) on the lookout for passengers; swarms of mopeds; buses belching fumes: all these contribute to the chronic traffic congestion in the notably unromantic metropolis which Denpasar (population 300,000) has become since it was made capital of Bali in 1958. Thanks to the considerable foreign earnings from tourism, the little market town which greew up around the raja's palace of Permecutan has become one of the most affluent cities in Indonesia. Denpasar means "east of the market"; locals, however, usually call it Badung, a name which refers not only to the former seat of the raja, but the whole principality and the modern administrative district which extends from the Bukit Badung peninsula up to the volcanic Catur massif.

57

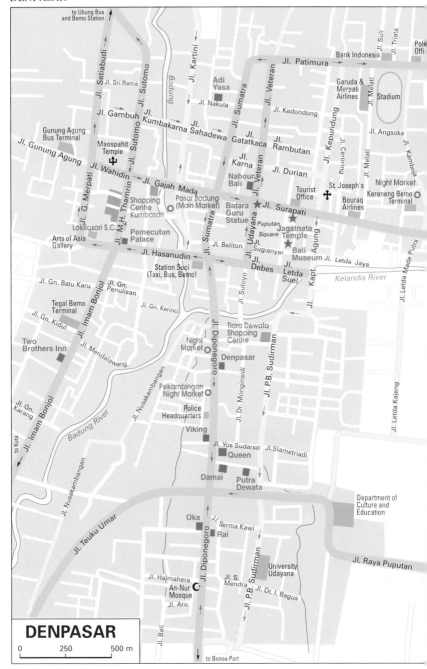

DENPASAR

0   250   500 m

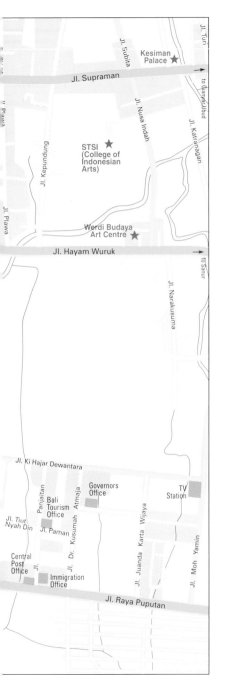

The rajas and nobility of Badung traditionally came from the Ksatriya caste, which today continues to form the elite of Denpasar – from administrative officials to hotel owners. However, the bulk of the population is by no means so homogeneous. The inexorably advancing, insatiable city is swallowing up the surrounding rice-paddies and villages. It has already reached the Bay of Benoa to the south and the artists' village of Batubulan to the north, and acts as a magnet to draw people in from the countryside and villages. Immigrants don't come only from Bali. Even in the 1930s, Dutch colonial rule attracted an influx of Moslem traders of Buginese, Indian and Arab origin to Denpasar. Recent decades have seen their ranks swollen by large numbers of Moslems from Java and Madura; they daily answer the muezzin's call to prayer at the mosques of Raya Masjid and An-Nur Masjid on Jalan Diponegoro.The Javanese can often be seen peddling their wares in the streets or operating mobile shops and cookshacks called *warungs.* Industrious Chinese businessmen, both Buddhist and Christian, belong to the commercial elite of Denpasar. On the flat roofs of their tall office buildings, next to the satellite dishes, you sometimes see splendid gilded pagoda-like shrines to their ancestors. It would be very risky to believe in no god at all, since atheists get lumped together with Communists.

The younger generation, estranged from traditional village life, seek a new cultural orientation in the westernized lifestyle of Kuta on the one hand, and – perhaps in a more lasting way – from the Indonesian metropolis, Jakarta, on the other. The *lingua franca* of the Indonesian archipelago, derived from traders' Malay, is the official language, Bahasa Indonesia. Spreading out from Denpasar through schools and universities, cinema and television, it is gaining supremacy over the native tongues of the island. Indonesia's national motto of "Unity in

Diversity" (*bhinneka tunggal ika*) is beginning to take root in Bali's young capital. The different caste-based languages, which in rural Bali separate princes from rice farmers the moment they open their mouths, no longer have much significance in city life. Here, videos are more popular than shadow-puppet plays; and the principle of individuality is coming to take precedence over the all-embracing divine order of the Hindu cosmos. At the same time, the deeply traditional countryside is receiving a new infusion of energy and ideas from Denpasar – in art and religion, dance, music and painting. Following the example of India, Brahman theologians are attempting to focus Balinese Hindus' belief in a pantheon of many gods into a more monotheistic view concentrated around the Supreme Being of Sanghyang Widhi Wasa, while trying to play down animistic tendencies in folk

Above: The four-faced Batara Guru stands in Puputan Square. Right: The Art Center at twilight.

religious belief, which derive from before the advent of Hinduism.

At the State College of Dance, STSI (*Sekolah Tinggi Seni Indonesia* on Jalan Nusa Indah) and the SMKI (*Sekolah Menengah Karawitan Indonesia* in Batubulan, also known as KOKAR), new choreography is developed for the old temple dances, as well as completely new dances which are performed throughout the year on the large stage of the Werdi Budaya Art Center (formerly Abiankapas), most impressively during the *Bali Arts Festival* in June and July. Among the programs are also performances of the *Ramayana* ballet, reflecting a classical Javanese influence, and competitions between *gamelan* orchestras.

A Walk Round the City

City life in Denpasar centers around **Puputan Square.** The name recalls the *Puputan*, or mass ritual suicide of the entire royal court of Pemecutan on September 20th, 1906; it thus commemorates the heroic self-sacrifice of the ruling class of Bali faced with the superior arms of the Dutch soldiers who had been sent on a punitive expedition against the Raja of Badung for having ordered the looting of a Chinese merchant ship which had gone aground on the coast (see p. 27-28). In the center of the square stands a bronze **memorial** to those who lost their lives in the fight for liberation from the Dutch at the end of World War II.

In the northwest corner of Puputan Square, at the busy intersection of Jalan Gajah Mada and Jalan Udayana, the four-faced **Batara Guru** on his pedestal surveys the hectic city traffic in all four cardinal directions. The 15-foot (5 m) high stone statue is dedicated to Shiva, the "Great Teacher." The face looking eastward is that of Iswara (Indra), while Brahma looks to the south, Mahadewa to the west and Vishnu to the north. The last-named is easy to recognize by his insignia, the shell horn and the Wheel of Life (*cakra*).

On the east side of the square rises the modern **Pura Jagatnata**, the "Temple of the Lord of the World." Inside, standing in the middle of a lotus-pond, there is a seven-tiered throne of stone bearing a gilded statue of Sanghyang Widhi Wasa, the Supreme God.

Adjoining the Jagatnata temple to the south is the **Bali Museum.** This was established by the Dutch colonial government in 1932 as an ethnographic museum, and displays archaeological finds, native handicrafts, dance-masks and paintings, as well as illustrating the main architectural styles of Balinese temples and palaces. It is well worth a visit, especially before starting a tour of the island.

The museum's central building is a replica of a palace in the East Balinese Karangasem style. In front of it stands a row of original stone sculptures of musicians, dating from the 16th century. Inside, finds from the Neolithic period are on display, as well as models showing

various initiation rites, including tooth-filing. The building next door (opposite the Kulkul Tower, with its huge drum) is a replica of the palace of Buleleng in northern Bali. It contains, among other things, valuable figures of the dragon-like Barong, carved Topeng dance-masks, old shadow-puppets (*wayang kulit*), traditonal *ikat* woven fabrics and an excellent collection of *kris* knives. The third museum pavilion shows the palace architecture of the Rajas of Tabanan (West Bali). It houses a collection of ivory carvings and Bronze Age finds from Gilimanuk.

One of Denpasar's busiest shopping streets is **Jalan Dr. Wahidin/Jalan Gajah Mada,** with the bustling vegetable and textile market of **Pasar Badung** and the large **Kumbasari Shopping Center** on the river Badung. Right beside the Kumbasari complex, the **Pasar Malam** (night market) opens in the late afternoon and is a favorite spot for anyone looking for a good and cheap evening meal. Other night markets worth visiting for local color and a complete range of Javanese and Balinese culinary specialties can be found on the east side of city, in the **Kereneng Bemo Terminal**, or the **Pekambingan Market** on **Jalan Diponegoro**, a major commercial thoroughfare.

Near the intersection of Jalan Dr. Wahidin and Jalan Dr. Sutomo you come to the oldest Hindu temple in the city, the 14th-century **Pura Maospahit**, dating from the early years of Javanese colonization. Its entrance, in the traditional *candi bentar* (split gate) form, is guarded by statues of the mythical bird Garuda and the wind-god Batara Bayu.

Another paradise for shoppers is the continuation of Jalan Dr. Sutomo, called **Jalan Thamrin** and dominated by the **Lokitari Shopping Center**. Not far from here, on Jalan Hasanuddin, stood the palace of the aristocratic Pemecutan family, which was destroyed during the Dutch invasion of 1906. It was later rebuilt and became the **Pemecutan Palace Hotel**, where today a *gamelan* orchestra in the lobby welcomes guests. Adjoining the hotel garden, the former palace temple, the **Pura Pemecutan**, has been faithfully reconstructed.

If you leave Puputan Square and walk eastwards along Jalan Surapati, you soon come to a side street called Jalan Kepundung. There you will find the Catholic church, **Gereja Katolik St Joseph,** whose interior decoration combines Christian iconography with Balinese art forms in a very unusual way. Apart from Catholics, Denpasar has a full range of Christian congregations, including Protestants (Jalan Debes), Seventh-Day Adventists (Jalan Surapati) and the adherents of the Pentecostal Church (Jalan Karna), ever ready to raise their voices in joyful song.

Returning to the main street, keep heading east and you will eventually come to Jalan Nusa Indah (formerly Jalan Bayusuta) and the **Werdi Budaya Art Center**, Denpasar's venue for festivals and exhibitions. Anyone looking for high-quality souvenirs will find paintings and woodcarvings, demonstrating a representative cross-section of Bali's artistic production, at the exhibition and sales center next door. A whole room is dedicated to Walter Spies, the German-born artist who made his home in Bali, with examples of his photography as well as reproductions of his paintings.

North of the Art Center is the district of **Kesiman**, the one place left which still gives an idea of Denpasar's erstwhile village atmosphere before the advent of reinforced concrete. Look for the old brick **Raja's Palace** with its handsomely ornamented ancestral temple, the **Pura Kesiman**.

The best of modern Balinese architecture is to be seen in the new government district in the southeastern suburb of **Renon**, bordered by Jalan Tantular and Jalan Niti Mandala. This is where the official residence of the Governor is located, together with various ministries, the Central Post Office, the Immigration Office, and the Tourist Office.

KUTA AND LEGIAN

People who bemoan the decline of Balinese culture and criticize the tourist invasion have only one good thing to say about Kuta: it can guarantee genuine and phenomenal blood-red sunsets. And since there are no seasons in the tropics, this wonderful free show takes place punctually every evening at six o'clock. But opinions are more divided about Kuta's wide, 3-mile (5 km) long beach. If you come here looking to spend your day in peace, you are out of luck – you will face a never-ending stream of mobile souvenir shops, boys selling cool drinks, girls selling sarongs and women offering you a massage. (Don't worry, Kuta is not like Thailand's Pattaya. You really do get a massage – nothing more!) The latter,

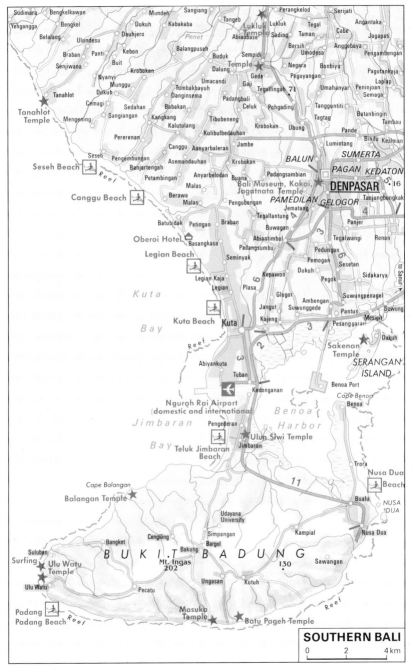

Sudimara · Bengkelkawan · Mundeh · Sangiang · Perangkelod · Serijati · Angantaka
Yehgangga · Bengkel · Dukuh · Kabakaba · Tangeb · Lukluk · Lukluk · Tegal · Cabe · Jagapati
Belalang · Ulundesu · Dauhjero · Abianbase · Sading · Taman · Anggebaya · Pengambengan
Braban · Kebon · Balangpuseh · Buduk · Sempidi · Bersih · Umodesa
Panti · Buit · Dalung · Temple · Negara · Bonbiyu · Pagutankaja
Senjiwana · Nyanyi · Krobokan · Gede · Peguyangan · Umahanyar · Peninjoan · Lapal
Munggu · Umacandi · Gaji · Tegallingah 71 · Semaga
Tanahlot · Dukuh · Tumbakbayuh · Padangbali · Pohgading · Tangguntiti · Batanbingin
Tanahlot · Cemagi · Sedahan · Babakan · Celuk · Tagtag · Tambau
Temple · Mengening · Sangiangan · Kangkang · Tibubeneng · Krobokan · Ubung · Pande · Bindu · Kesiman
Kalutulang · Kulibulbedauhan · Lumintang · SUMERTA
Pererenan · Canggu · Aanyarbaleran · Jambe · BALUN · PAGAN · KEDATON
Seseh Beach · Seseh · Pengembungan · Asemandauhan · Krobokan · Padangsambian · Bali Museum, Kokai, · DENPASAR · 5.16
Banjartengah · Buana · Jagatnata Temple · PAMEDILAN · GELOGOR · Tanjungbongkak
Canggu Beach · Petambingan · Anyarbelodan · Pengubengan · Jematang · 4
Malas · Berawa · Tegallantung · Buwagan · Panjer
Batubidak · Petingan · Braban · Abiantimbul · Tegalwangi · Renon
Malas · Padangsumbu · Pedungan
Oberoi Hotel · Basangkasa · Seminyak · Pemogan · Sesetan
Legian Beach · Dukuh · Pegok · Sidakarya
Legian Kaja · Kepawon · Glogor · Suwungpenagel
Legian · Plasa · Jangut · Ambengan · Pantus · Suwung
Kuta · Kuta Beach · Kuta · Kajeng · Suwunggede · Pesanggaran · Mesigit · Dukuh
Bay · 3
Abiyankuta · 2 · Sakenan · *SERANGAN*
Tuban · Temple · *ISLAND*
Kedonganan · Benoa Port
Ngurah Rai Airport · Cape Benoa · Benoa
(domestic and international) · *Benoa*
Jimbaran · Pengederan · *Harbor*
Bay · Teluk Jimbaran · Ulun Siwi Temple · Trora
Beach · Jimbaran · Nusa Dua Beach
Cape Balangan · Bualu · *NUSA DUA*
Balangan Temple · Nusa Dua
Udayana University · *BUKIT BADUNG* · Kampial
Bangket · Cengiling · Simpangan · Sawangon
Suluban · Bakung · Bargol
Surfing · Ulu Watu Temple · Mt. Ingas 202 · 130
Ulu Watu · Ungasan · Kutuh
Pecatu
Padang Padang Beach · Masuka Temple · Batu Pageh Temple

SOUTHERN BALI

0   2   4 km

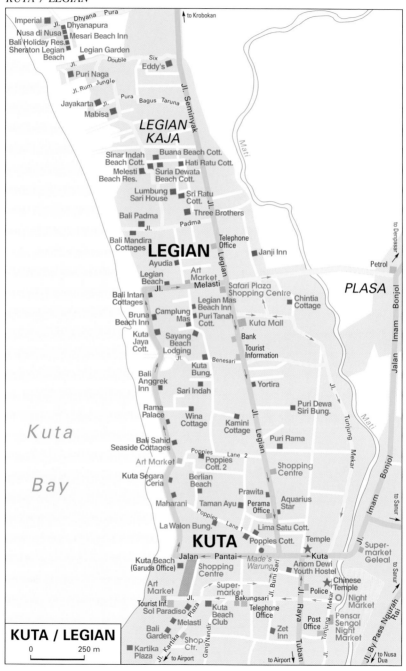

KUTA / LEGIAN

0   250 m

women with strong hands ready to knead tight muscles into submission, became so numerous in the 1980s that they were issued with a kind of licence-plate: their registration numbers are painted in bright red on their straw hats. Either you'll hate the whole beach scene or you'll find ways to enjoy it: for example, by employing "your own" *Ibu Massage* to knead you from head to toe for a discount price every morning. Later in the day, without having to interrupt the grilling process by standing up from your beach towel, you can feast on delicious fresh pineapple, or have an ice-cold beer is brought to you on a tray. Fancy a pair of those trendy flared pants that are all the rage in Legian? The whole boutique will come to you. Woodcarvings from Ubud, silver jewelry from Celuk – you can buy anything you want on the beach. The only thing in short supply is shade, but at least there's a big selection of straw hats. If you are blessed with a sense of humor, you can have a lot of fun with the people who come to sell you things, and pick up a few words of Bahasa Indonesia into the bargain.

The stars of Kuta Beach are the surfers – and no longer just the Australians: the local village kids have now mastered the art of riding the waves and are just as good, if not better. You find the best waves on a coral reef lying offshore, from March to July. If you are new to surfing but are willing to take your chances, you can rent a second-hand board from one of the water-sport shops in Kuta – but whether you actually manage to get a turn on one of the breakers is another matter, because there are always a lot of crafty old hands just waiting to get up on a really good wave.

And when you are in the sea, do not underestimate the strength of the undertow, which every year claims more victims than the sharks. That is why lifeguard stations have been set up on the beach. When you are swimming, stay near the beach, inside the reefs. Once you are out beyond the third wave, it gets pretty dangerous.

If you are looking for quiet and solitude on the beach, you only have to walk a little way further along the coast to the northwest. Beyond Legian, you've virtually left the noise and crowds behind, and once you've passed the Oberoi Hotel you're alone with the roar of the surf. The beaches by the villages of Canggu and Seseh are still untouched by tourism. In theory it would be possible to walk as far as the sea-temple of Tanahlot, a good 8 miles (13 km); but in practice you would have to cross several estuaries, which are fairly deep at high tide, and not everyone may want to try.

Travelers who visited Kuta in the early 1960s – usually backpackers on a low budget – found nothing there but a handful of fishermen's huts and farmsteads, which looked idyllic enough under the coconut palms, but were pretty impoverished. Only a few modest successors to the legendary Kuta Beach Hotel of the 1930s catered to beach-loving vacationers; apart from these, the nearest overnight accommodation was 6 miles (10 km) away in Denpasar. But the inhabitants of Kuta reacted quickly to the increasing demand and built simple *losmens* (basic but clean apartments, from the French *logement*) for the thousands of travelers who arrived to stay for longer periods in the 1970s – all on the overland quest for Paradise, which in those days was believed to lie somewhere between Afghanistan and the South Pacific. Today there are more than 300 simple *losmens* for visitors on a limited budget. In addition, there are something like 60 bungalow establishments in the middle price-range, and a good dozen luxury hotels, such as the Pertamina Cottages near the airport or the Oberoi Hotel north of Legian.

If you take an afternoon stroll down **Jalan Legian**, you may well get the feeling that the tourism boom carries within

itself the seeds of its own destruction. The 2-mile (3 km) long main street linking the once-separate villages of Kuta and Legian is jammed with smelly, honking *bemos,* taxis, rental cars and mopeds, through which death-defying cyclists weave their way. The fact that this is a one-way street does nothing to improve matters. On the other hand, Jalan Legian offers everything a vacationer's heart could desire: money-changers, car and motorcycle rental firms, travel agents offering "cremation tours," video shops, fashion boutiques, hand-woven ceremonial cloths from Sumbawa, batik bikinis from Denpasar, transparency-film kept cool in the fridge, "Australian Bars," "Swiss Restaurants," open-air discos and, last but not least, call-boys for lonely hearts. Along the back streets leading down to the beach are row upon row of *losmens.*

Crazy as this gold-rush mentality may

Above: On the beach at Kuta. Right: One of the legion beach peddlers.

seem, there is no getting away from the fact that it has made the citizens of Kuta a great deal more prosperous than the rest of the island. A large part of the capital invested comes from Kuta itself, and profits are immediately re-invested – in sharp contrast to the international luxury hotel centers in Sanur and Nusa Dua. On the debit side of this boom are theft, prostitution and drug-dealing; however, the police have got things reasonably under control – at least during the day. After dark the "Anglers" get to work, sophisticated thieves whose speciality is silently fishing your valuables out through the gratings over the windows.

The direct route to the beach takes you along **Jalan Pantai Kuta**, which gets hopelessly jammed around sunset. Here, people in search of the meaning of life, or those who think they've found it, meet at any time of day or night in **Made's Warung.** While other trendy spots in Kuta come and go almost weekly, Made's has remained for 20 years simply *the* place, an institution sacred to the international

banana-pancake brigade. Sitting over Australian jaffles, Javanese gado-gado, Italian capuccino, German apple strudel, or English gin-and-tonic, and watching the world go by along Jalan Pantai is the classic way to start or end the day. When Made's closes around midnight, "Kuta society" moves over to the Indian **New Goa** in Legian.

If you want to eat American-style in Kuta, don't despair: there's a Kentucky Fried Chicken outlet in the Gelael Supermarket on Jalan Imam Bonjol. For those with more adventurous palates, there's a wide range of Asian and international cuisine available; make sure not to miss out on the fresh seafood, from tuna to lobster.

The culinary arts of Indonesia are practiced every evening in the **Pasar Senggol Night Market** (near the Post Office), at prices welcome to any budget-conscious traveler. This is the right atmosphere in which to try Balinese *babi goreng*, Javanese *sate ayam* or Chinese *cap cay*. A more unexpected blend of Balinese,

Mexican, and Australian cuisine (the latter represented by fish and chips) is stylishly served up at the "established" **Poppies** restaurant on Poppies Lane. Famous throughout the island for its excellent Mexican tacos and enchiladas is **TJ's**, a little further down the same street, towards the beach. You can get a pizza right next door at **Fat Yogi**, while **Il Pirata** serves them 24 hours a day. Japanese secretaries on a few days' holiday buy their take-out snacks at **Takitate Bento** on Jalan Legian. An amazing variety of coffee is offered at **Benny's**, which is especially popular for brunch; try the *Kopi Bali,* a native product from the highland interior of the island. Beware of omelettes with ingredients described as "special" or "magic": these contain hallucinogenic mushrooms which have an effect similar to LSD.

From 10 pm onwards, disco fever takes over in Kuta and Legian. Old Bali hands collect at the **Gado-Gado** or the **Double Six** in the north of Legian, right on the beach.

67

A considerable number of up-market drop-outs from Europe and America have settled in and around Kuta. Many of them are involved in fashion design and provide inspiration for the astonishing variety of designs and fabrics on sale in the innumerable textile shops – from the open-air stalls on Jalan Pantai, where you have to haggle with skill and persistence, to the yuppie boutiques on Jalan Legian with their fixed prices. The most popular souvenirs include leather goods, bags and baskets woven in rattan, jewelry, paintings, wood-carvings, ceramics, and brand-new "antiques" from the neighboring islands of Lombok and Sumbawa.

BUKIT BADUNG

A narrow isthmus, edged with mangrove swamps, connects the peninsula of Bukit Badung to the mainland of Bali. In

Above: The entire southwest coast, including the Bukit Badung peninsula, is a surfers' paradise.

contrast to the well-irrigated and fertile rice-growing country around Denpasar, it is a dry, porous, riverless plateau; a lump of limestone rising 600 feet (200 m) out of the sea – the name Bukit simply means "hill." Only between October and April is there enough rainfall to support agriculture naturally; during the dry season, the inhabitants have to draw water from cisterns. The soil is poor; bushes and cactus are the main vegetation, and the roads are bordered by acacias and kapok trees. Until the last century the sparsely-populated peninsula, riddled with limestone caves, was reserved as a hunting-ground for the Rajas of Mengwi and Badung. On the west and south coasts, high cliffs drop dramatically to a rocky shore on which the great, long rollers of the Indian Ocean break continuously, attracting surfers from all over the world. At the southwest corner, perched spectacularly above a sheer, white chalk cliff, is the sea-temple of Ulu Watu, which is well worth a visit. The east coast has magnificent sand beaches, and it is here that the ambitious Nusa Dua hotel project took shape in the 1980s, almost seeming to grow out of the bare earth. This backward region, whose people once lived from fishing, salt-panning and plundering wrecked ships, has recently experienced a rapid transformation into a dream destination for international package tourists. Even some departments of Udayana University have been moved here as part of a long-term plan to urbanize what used to be the poorest area of Bali.

At the neck of the peninsula lies the fishing village of **Jimbaran**. The impressive catches landed every morning from large oceangoing boats on Jimbaran's western shore go straight to the kitchens of the big hotels in Sanur and Nusa Dua. The fine sand beach of **Teluk Jimbaran** (Jimbaran Bay) is nearly 3 miles (5 km) long; new hotels are under construction here which will open up the area for tourism. A long coral reef, submerged offshore, keeps all boats except for small *prahus* with brightly-colored sails out of the calm waters of the broad, crescent-shaped bay. The fishermen are happy to take paying passengers aboard.

Towards sunset, you should pay a visit to the attractive old village temple of **Pura Ulun Siwi,** which was built in the 17th century, under the Mengwi dynasty. It is maintained by rice-farmers and is the most important of the Subak shrines in Bali, dedicated to the rice-goddess Dewi Sri. Inside, you can see sacred dance masks of Barong and Rangda, as well as a soaring, eleven-tiered *tumpang meru* dedicated to Shiva.

The roads across the peninsula are still narrow, winding and full of potholes. Going south towards Ulu Watu, after the turn-off to the Udayan campus, motorcyclists can bear northwest at the village of **Bakung** and proceed along a rough road to the fishing village of **Cengiling**. From here, a short walk brings you to the cave-temple of **Pura Balangan**, on the shore of an isolated sandy bay. At the northern

end of this bay there is also a small Chinese temple, the **Pura Konco**.

From Bakung, a rutted path leads due south to a little sea-temple called **Pura Masuka,** standing high up on a breathtaking cliff. A little to the east of Bakung, in the village of **Ungasan**, another equally rutted path leads off to the cave temple of **Pura Batu Pageh**, in a cave at the foot of a high cliff.

Continuing on the road to Ulu Watu, you pass **Gunung Ingas** which, at 663 feet (202 m), is the highest point of land on the peninsula. The winding road runs westward through Pecatu and finally arrives at the **Pura Luhur Ulu Watu**, the "temple atop the high cliffs." *Nge luhur* can also be translated as "the attainment of *moksa*," "enlightenment"; for it is here that the 16th-century Hindu religious teacher and reformer Pedanda Bau Rauh, is said to have achieved the highest state of bliss through years of meditation. The temple is dedicated to the goddess of the sea, Dewi Danu, and the best time to visit it is when the sun is sinking into the ocean and the pale coral stone of the temple is bathed in a pink glow. The whole cliff, which drops a dizzying 660 feet (200 m) into the Indian Ocean, is worshipped as the goddess's ship of stone. The temple, which is one of the most important in Bali, is said to have been built in the 11th century by a Brahman named Kuturan, on the site of a pre-Hindu sacrificial altar. Ulu Watu is one of the nine "directional" temples which protect Bali from all sides, guarding the southwestern extremity of the island.

A flight of 70 steps leads up to a split *candi bentar* gate, decorated with the heads of demons. Its curving form is meant to represent the wings of the sacred bird Garuda, the mount of the god Vishnu. Behind it lies the temple forecourt (*jaba sisi*); from this, a covered doorway leads to the central courtyard. The Kori-Agung gate gives onto the Holy

of Holies (*jeroan*); its arched entrance is rather an anomaly on Bali. It is flanked by two stone statues of the elephant-headed god Ganesha, in the same dancing pose that his divine father, Shiva, adopts as *Nataraja* (King of the Dance). Positioned above the archway is a much-weathered Kala-Boma face. In the inner courtyard stands a three-tiered *tumpang meru* dedicated to Shiva, flanked by two limestone figures of watchmen armed with cudgels.

The simple, straw-roofed shrines are in themselves not particularly impressive, but the view over the cliffs and the sea is spectacular. On a clear day you can see as far as Cape Bantenan on Java, some 37 miles (60 km) distant. Located much closer are some excellent surfing beaches: a little more than a mile (2 km) away is **Suluban**, with restaurants and *losmens* on the beach; then comes **Pa-**

Right: The temple of Pura Luhur Ulu Watu perches high above the waves.

dang-Padang, then **Balangan**, further to the north.

NUSA DUA

At the northeast corner of the Bukit Badung peninsula a long, flat spit of land thrusts out into the Bay of Benoa. Its landward side is fringed with mangrove swamps, but the ocean side has a magnificent sandy beach. Until about ten years ago, fishing and harvesting coconuts were the main sources of income for the local population. The little port of **Tanjung Benoa**, at the end of the spit, was once inhabited mainly by Chinese merchants – a Chinese temple still bears witness to this – and by Buginese sailors, whose descendants still gather every Friday in a small mosque.

Then, in 1970, tourism experts from the World Bank set their sights on the Hindu village of Bualu and its deserted 2-mile (3 km) beach. Their vision, which in due course became reality, was the development of a luxury hotel complex for multinational investors, a mere 8 miles (13 km) from Ngurah Rai, Bali's international airport, and christened **Nusa Dua** (Two Islands). The first of these glitzy establishments, the **Buala Club Hotel**, opened its doors in 1979, doubling as a practical training ground for the neighboring college of hotel management. By 1992, seven more luxury hotels had been put up, providing thousands of beds for sun-seekers from all over the world who are prepared to spend freely to enjoy the priceless days of their vacation. Cynics describe Nusa Dua as a "beach ghetto," for this artificial paradise, with its elegantly landscaped gardens laid out beneath coconut palms, is fenced and guarded. By buying up large areas of land and fencing them off, the developers have carefully avoided the unsightly spread of *losmens* such as one sees in Kuta. Sports-minded visitors will find a wide range of activities on offer at Nusa

Dua, including tennis, riding, scuba-diving and snorkeling, parasailing, windsurfing and, of course, surfing. And anyone who misses the crowds can simply catch the hotel shuttle bus to Kuta.

SANUR

The blue lagoon of Sanur is protected from the ocean breakers by a coral reef. Its waters are therefore delightfully calm most of the time, and ideal for windsurfing or snorkelling – the vivid colors of the little fish that swim among the coral are quite breathtaking. However, at low tide the sharp edges of the coral can be a problem if you want to bathe. Ever-popular are snorkeling excursions along the reef, which is generally reached by means of the boats called *jukungs*. These are outriggers with brightly colored sails, in which the fisherman go out at night, equipped with kerosene lamps, to catch prawns; by day, you can find them at the landing-stage at the end of Jalan Hangtuah, near the Alit's Beach bungalows.

There are also boat-trips to Serangan, Lembongan and Nusa Penida.The more courageous can try parasailing, and get a birds-eye view of the 3-mile (5 km) long Sanur beach.

In contrast to the turbulent life of Kuta, Sanur is considerably quieter and more civilized – you won't find "Aussie pubs" here – and, furthermore, more expensive; it therefore tends to attract a slightly older crowd. Early risers are treated to a picturesque sight at about 6 am, when the sun rises over the island of Nusa Penida.

In the 1930s, Western artists and lotus-eaters "discovered" Sanur's sand beach, an island hideaway paradise under the palms. Among the first of these settlers were the Germans Walter Spies, a painter, and Vicki Baum, author of *A Tale from Bali*, and the American anthropologists Jane Belo (author of *A Trance in Bali*) and Margaret Mead. Mead was drawn to Sanur by her interest in the local Brahmans; for the Balinese hold this traditional pedanda community to be the home of the "Black Barong," whose dan-

over Bali, was converted into the **Museum Le Mayeur**. It can be found near the beach, south of the Diwangkara Hotel. The artist appears to have been more than a little fascinated by bare-breasted Balinese girls, and must have been happy to escape from the inhibitions of Europe: he married his favorite model, the talented native dancer, Ni Polok, who lived on until 1985.

In the 1960s the president of Indonesia, Sukarno, who was himself half-Balinese, decided to open up the island to tourism as a means of bringing in much-needed foreign currency. The necessary capital investment was provided by the Japanese as reparations for their occupation of the island during World War II. Thus it was that in 1966 Sanur saw the opening of the ten-storey Bali Beach Hotel, the first modern hotel on the island to meet international luxury standards. It had tennis courts, a bowling alley and a 6-hole golf course, and catered predominantly to Japanese visitors. The building's roof supports an elegant restaurant with panoramic views. Burned to the ground in 1993, the hotel reopened as the **Grand Bali Beach Hotel** in 1994.

Newer, pricier and more exclusive is the **Bali Hyatt**, member of the American luxury chain, situated further down the beach to the south. Its design is strongly influenced by Balinese architecture, even down to the swimming pool, which features a replica of the grotto of Goa Gajah. Furthermore, this efficiently-run hotel also has the most fashionable disco in Sanur, freuqented by an international clientele.

gerous magic power required constant appeasing. Nowadays the hearts and minds of local tradespeople are more readily influenced by the magic of a credit card produced from the pocket of a pair of batik bermuda shorts. Nonetheless, the temple of **Pura Dalem Kedewatan** in Sanur (near the Bali Beach Hotel), is frequently the scene of religious processions; and the local Brahmans, known far and wide for their knowledge of the *vedas* and in questions of offerings to the gods, are often sought out by devout Hindus with questions about religious or ceremonial matters. Unique to this village is a temple dance featuring the *kris,* performed only by women – and only on rare occasions.

Before World War II, the post-Impressionist Belgian artist Adrien Jean Le Mayeur set up a studio in Sanur. After his death, his house, including an extensive collection of antique sculpture from all

Another luxury establishment is the **Sanur Beach Hotel**, with well-tended gardens, several restaurants, an open-air stage on which classical Balinese dances are performed every evening, and a first-class buffet beside the pool. Owned by the Indonesian state airline, Garuda, it has more than 400 rooms and is located at the southern end of the beach.

Right: Outriggers waiting for the next trip out from the beach at Sanur.

Most of the hotels, restaurants and souvenir shops are colleted along **Jalan Tanjung Sari,** which runs parallel to the coast. As you might expect in a high-class beach resort, both quality and prices are noticeably higher than in Kuta. On the beach, at the end of Jalan Segara Ayu, the villagers of Sanur run the **Beach Market,** a cooperative venture selling handicrafts, and batik clothes, as well as beautifully painted paper kites – kite-flying is a favorite pastime among the boys of the village.

Expedition to Serangan

The little island of Serangan lies some 1 1/4 miles (2 km) off the southern end of Sanur beach. The shortest crossings are from **Mesigit** or **Suwung,** from where motorized *jukungs* take passengers over to the island. Resident here are about 2,000 people, most of them Moslems. The main village is **Dukuh,** in the north. The islanders' chief source of income is breeding sea turtles (*penyu*). Off the

beach at Dukuh, the turtles are fattened up in underwater bamboo cages. The meat from these creatures is appreciated both by the native Balinese and by the tourists; it's eaten either grilled on a skewer, as *sate*, or ground, as *lawar*. Unfortunately, the turtle farms of Serangan are unable to produce enough to meet the growing demand of the restaurant trade, so fishermen supplement their incomes by catching the animals in the wild, around the islands of eastern Indonesia; as a result, sea turtles are threatened with extinction. If you eat sea turtle in Bali, therefore, you are contributing to the disappearance of yet another species from our planet! Fewer and fewer specimens of this armor-plated reptile come up on the beach at Dukuh every year to lay their eggs; those who do are often caught and brought to the market at Denpasar,along with the eggs, which are themselves regarded as a culinary delicacy.

Another important source of income on the island are shells, which divers bring up from the sea bottom. The shells

NUSA PENIDA

0   4 km

are polished to a high gloss and touted by peddlers who know no restraint in the fervor of their pursuit of a quick rupiah.

Every year, for the festival of *Manis Kuningan*, thousands of visitors come to the **Sakenan Temple** at the northwestern tip of the island to make offerings to the rice-goddess Dewi Sri and pray for the fertility and prosperity of their families, fields and livestock. In a ceremonial procession of boats, tall Barong-Landung figures are carried over the waves in order to appease the sea-demons – for the Balinese people have a deep-rooted fear of the ocean and its unpredictable, capricious moods.

NUSA LEMBONGAN

Some 12 miles (20 km) from Sanur lies a group of three islands: Nusa Lembongan, Nusa Ceningan and Nusa Penida. ("Nusa" means island). Ceningan is the smallest; Penida is by far the largest; and Lembongan is, of the three, the most interesting for tourists. If you are going

from Sanur, the most comfortable (and safest) trip is in the passenger launch operated by Bali International Yacht Club. Charter motorboats also operate from Nusa Dua, or you can take a fishing boat from Kusamba or Padangbai, further up the coast near Klungkung.

If you charter a motorized *jukung* in Sanur – the larger the better – it will take about an hour and a half to reach Lembongan across the Straits of Badung (Selat Badung). You will be put ashore at **Jungut Batu.**

Measuring only 2 1/2 miles long and 1 1/2 wide (4 km by 2.5 km), the island can easily be explored in half a day. But few people do: the white coral sand of the beach near the landing-stage is much too inviting. Divers and snorkelers can spend many happy hours in the crystal-clear waters round the coral reef a little way offshore; and the channel between Lembongan and Ceningan is also known as a first-class area for snorkelling. You can rent a full spectrum of equipment, including surfboards. A favorite spot with surfers are the breakers over the coral-covered hulk of a wrecked ship.

There are already more then a dozen simple *losmens* in Jungut Batu, as well as some *warungs* and basic restaurants. Fish dishes are particularly good value; meat, by contrast, has to be brought in from the mainland.

The prominence of jaffles on local menus indicates that hungry Australian surfers make up the bulk of the guests. Yet even more important than tourism as a source of income for the 5,000 predominantly Hindu islanders is the cultivation of sea-grass (*siwi*), which is grown in plantations near the main village of the island, in exceptionally clear water, destined mainly for use in the cosmetic industry. However, the state tourism planners fear that the rather unpleasant smell will put off potential package tourists, and are asking the sea-grass growers, in all seriousness, to move to Sulawesi.

The interior of the low-lying island is dry and rocky, overgrown with cacti and scrub in which lizards scuttle about. Anyone seeking peace and quite will certainly find it on this island. There are neither mopeds nor *bemos*; the whole place is one big pedestrian zone, and no one will try to sell you wood-carvings, paintings or sarongs on the beach. One can only hope that the assembled demons of Bali will descend in force upon the investors and developers who propose to turn the place into another Kuta.

Offerings to the sea gods are made in a **sea temple**, hidden among the mangroves on the coast north of Jungut Batu.

It is only half-an-hour's walk to the old Hindu village of **Lembongan**, the island's "capital." As well as a few little temples built from bright coral stone and some small shops, this unspoiled village has a curiosity to offer: a subterranean labyrinth, which a villager built beneath his house, presumably to keep away demons. Called **Rumah Goa**, which means "House of Caves," it is open to visitors.

NUSA PENIDA

Mainland Balinese believe the island of Nusa Penida – 12 miles long and 7 1/2 miles wide (20 km by 12 km), and known simply as Nusa to the locals – to be the home of a malevolent and dangerous demon called Ratu Gede Macaling. Under the name of Jero Gede. he appears in *Barong-Landung* dances as a towering black figure, who, in the dualistic Balinese world order, functions as the opponent of all that is light, good and creative. The Rajas of Klungkung (the adminstrative region which includes Penida) used to banish miscreants to this island.

With its dry limestone landscape, where lack of water makes rice cultivation impossible, Nusa Penida has none of the charm one associates with Bali. The highest point on the island is **Bukit Mundi** (1,736 feet / 529 m).

There are easily accessible beaches in the north and northeast of the island, whereas the south coast is made up of sheer cliffs, rising to 650 feet (200 m). In the 1920s, Walter Spies discovered a rare species of greenish-colored bat here; while the island's avian denizens include the white cockatoo and Rothschild's mynah.

The fishing boats which ferry locals to and from Kusamba in eastern Bali will land you on the flat north coast near the little market town of **Toyapakeh**. There you will find a beautiful white sand beach, fringed with palms and looking across to the island of Lembongan; but the few tourists who stray here cause such a sensation among the village children that a quiet, undisturbed swim is out of the question.

Fishing and seaweed-growing are the main sources of income for the predominantly Moslem inhabitants of Nusa Penida's north coast. Along the main road, which runs along the beach leading east, and is trafficked by *bemos* every morning, lies the inhospitable dwelling of the

monster Jero Gede, the **Pura Dalem Pe-nataran Ped**. The island is too poor to afford a temple of any great splendor; the shrine to the dreaded black demon Me-caling stands in the middle of a pond overgrown with green slime. Every three years, pilgrims from all over Bali come to make offerings at the festival of *Usaba*.

To date, the only accommodation on Nusa Penida is to be found in the main town of the island, **Sampalan,** in the form of the simple, government-owned Pemda Bungalows. You will find them near the little harbor of **Mentigi**, which is always crowded with outriggers from Kusamba and Padangbai. In the market of Sampalan, you can buy the local spe-ciality, grilled tuna fish.

If you want to explore the interior of the island, you need to be able to speak a little Indonesian, since tourists are practi-cally unknown here. The condition of the roads is almost beyond belief to a West-

Above: Coconuts can only be harvested with the help of a rope.

76

erner. A few rickety *bemos* manage to struggle along them; mountain bikes are a more appropriate form of transport-ation. If you have rented a motorcycle in Bali, you can bring it over with you on the *jukung*; you won't regret it. Occasion-ally motorcycle taxis will offer to taxi you about as a pillion passenger, but this means taking your life into your own hands!

About 2 1/2 miles (4 km) southeast of Sampalan, a path branches off to the sacred cave of **Goa Karangsari**, where, needless to say, a demon is believed to live. To look at this gigantic stalactite cave, you have to be guided by one of the local children – but negotiate a fee in ad-vance! They will also provide powerful kerosene lamps, without which you will not be able to see the innumerable bats which flit about above you. In one branch of the extensive network of limestone ca-verns there is supposed to be a subter-ranean lake. Emerging into the sunlight again, you will find a beautiful beach of pale sand near the fishing village of **Su-wana**. There is another beach at **Karang**, further to the southeast, but this is rather inaccessible. You approach it through Pejukutan. Near Suwana stands a sea-temple: the **Pura Batu Medau.**

In the middle of the island, at **Batu-kandik,** there is a religious site, pres-umed to be pre-Hindu, with a primitive stone sculpture of a mother-goddess with enormous breasts; it lies 4 1/2 miles (7 km) east of the village of **Batumadeg,** which is occasionally served by *bemos*. From the village you can also take the road through **Sebuluh** to the wild and ro-mantic southwest coast, with its im-pressive 650 feet (200 m) high chalk cliffs. Fishermen have established lofty platforms, built into the sheer cliff-face, from where they put out their lines. The villagers living up on the limestone pla-teau have no immediate water-supply and have to make their way down hair-raising paths to collect fresh water from springs.

DENPASAR

If you can avoid Denpasar, you should do so. It is only worth visiting for the museums, or if you have official dealings with the authorities (for example, if you need to get a motorcycle license).

Accommodation

LUXURY: **Putri Bali Hotel**, Lot N-3, Nusa Dua, Denpasar, tel. 0361/771020.
MODERATE: **Natour Bali Hotel**, Jl. Veteran 3, tel. 225681, attractively furnished, from US$ 48. **Pemecutan Palace**, Jl. Thamrin 2, tel. 223491, historic setting, near terminus for *bemos* to Kuta; higher-priced accommodation also available; from Rps. 20,000.
BUDGET: **Adi Yasa**, Jl. Nakula 11, tel. 222679, once popular with backpackers, from Rps. 10,000; **Losmen Marhaen**, Jl. Diponegoro, Gang VII/4, tel. 223781, from Rps. 10,000.

Restaurants

The restaurant in the **Bali Hotel** has a good Rijstafel. Otherwise, you can find good-value Chinese restaurants on Jl. Gajah Mada, such as **Hongkong**, self-service; Indonesian *warungs* on Jl. Teuku Umar, such as **Simpang Enam**, Balinese, Indonesian, Chinese; and the same on Jl. Diponegoro, such as **Melati**, with Javanese specialties. The **Café Amsterdam**, on Jl. Diponegoro, specializes in baked goods, ice cream and steaks.

Museum

Bali Museum, Puputan Square, open daily except Mon 8 am-5 pm, Friday until 3:30 pm; (200 Rps.)

Shopping

Shops selling everything that Bali has to offer – and at rather lower prices than in Kuta – can be found on Jl. Gajah Mada and Jl. Kartini. Opening hours are usually 9 am - 1 pm and 5 pm - 8 pm.

Useful Addresses

The **Post Office** is in Renon, a little way from the city center, on Jl. Raja Puputan. Just around the corner on Jl. Panjaitan is the **Immigration Office**. One block to the north, on Jl. Raja Puputan, is the Balinese **Tourist Bureau**. There is a **telephone office** next to the Post Office in Renon, and another on Jl. Diponegoro south of Jl. Yos Sudarso. There is no **British Consulate**, but British matters are handled by the **Australian Consulate**, Jl. Raya Sanur 146, tel. 235092, fax 231990. This consulate also looks after citizens of New Zealand and Canada. The nearest **U.S. Consulate** is in the resort town of Sanur, Jl. Segara Ayu 5, tel. (0361) 288478. The **hospital (RSU)** which has emergency and intens-

ive-care units, is in the south of town, in Sanglah, on Jl. Kesehatan Selatan 1, tel. 227911.

KUTA / LEGIAN
Accommodation

In Kuta and Legian, there are more than 300 losmens and other basic accommodation from Rps. 10,000 (about £3.60 or US $ 5.90) upwards – as well as a number of attractive medium and luxury hotels. The rapid boom has admittedly also produced some rather charmless establishments. Anyone travelling on a limited budget should carefully check the hygiene (get them to show you the *mandi* or shower) and the location (close to beach and restaurants, but not to construction sites or the noisy main streets). With care, even a little money will get you comfortable and attractive lodgings.

Legian is a bit quieter than Kuta. The hotels in the center between the Kuta Beach Hotel and Legian Beach Hotel often have a view of the sea, but are separated from the beach by a road. Prices quoted are always for a double room.

LUXURY: **Bali Oberoi**, Jl. Kaya Ayu, Legian, P.O. Box 351 Denpasar, tel. 751061, fax 752791, on a quiet beach north of Legian, from US$ 150; **Kartika Plaza**, Jl. Kartika, Kuta, P.O. Box 84 Denpasar, tel. 751067, fax 752475, on the beach, from US$ 80; **Pertamina Cottages**, Kuta Beach, P.O. Box 121 Denpasar, tel. 751161 fax 752030, on the beach, close to the airport, from US$ 110.
MODERATE: **Bali Intan Cottages**, Jl. Melasti 1, Legian, P.O. Box 1002 Tuban 80361, tel. 751770, fax 751891, near the beach, from US$ 70; **Bruna Beach Inn**, P.O. Box 116 Denpasar, tel. 751565, fax 753201, near the beach, central location, from US$ 17; **Hotel Jayakarta**, Jl. Pura Bagus Taruna, Legian, P.O. Box 244 Denpasar, tel. 751433-6, fax 752074, on the beach, from US$ 75. **Kuta Cottages**, Jl. Bakungsari, P.O. Box 300 Denpasar, tel. 751101, near the beach, from US$ 22; **Legian Beach**, Jl. Melasti, Legian, P.O. Box 308 Denpasar, tel. 751365, on the beach, from US$ 82; **Nusa di Nusa**, Seminyak, P.O. Box 191 Denpasar, tel. 751414, fax 751746, north of Legian near the beach, very quiet location, from US$ 35; **Poppies Cottages**, Poppies Lane, P.O. Box 378 Denpasar, tel. 751059, in the middle of Kuta, with garden and swimming pool, from US$ 95.
BUDGET: **Anom Dewi Youth Hostel**, tel. 752292, on a side street in the middle of Kuta, from Rps. 10,000; **Baleka Beach Inn**, Legian Kaja, tel. 751931, north of Legian, with swimming-pool, from Rps. 20,000; **Berlian Inn**, Poppies Lane, Kuta, tel. 751501, central location, from Rps. 15,000; **Kempu Taman Ayu**, near Poppies Lane, Kuta, central, but fairly quiet, from Rps. 9,000; **La Walon Bungalows**, tel. 757234, Poppies Lane, Kuta, central, from

Rps. 55,000; **Three Brothers Bungalows**, Legian, tel. 751566, spacious, accommodation in various price categories, quiet, has long been a well-kept secret, from US$ 15.

Restaurants

New places are springing up all the time. The choice ranges from good, simple Asian dishes from the wok to Swiss *röschti*, French *nouvelle cuisine* and American fast food. Here are just a few examples in addition to those already mentioned in the section on Kuta:

If you are not breakfasting in your hotel, try **Za's Bakery** in Jl. Legian or the **Treehouse Restaurant** in Poppies Lane, both in Kuta; or, in Legian, **Warung Kopi**, which also serves Indian vegetarian food.

For a modest sum you can eat **Nasi Campur** in the *warung* of the same name on Jl. Raya Kuta.

Both beer and pepper steaks are reasonably priced at the **Blue Pub** on Jl.Legian, while **Yannies** is better known for the tame owl which flaps around than for its hamburgers. The fish and seafood are good at both branches of **Bali Indah**.

If you are not put off by the Australian atmosphere, **Waltzing Matilda** serves excellent shrimp. Also excellent is the Thai restaurant **Sawasdee**, on Jl. Pura Bagus Taruna. Their fish soup spiced with lemon-grass has brought tears to the eyes of many a strong man.

In fact, the whole Jl. Pura Bagus Taruna has become a culinary center catering to a wide range of palates. Homesick Europeans can enjoy excellent fare at the **Swiss Restaurant**. Very popular here, for its ambience as well as for its food, is the **Bamboo Palace Restaurant**.

Entertainment and Nightlife

Since the "in" bars change every week, and there's an unbelievable proliferation of bars, dives, and discos, one can only follow general guidelines when venturing out into the night. If you like noise, head for the loud discos and bars on Jl. Buni Sari and Jl. Legian. Those who prefer something quieter and more civilized should look in the side streets or seek out a quiet pub down near the beach.

Anyone who keeps her eyes open will notice that in Legian, particularly, the cultural and religious life of the Balinese continues apace, regardless of the "white noise" of the tourist crowds. In the banjar center, near the Warung Kopi, *gamelan* orchestras practice loudly and enthusiastically for festivals and ceremonies. There, you can also learn when the Barong is next going to attend to the spiritual purification of the town.

Shopping

In Kuta and Legian, you can find an incredible variety of goods on sale, from mass-produced items for the tourist market to individual specimens of beautiful craftsmanship. Locally, textiles are the main artisan products. In Kuta, there are several shops which only sell clothes in black and white. Increasingly, the really smart shops are moving to Legian. European designer goods are usually sold for their full, marked prices; everywhere else, bargaining is the order of the day.

If you want to have something made to order, it is essential to take a pattern or a piece of clothing to be copied. You should look carefully at how well the seams are done. Leather clothes can also be bought off the peg or made to measure. If you are having something made, you should order it at the beginning of your holiday, because alterations are often necessary. As you travel around the rest of Bali, it is a good idea to use Kuta prices as a standard of comparison. In other places everything should be rather cheaper, especially the average tourist souvenirs.

Useful Addresses

The **Post Office** is located on a little side street called Jl. Tujung Mekar, near the night market, in the southeast of Kuta. Public **telephone offices** in Kuta: on Jl. Bakung Sari, right beside the supermarket, or on Jl. Legian near the Mini restaurant; in Legian: Jl. Legian between Jl. Melasti and Jl. Padma. The **Tourist Office** is on Jl. Bakung Sari, east of Jl. Buni Sari, tel. 751419.

The office of **Garuda Airlines** is in the grounds of the Kuta Beach Hotel at the western end of Jl. Pantai Kuta, tel. 751179.

The **Swiss Consulate** is on Jl. Legian Kelod in Kuta, tel. and fax 751735.

Transportation

To get around Kuta/Legian or go elsewhere, you can hire a bemo or a taxi at any time of day at any intersection of Jl. Legian or on the beach road. (Negotiate the price in advance.) Sample price for a taxi-ride from the airport to the Oberoi Hotel: Rps. 15,000. *Bemos* operate regularly from the *bemo* station at the little roundabout on Jl. Pantai Kuta to Denpasar (Rps. 700) and to the airport. For other destinations, you have to change at Denpasar.

Denpasar is also the starting point for long-distance bus journeys, e.g. to Jakarta. From Jl. Legian in Kuta, the *Perama* bus company runs regular services to other destinations of interest to tourists. Examples: Airport Rps. 3,500; Ubud Rps. 6,000; Lovina Beach Rps. 12,000; Candi Dasa Rps. 7,500; Senggigi, on Lombok Rps. 17,000; Bangsal on Lombok, the harbor for Gili Air island, Rps. 20,000.

Rental Vehicles

Because there is so much competition between hire-firms, Kuta/Legian is the best place to rent jeeps, motorcycles, mopeds or bicycles. The general rule is: if you hire for a longer period, you can get a reduction on the daily rate.

Sample prices: jeep for one day, Rps. 42,000; for one week, Rps. 38,000 per day; for longer, Rps. 35,000 or less per day; equivalent prices for motorcycle Rps. 12,000, Rps. 10,000 and Rps. 8,000. Regular bicycles are around Rps. 3,000 per day. If you are hiring a motorcycle for a longish period, you should allow a few days to try it out, in order to sort out any mechanical problems. If you want to ride to Lombok on a motorcycle, make sure that your permit is valid for Lombok as well as Bali. If it is not, you will be relentlessly turned back at the ferry.

Gas (petrol) stations can be found on the road north out of Legian and on the road out of Kuta, heading for Sanur.

NUSA DUA
Accommodation

With one exception, all the hotels within the enclosed area of Nusa Dua are *LUXURY:* **Bali Sol**, P.O. Box 1048 Tuban, tel. 771510, from US$ 78. **Club Bualu**, P.O. Box 6 Nusa Dua, tel. 771310, from US$ 70. **Club Méditerranée**, P.O. Box 1 Nusa Dua, tel. 771520, from US$ 100. **Nusa Dua Beach**, P.O. Box 1028 Tuban, tel. 771210, fax 771229, from US$ 120.

MODERATE: **Lancun Guesthouse**, tel. 771983, from US$ 25.

Outside the area, in Tanjung Benoa, there are a few *losmens*. The cheapest is **Homestay Asa**, Jl. Pratama, tel. 772456, from Rps. 17,000.

Restaurants

Every hotel has its own restaurant. The outstanding ones are the **Benoa Harbor Restaurant** in the Club Bualu and the **Ulam** in the village of Bualu. If you want something simpler and cheaper, you have to go to Tanjung Benoa. Even the restaurants at the periphery of the hotel zone are relatively expensive by Balinese standards.

SANUR
Accommodation

LUXURY: **Bali Hyatt**, Jl. Tanjung Sari, P.O. Box 392 Denpasar, tel. 281234, very big hotel complex, but beautifully integrated in the landscape, double rooms from US$ 100.

Diwangkara Beach, Jl. Raya Sanur, P.O. Box 120 Denpasar, tel. 288577, somewhat hidden beside the sea, from US$ 55.

Sanur Beach, Jl. Semawang, P.O. Box 279 Denpasar, tel. 288011, fax 287566, from US$ 135.

MODERATE: **Alit's Beach Bungalows**, Jl. Hang Tuah 41 Pantai Sanur, P.O. Box 102 Denpasar, tel. 288567, close to the beach, from US$ 44.

Gazebo Cottages, Jl. Tanjung Sari, P.O. Box 134 Denpasar, tel. 288300, has a somewhat faded charm, on the sea, from US$ 35.

Santrian Beach Resort, Jl. Semawang, P.O. Box 55 Denpasar, tel. 288009, fax 288185, two pools, from US$ 70; **Sindhu Beach**, Jl. Pantai Sindhu, P.O. Box 181 Denpasar, tel. 288441, on the sea, from US$ 40.

Swastika Bungalows, Jl. Batujimbar, tel. 288693, beautiful garden, two pools, but not right on the sea, from US$ 30.

BUDGET: **Abian Srama**, Jl. Bypass, tel. 288792, from US$ 15.

Three hotels on the far side of the main through road, inland on Jl. Segara offer the cheapest accommodation: **Rani** (from Rps. 20,000), **Taman Sari** (from Rps. 20,000), and **Sanur Indah** (from Rps. 20,000).

Restaurants

All the big hotels have restaurants with correspondingly high prices. For homesick Europeans, there is Italian cuisine in the **Trattoria da Marco** and Swiss food (what else?) in the **Swiss Restaurant**. If you like fish, **Lenny's** and the **Kulkul Restaurant** are to be recommended. There are two East Asian restaurants on Jl. Danau Tamblingan: the **New Seoul Korean Restaurant** and the **Japanese Restaurant**.

If your stomach has got used to local food, the best and also cheapest meals can be had at a food-stall on the jetty where the boats leave for Lembongan, or in the inconspicuous little **Wayan's Warung** at the intersection of Jl. Tanjung Sari and Jl. Pantai Karang.

Useful Addresses

Post Office, Jl. Segara, inland. In the Bali Beach hotel complex, you will find offices of the following **airlines**: Cathay Pacific, Continental, Garuda, KLM, Malaysian Airlines, Qantas, Singapore Airlines and Thai Airways.

The **United States Consulate** is at Jl. Segara Ayu 5, tel. 280228, fax 287760.

Museum

North of the Bali Beach Hotel, the **Museum Le Mayeur** is open daily except Mondays from 8 am-2 pm, on Fridays only until 11 am, and on Saturdays only until 12 noon. Entrance: Rps. 1,000. The museum displays mainly paintings by the Belgian artist Adrien Jean Le Mayeur.

CULTURE AND KITSCH
IN BALI'S HOLY LAND

BADUNG

TABANAN

TANAHLOT

GIANYAR

UBUD

BANGLI

Central Bali is the cultural heartland of this devoutly Hindu island. Here, away from the main roads, you will find ancient temples, picturesque rice terraces, and villages which still nurture a peasant way of life. The rice goddess Dewi Sri has shown favor to the people of central Bali; there are up to three rice harvests a year. There's plenty of water for irrigation; countless streams run down from the volcanic massifs of Batur, Catur and Batukau, cutting deep valleys in the rich red loam as they flow toward the sea. The course of these rivers also dictates the pattern of the roads: building bridges is expensive, and so cross-country connecting routes are rare. Administratively speaking, central Bali is made up of the districts or "regencies" of Badung and Tabanan in the west, and Gianyar and Bangli to the east.

BADUNG

About 12 miles (20 km) north of Denpasar, on the road to Singaraja, stands the residence of the once-powerful Raja of Mengwi, whose empire declined at the end of the 19th century. On the way to

Previous pages: At work in the terraced rice paddies. Left: Returning from the temple.

Mengwi, you'll first pass through the village of **Ubung**, famous for its potters. The busy main road, which, as far as Kapal, also carries heavy truck traffic heading for Java, soon reaches **Sempidi**, a village with three beautifully decorated temples, Pura Desa, Pura Dalem and Pura Puseh. **Lukluk,** the next village on this stretch, is proud of its Pura Dalem temple, which has brightly painted reliefs depicting scenes from the world of farmers and craftsmen.

A further 10 miles (16 km) on is the village of **Kapal,** which is in fact famous for producing traditional clay figures and stone sculpture – but figures of the Hindu gods are also cast in cement and painted with gaudy acrylic lacquer to produce Bali's answer to the garden gnome. There is a big demand for new religious statuary, since the damp, warm tropical climate has weathered many ancient figures almost beyond recognition. All over the island, temples are being restored and their courtyards and gardens beautified with Garudas, Rangdas and demons from Kapal. Alongside this, there's quite a market for more prosaic ceramic products, such as drainpipes and toilet bowls.

The **Pura Puseh** at Kapal does have some interesting reliefs with scenes from the *Ramayana*, but the real architectural

83

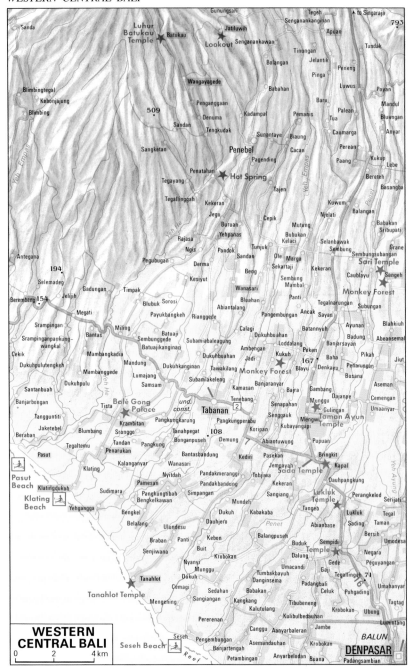

WESTERN
CENTRAL BALI
0   2   4 km

jewel is to be found a few hundred yards south of the village's main street (about 15 minutes on foot): this is the splendid **Pura Sada,** the ancestral and state temple of the Rajas of Mengwi. Probably built in the 14th century, its entrance is guarded by an ancient, spreading banyan tree, whose thick roots conceal a stone throne for the demons of the underworld. In the walled forecourt there are two *bales* for the preparation of sacrificial offerings and for meetings. A covered gateway leads to the *jeroan* or inner temple courtyard. This is dominated by an eleven-tiered, brick-built *candi* (also called a *prasada*), which was restored in 1949 and hearkens back to the East Javanese Majapahit style. It represents the mountain of the gods, which is held to be the seat of Shiva and was the ritual center of the Mengwi rajadom – its phallic shape was meant to represent the vitality and procreative force of the deified raja. While the first of the roofs (the *tumpang*) is decorated with Kala-Boma heads, the mighty base of the temple tower is adorned on all four sides and corners with the directional gods or *Nawa Sanga*, which the Hindus of Bali adopted from Indian Mahayana Buddhism.

There are a remarkable number of stone thrones in the *jeroan*, 57 of them in all. The **Mekel Masatia**, a group of three larger thrones (on the right as you enter), appear to be a reminder of the Hindu custom of widow-burning (*sati*), which as recently as the beginning of this century was finally banned by the Dutch. According to another legend the three large thrones are dedicated to the leaders of 54 servants who are said to have accompanied the ashes of an East Javanese raja to Bali, long, long ago.

Mengwi

The village of Mengwi, once the center of power in the region, can still be proud to possess one of the most beautiful temples in Bali, the **Pura Taman Ayun**. If you want to enjoy it in peace, you must get up early (accommodation is available in Mengwi at the Homestay of I Ketut Arya); after 10 am it is overrun with coachloads of tourists. *Taman ayun* means "floating garden," which describes the place very accurately: built around 1740, the royal temple of the Mengwi rajas, who were members of the Ksatriya caste, stands on an island surrounded by still water, blanketed with lotus blossoms, that is more like a small pond than a stream. Its banks are verdant with flowering trees, including frangipani, mangosteen, rambutan and durian. The temple's inner courtyard, or *jeroan*, is enclosed by another, smaller moat.

The whole complex reflects the Hindu concept of the world held by the powerful 18th-century Mengwi rulers: the orientation is northwards, in the *kaja* direction of the mountains, the volcanoes and the sacred lake of Bratan, whose waters feed the rivers Sungi and Petan. The corresponding sea-temple in the south of Bali is the Ulun Siwi on the isthmus leading to the peninsula of Bukit Badung, south of Denpasar; it wards off sea demons. Between mountains and sea, in the Pura Taman Ayun, the rajas of Mengwi, supported by the *pedandas* with their vedic wisdom, kept the cosmic powers of creation and destruction in harmonious equilibrium through sacrificial ceremonies. But this fine balance was disturbed when, in 1891, the rival rajadoms of Klungkung, Badung, Tabanan and Bangli attacked Mengwi, defeated it, and proceeded to divide up the territory which they had coveted for its fertile rice paddies, the rich coffee plantations in the northwest, and not least for its lucrative trade in opium. Yet the inhabitants of this region still preserve a sense of identity which has its origins in the great days of the Mengwi raj.

Industrious women purvey fruit and lemonade in *warungs* at the entrance to the

causeway which leads over the water to the temple island. In the first courtyard there is a large open-sided hall with a tiered roof, which is used for meetings and dance performances. A flight of seven steps leads up to a *candi bentar* gate through which one reaches the second courtyard. In it stands a tall *kulkul* (bell tower) which you are allowed to climb in order to get a view of the attractive, terraced temple grounds.

Another staircase brings you to the slightly elevated *jeroan*, or Holy of Holies, first taking you through a gateway reminiscent of south Indian temple towers and then over a small bridge across the inner moat. On the west (left) side of the courtyard are several *bales*; in the middle a stone lotus-throne for the trinity of gods, Brahma, Vishnu and Shiva; and on the east side a row of pagoda-like *merus*. The three *merus* of dif-

ferent heights standing diagonally behind the *padmasana* (lotus-throne) are said to be dedicated to the mountain deities; a nine-tiered *meru* is for the "Lord of Lake Bratan," an eleven-tiered one for the "Lord of Agung," and another nine-tiered one next to it for the "Lord of Batur." Finally, by the end wall of the *jeroan* stands a *meru* with eleven straw-thatched roofs, dedicated to the "Lord of Mount Batukau." In the northeast corner the rice-goddess Dewi Sri – here called Ulun Siwi – has her own eleven-tiered *meru*.

The wooden wall of the **Bale Murdha**, the meeting hall of the village elders to the right of the gate, has recently been decorated with a colorful painting. But much older are the reliefs on the base of the **Bale Pawedaan** (the priests' pavilion) in the center of the west wall: these portray a scene from the *Ramayana*, in which nymphs attempt to distract Prince Arjuna from his meditation.

After visiting the temple you can be taken on a little ferry, pulled by ropes, across the river to the delightful **Man-**

Above: A pause near the Pura Taman Ayun in Mengwi. Right: Plinth decoration in the holy of holies of the Pura Taman Ayun.

dala Wisata Garden Restaurant on the west bank. The Indonesian and Chinese specialities on the menu are not cheap, but they are good.

Sangeh

Seven and a half miles (12 km) northeast of Mengwi lies the famous, not to say notorious, **Monkey Forest of Sangeh.** A visit to the **Bukit Sari temple**, founded in the 17th century by a raja of the Mengwi dynasty, can be an unforgettable experience: it is surrounded by a hedge of nutmeg trees (*pala*), which are very rare on Bali, and provide a home for three tribes of monkeys. These descendants of Hanuman, the monkey-god who, in the *Ramayana* epic, defeated the demon Ravan in Sri Lanka, are regrettably lacking in all sense of propriety. They have no inhibitions about attacking unsuspecting tourists, grabbing their hats or glasses, even handbags and cameras, and scampering up into the highest branches with their loot. It is pointless trying to fight back, but do not despair: just as a mouse is tempted by cheese, these sacred monkeys can be lured down with peanuts and bananas. When these greedy sons of Hanuman grab for the food with both hands, they drop their booty – the numerous locals who sell you the nuts obviously do pretty well from their partnership with the monkeys.

Once you are through this "Thieves' Alley," nothing more stands between you and the temple. Its pride is a large stone statue of Garuda. This creature, half-bird, half-man, is the steed of Vishnu; in Hindu mythology he is the opponent of the *Nagas*, the serpent-gods who represent the element of water.

Marga

In Marga, just 6 miles (10 km) north of Mengwi, there is a **memorial** to the freedom-fighters who, in November, 1946,

met a martyr's death when hopelessly outnumbered in a final battle against Dutch colonial troops. The 94 small *stupas*, looked after by a Buddhist monk, recall the sacrifice made by these Balinese, among whom were Christians and Moslems as well as Hindus. The Dutch seem to have operated under a strange moral double standard; after their own country had finally been freed from the shackles of Nazi occupation, they proceeded to resort to military force in reoccupying their former Indonesian colonies once the Japanese had withdrawn. Not until the U.S.A. threatened to suspend economic aid for rebuilding efforts in their war-ravaged mother country did the Dutch bring their colonial campaign in Indonesia to an end. The airport at Denpasar is named after I Gusti Ngurah Rai, who led the Balinese guerillas and was among those who died at Marga.

Three miles (5 km) south of Marga is the village of **Belayu**, where you can watch women weaving precious ceremonial shawls (*songket*).

TABANAN

Tabanan may be only a small town, but it is the capital of the regency, or administrative district, of the same name. The last raja of the prosperous state of Tabanan, which was abolished by the Dutch in 1906, had his residence in the **Puri Tabanan**. This was built in the 17th century by descendants of the East Javanese nobility who had come to Bali in the 14th century with the army of Gajah Mada. Hence the town's long artistic and artisan tradition. Classical literature is highly respected and kept alive: groups regularly meet to recite its texts, and there are even classical poetry competitions.

The famous dancer I Ketut Marya ("Mario," who died in 1968), received his dance training in Tabanan around the beginning of this century and later went on to create new dances such as the *Ke-*

Above: Chinese porcelain plates adorn the Raja's Palace in Krambitan. Right: The sea-temple at Tanahlot.

byar Duduk and the *Trompong*. Walter Spies photographed Marya in the 1930s, and immortalized him in the book *Dance and Drama in Bali,* which Spies wrote together with the Dutch writer Beryl de Zoete, and which was published in England in 1938. The town hall is named **Gedong Marya** in honor of this gifted dancer and teacher.

In the painter and ceramicist Kay It (who died in 1977), Tabanan produced the most important impressionist artist in Indonesia. His paintings are displayed in the museum in Ubud, and the gardens of the Bali Hyatt hotel in Sanur are adorned with his sculptures.

But even artists have to eat – rice. The **Subak Museum** on the west side of Tabanan presents graphic displays explaining the complex organization of the irrigation associations of Balinese rice-growers, as well as the different stages of rice cultivation (*sawah*), and the implements the farmers use. There is even a model kitchen with traditional Balinese utensils from the pre-microwave era.

Krambitan

West of Tabanan lies the artists' village of Krambitan, whose name is thought to be derived from *karawitan,* meaning "fine arts." Painting, music and dance are all living traditions here, as is wood-carving; and the neighboring village of **Penarukan** is well known for its carvings in the soft volcanic stone. The painters of Krambitan work in the time-honored *Wayang* style, portraying the figures so familiar from shadow-puppet plays in silhouette, in the natural colors of red, black and ocher.

The signature dance style of Krambitan is called *Tektekan*, a kind of processional dance of exorcism in which the performers carry large cow-bells, rattles and bamboo drums through the village. You can arrange to see it performed in the **Bale Gong,** the main hall of the old

royal palace of **Puri Anyar**, richly decorated with gilded wood-carvings and Chinese ceramics. This former feudal seat, dating from the 17th century, still belongs to the seventh generation of a branch of the Tabanan dynasty, and these descendants of the rajas now run it as a hotel. You can spend the night in one of its elegant rooms, and pretend you are a Balinese aristocrat, surrounded by valuable paintings, sculpture and porcelain.

Less than 4 miles (6 km) southwest of Krambitan, the black sand beach of **Pasut** invites you to swim in the powerful surf. And **Klating beach** is also within reach, 3 miles (5 km) to the south.

TANAHLOT

One of the most famous buildings in the Tabanan regency, if not in the whole of Bali, is the **sea-temple of Tanahlot.** Photographers have a virtual responsibility to visit at sunset, when the silhouette of the temple is etched in sharp detail against the glowing red of the eve-

ning sky. Japanese camera and film manufacturers should actually erect a shrine of thanksgiving to the gods of the sea at this picturesque temple on its rocky island – scarcely another monument in southeast Asia can claim to have been more often documented on film. Alas, it is not a place to come for quiet meditation; endless soft-drink and souvenir shops, and enterprising street vendors line the 300-yard path from the car-park to the sea – you'll be ignored only by the black-and-yellow striped snakes, apparently harmless, which doze in holes in the cliffs above the high-water mark.

When the tide ebbs, enabling tourists to walk across to the island of Tanahlot (meaning "land in the water"), the snakes also slither over to the temple, where they are worshipped as virtually sacred messengers of the serpent- and water-god Basuki, who is "Lord of the Temple" of Tanahlot. It is to him that the Hindus of Bali make offerings in the tall, five-tiered pagoda shrine, which is officially dedicated to the supreme trinity of Shiva, Brahma

and Vishnu. There is also a three-tiered *meru* dedicated to the Javanese yogi and religious reformer Nirartha (also called Pendanda Bau Rauh), who may have founded Tanahlot in the 16th century. Next to this merus, a sacrificial column (*paibon*) and two *bales*, for the preparation of offerings, vie for space on this small, rocky island, pounded by surf.

On the way back to the Tabanan-Denpasar road, you can detour over to **Pamesan** (Pejaten), near Nyitdah, and admire the skilled potters of the village, who also produce remarkable glazed ceramics in the Chinese style.

A little further north, in **Kediri**, the big livestock market (*pasar hewan*) is worth a visit: there are black pot-bellied pigs, cattle, ducks and hens galore – the latter often tied together by the legs in handy bundles of a dozen at a time, much to the horror of western animal-lovers.

Above: Moss-covered temple figures in the Pura Luhur Batukau. Right: Carrying loads calls for a level head – in every sense.

Pura Luhur and Gunung Batukau

If you hear the call of the mountains, it is not far to Gunung Batukau, the "Coconut-Shell Mountain," an extinct volcano which rises to 7,465 feet (2,276 m). At its foot lies the Pura Luhur, the ancestral temple of the Tabanan dynasty. This is one of the nine directional temples of Bali, and faces west. From Tabanan you drive northwards past lush green rice-paddies as far as **Wanasari** and then branch off in a northwesterly direction to **Yehpanas**. The place-name means "hot water," and with good reason: the sulphur springs are extremely hot, and anyone who immerses herself for more than ten minutes runs the risk of collapsing.

The little road continues northward through thickly wooded volcanic uplands, dotted with fruit plantations. In **Wangayagede**, the last village before the paved road gives way to dirt, ambitious climbers can hire an expert local guide to accompany them to the summit of Gunung Batukau.

For mere sightseers, the objective is soon reached: the **Pura Luhur Batakau** stands at a height of 2,300 feet (700 m) in a clearing on the edge of the seemingly impenetrable tropical rain-forest. The site is not particularly large; the largest shrine is a seven-tiered pagoda dedicated to Di Made, a raja who ruled over Bali from Gelgel, in the south of the island, in the second half of the 17th century. The rajas of Tabanan worshipped their ancestors in a three-tiered *meru*. On a miniature island in a small pond nearby there are two shrines, one dedicated to the water deity of Lake Tamblingan, and the other to the "Lord of Batukau."

The route up to the summit of Batukau is steep and slippery; you should allow six hours for the climb. Those interested in botany will find tree-ferns and thorn-palms in their primeval forest setting, a sight all too rare in densely-populated Bali. Of course, there's no cross atop this overgrown summit, but there is an ancient, moss-covered stone throne for Shiva in his guise as Mahadewa, great god and ruler of the world. The descent is pretty rapid – sometimes too rapid when it starts to rain and the earth path is transformed into a veritable mudslide.

One of the finest panoramic views in Bali can be enjoyed from **Jatiluwih**, a little rice-growing village at an altitude of 2,300 feet (700 m). There are already plans to build *losmens* here. Jatiluwih is situated on a small, winding road which starts in Wangayagede and ends at Apuan, on the road from Tabanan to Bedugul (Lake Bratan).

GIANYAR

The Gianyar regency, which reaches from Batubulan in the west to Tegalbesar in the east, and Punggang in the north, is home to the most famous of Bali's artists' and artisans' villages. The fertile agricultural land produces an abundance of rice, sweet potatoes (*ubi*), soy beans, coconuts (*kelapa*), tobacco and vanilla; and freshwater fish are bred and housed in its ponds. At higher altitudes, in the area

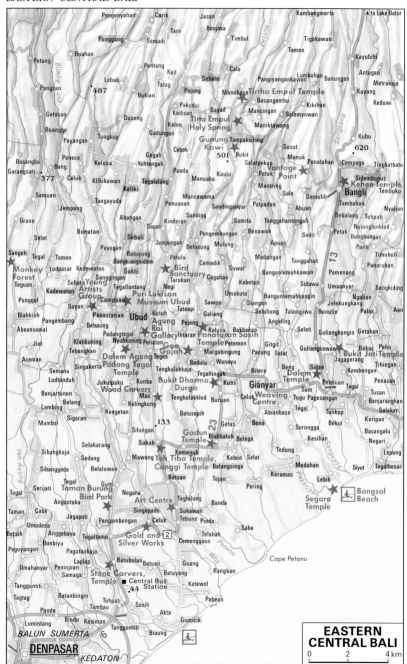

EASTERN
CENTRAL BALI

0   2   4km

around Taro, Bali's best coffee (*kopi*) is harvested.

Gianyar offers so many attractions that the selection of destinations must be left to individual preference. But the one "must" for visitors is the district around Ubud, the cultural and artistic focal point of the island, where hundreds of painters, wood-carvers dancers and musicians live and work.

Batubulan

Every morning at 10 am there is a rush-hour in Batubulan, a few miles northeast of Denpasar: it's *Barong* time! Three dance groups make a living in Batubulan by performing traditional trance dances. Audiences are always fascinated by these dance-dramas, performed in front of a temple backdrop, and representing the eternal struggle between Good and Evil. Good is represented by the Barong, half-serpent, half-dragon, and Evil by the wicked witch Rangda, with her sharp fangs and overlong finger-nails. The cast of characters also includes charming pricesses with flowers in their hair and dressed in magnificent brocade gowns; bold princes and wild boars; mischievous monkeys and priests versed in magic; and finally courageous warriors in black-and-white checked sarongs, who fall under the curse of the Evil One and then – in the climax of the drama – turn their bewitched *krises* against themselves, all to the accompaniment of melodious *gamelan* music. In the end the Barong intervenes and drives away the evil sorceress Rangda, thus restoring equilibrium to the cosmos.

In addition to this, Batubulan is known – as is the neighboring village of **Tegal-tamu** – for carvings made from the volcanic tufa stone, which are on sale in souvenir shops all along the main street. There is even a lovely sand beach only some 2 1/2 miles (4 km) away, at **Gumicik**.

Celuk

Have you got your credit card at the ready and your pockets full of dollars? If so, then there is nothing to stop you paying a visit to the gold- and silversmiths' center at Celuk. Hard currencies are preferred; price-tags on the expensive items lead one to believe that the prices are fixed – and evidence of the fact that many customers pay them without bargaining can be seen in the stately villas of the shop owners along the well-paved road. It is more interesting to wander round the back streets and watch the smiths at work with their precious metals in little workshops; and here, the rings, necklaces, brooches and earrings are much cheaper. A walk of just 50 yards can mean a difference in price of as much as 300 percent! The silversmiths work not only on traditional models, in the so-called "Raja style," but also from drawings by western designers – quite a number of ex-hippies are now active in the international jewelry trade.

In the neighboring village of **Singa-padu**, the bird park **Taman Burung**, extensive (5 acres/2.5 ha) and well-tended, is home to more than 1,000 exotic birds from Asia, New Guinea, Australia, and Africa, including the rare *komodo waran*.

Sukawati

The name of the busy market town of Sukawati, east of Celuk, is said to be derived from *sukahati,* which means something like "my heart likes it" – apparently a recollection of the magnificent temples and palaces that a powerful raja named Agung Anom is supposed to have built here in the East Javanese Majapahit style. Sadly, the earthquake of 1917 removed every trace of them.

The **Pura Penataran Agung** in the center of the town was rebuilt; and is still today a place of pilgrimage for the noble families of the district.

There are two rather curious stone statues of Dutchmen in tropical helmets, sitting on elephants and guarding the *candi bentar* gate of the temple of **Pura Pelinggih Sunya Loka.**

Famous throughout Bali are the Dalangs of Sukawati, who for generations have cultivated the art of puppet-making. They use cow-hide to make the figures for shadow-puppet plays, or *wayang kulit*, and often perform the plays as well. The products of the umbrella-makers (*tukang prada*) are still much in demand – less to keep off the rain than for processions and temple decorations.

Almost opposite the big fruit and vegetable market, which is held every morning, stands the **Art Center** (*pasar seni*). Here you can buy every imaginable kind of Balinese art and handicraft, from wood-carving to textiles and paintings. Many of the customers are wholesalers who resell the goods in beach resorts.

Above: Wood-carvers at work. Right: Garuda figures in the Pura Luhur Batukan.

Batuan

Over the years, Sukawati has grown together with its neighboring village to the north, Batuan, which has produced many important painters. An inscription dating from 1022 AD was found in Batuan's **Pura Desa** temple. This, and the fact that many village families belong to the legendary Buddhist clan of Griya Agung, are strong indications that Batuan may be one of the oldest centers of culture in Bali. It is the only place where the *Gambuh* is danced. Local wood-carvers make intricate masks for the *Wayang Topeng* (mask-dance) and the *Wayang Wong* (dance-theater), both of which are performed in the village.

In the 1930s, the native artists I Ngendon and I Patera were the first to start drawing with ink on paper, and thus to work exclusively in black and white. Around that time, under the influence of Walter Spies and Rudolf Bonnet, another new style emerged from the traditional Batuan school of painting: as well as the

94

classical religious themes, artists began drawing very detailed scenes from everyday life, depicting figures not in the traditional *wayang* style, in silhouette, but in anatomically correct perspective. Today, local painters portraying Balinese life go so far as to show bikini-clad girls on surfboards and tourists stalking through the village, camera at the ready; you can see this in, for example, the work of I Made Budi, displayed in the museums of Ubud and Denpasar. Copies of his museum pictures hang in the numerous picture-galleries along the main street.

About 1 1/4 miles (2 km) further north, near **Sakah**, you can go on walks through the rice fields and come upon beautifully situated and seldom-visited little temples: the **Pura Canggi** and the **Pura Yeh Tiba**, both dating from the 14th century. (Ask the way!)

Mas

Before leaving Sakah and heading eastwards to Blahbatu, it is worth detouring1 1/4 miles (2 km) north to the woodcarvers' village of Mas (meaning "Gold"), where the upper class can trace their ancestry back to one of the holiest clans of Bali: it was founded in the 15th century by no less a personage than the important Eastern Javan priest of Shiva, Nirartha (Pedanda Bau Rauh, see p. 90). The marriage of this Sanskrit scholar to a princess from Mas produced the founders of the four most important Brahman clans of Bali. That is why there is scarcely another village with so many *Ida Bagus* (members of the highest caste) among its inhabitants.

The temple of **Pura Taman Pule**, "temple with a magnificent garden," with its elaborately carved gates, is said to have been built on the site of Nirartha's dwelling. The senior pedande here is the keeper of the tantric flintstone (*vajra*) that belonged to the famous Javanese yogi.

Mas has produced some gifted woodcarvers, including such important artists as Ida Bagus Nyana, Ida Bagus Tilem and Ida Bagus Taman. Among the excellent mask-carvers are Ida Bagus Ambara and Ida Bagus Gelodog. Many of these master craftsmen draw their inspiration from the natural shapes of the tree roots from which they create people, animals and demons.

Whereas earlier Brahman artists devoted themselves exclusively to carving sacred works of art for temples and palaces, the enormous demand from tourists and exporters has called for new motifs, such as, for example, the brightly painted "wooden fruit." These are worked in tropical hardwoods like teak, ebony and jack-fruit; the most costly items are those carved in sandal-wood, since this has to be imported from other islands. The shops lining the main street are often very stylishly designed and stocked with high-priced wood-carvings (*topeng* masks, statues of gods, animals, flowers, fruit, etc.) If you have enough

time, you can even learn the art of Balinese wood-carving from one of the old craftsmen for a modest fee. Another wood-carving center is the village of **Kemenuh**, located on the road to Blahbatu.

Blahbatu

Formerly, one of the many princes of the Gianyar dynasty lived in Blahbatuh. His little palace is today occupied by the **Mantarai Budaya Orchid Farm**, near an important temple called the **Pura Gadun.** The latter contains a terrifying head, which represents the demon Kebon Iwa; using only his long fingernails, this malevolent figure is supposed to have created the cliff temple of Gunung Kawi, among other things.

Less than a mile (1 km) from Blahbatu is a favorite weekend picnic spot of the

Above: Relief showing a scene from the Ramayana. Right: Materials for ceremonial occasions.

Balinese to go at weekends: the waterfall (*air terjun*) of **Tegenungan** near the village of **Belangsinga**. South-east of Blahbatu is **Keramas** (famous for its *Arja* dance-troupe) and near **Medahan** there is a beach of black sand. There stands the **sea-temple of Masceti**, one of the nine ritually significant directional temples of Bali. It is also worth making a trip eastwards to the nearby beaches of **Lebih** with the **sea-temple of Pura Segara**, and **Tegalbesar,** formerly known as Siyut.

On the road from Blahbatu to Gianyar lies the village of **Belega**, whose carpenters have specialized in making bamboo furniture. In the neighboring village of **Bona** the leaves of the lontar-palm are woven into mats, baskets and sun-hats. The dramatic fire-dance, *Sanghyang*, and the *Kecak* are performed there regularly in the evening.

Gianyar

The regency capital of Gianyar is a heavily-trafficked market town without much in the way of tourist attractions, but it is nevertheless an important center of the Balinese textile trade. While here, it is worth looking out for the silk material known as *ikat.*The big stores also sell colorful Kuta-style T-shirts as well as batik shirts, which in this damp, hot climate are a good substitute for a jacket if you are invited out in the evening. In the factories on the western edge of the town, nimble-fingered but underpaid girls make sarongs from silk and cotton.

At the end of the 18th century, the Raja of Klungkung was weakened by attacks from Karangasem, and Gianyar was able to emerge as an independent rajadom. In 1900, the Dewa Anak Agung Manggis of Gianyar placed himself under the protection of the Netherlands, and was therefore spared when the Dutch invaded Bali in 1906. The **Puri**, his palace in the center of the town, is therefore still in excel-

lent condition; it is still home to the local aristocratic family, which continues to have influence at a national level (the palace can only be visited by special permission). Pagoda roofs in the Chinese style on some of the buildings are evidence of the contribution of the numerous Chinese merchants who lived in the prosperous Gianyar rajadom during its heyday. Their descendants still maintain one of the few **Buddhist temples** in Bali, on the road to Lebih, south of Alun-Alun, the main square.

About 4 miles (6 km) northeast of Gianyar, on the road to Bangli, stands the small but remarkable **Pura Dalem of Sidan**. As everywhere in Bali, this Dalem temple is intended to keep at bay the dangerous powers of the underworld and the spirits of the dead which have not yet been "purified" by ritual burning. It is dedicated to the Merajapati, the watchman of the kingdom of the dead. The fine reliefs on the base of the outer *Kulkul* tower show scenes from *Bhima's Journey into Hell* (see also Klungkung, p.

146). Terrifying figures of Rangda with pointed teeth and pendulous breasts flank the *candi bentar* gates inside the temple.

A little further north stands the ancestral temple of the rajas of Gianyar, the **Pura Merajan Agung** of Sidan. Some modern motifs have found their way into the reliefs: an aircraft and its pilot, a soldier with binoculars and a uniformed man on a bicycle. To the north, the classic triad of temples is completed by the **Pura Puseh Sidan**, facing towards the mountains; a "temple of origin" with a seven-tiered *meru*.

Kutri and Bedulu

Between Gianyar and Ubud lies a land of ancient culture, rich in archaeological finds and monuments of artistic importance. It lies between the rivers Pakerisan and Petanu ("blood river"), which rise near Penelokan in the Batur region. Traveling from the town of Gianyar to Ubud, you can visit Bali's three most important Durga shrines, one after the other

– the Bukit Dharma, the cave shrine of Goa Gajah, and the "Moon of Pejeng."

Bukit Dharma is the name of a sacred hill near **Kutri,** about 2 1/2 miles (4 km) west of Gianyar, on which the Javanese Queen Mahendradatta, the "wicked widow" of the Balinese king Udayana, is said to have been cremated in 1006 A.D. According to legend, Mahendradatta attempted, with the aid of black magic, to destroy her son, King Airlangga, together with all his retinue, by means of a plague. Many claim that she is the archetype of the dreaded witch Rangda. Be that as it may, the summit of the sacred hill, wooded with banyan trees, is crowned with a a weathered stone relief dating from the 12th century, portraying the six-armed goddess Durga. Durga represents the female energy of Shiva, who can be both destructive (Kali) and creative (Parvati).

Above: Entrance to the "elephant cave" of Goa Gajah. Right: Praying before the Yehpulu relief.

A few miles to the north, near **Bedulu,** is the **Goa Gajah**, or "Cave of the Elephant" – the name given to this cliff grotto by Dutch archaeologists who rediscovered it in 1923, probably inspired by the oversized ears of the gigantic demon-face carved in the rock around the cave entrance. If you have a flashlight with you, you can see a real elephant god in the cave's dark, T-shaped interior: in one of the 15 niches stands a four-armed figure, barely 3 feet (1 m) high, representing Ganesha, the elephant-headed son of the Hindu god Shiva.

This Shivaitic shrine, which was probably a place of meditation, dates from the 11th century and contains several stone *linggas*, or phallic symbols, which symbolize Shiva's procreative power. Buddhist monks have also left behind evidence of their activity in Goa Gajah: two severely weathered stone Buddhas, in the lotus position, sit beside a narrow path on the far side of a little stream in the southeast corner of the site. As if to demonstrate the island's multi-cultural charac-

ter, Balinese Hindus still come and place offerings before them. In 1954, a large bathing pool, about 1,000 years old, was excavated in front of the Elephant Cave. It is fed by six stone figures of water nymphs (*widadari*) spouting water.

Another historic bathing pool was discovered at **Yehpulu**, south of Bedulu; it can be reached on foot through the rice-fields, about half-an-hour's walk from Goa Gajah. There you will find a 30-foot (27 m) long **stone frieze** from the 14th century, unique in Indonesia. Its life-size figures carved from gray-brown lava stone include a yogi; an attacking bear; a hunter stabbing an animal; other hunters carrying their "bag" slung on a pole over their shoulders; and a rider on a horse, with a woman pulling the tail. These are probably figures from the Hindu epic *Mahabharata*, and may specifically relate to Krishna's hunt for the magic jewel of the bear Jambavat (Krishna is an incarnation of the god Vishnu). The relief is completed by a two-armed figure of Ganesha.

Pejeng

Until its conquest by the East Javanese general Gajah Mada in the 14th century, the area around Bedulu and Pejeng, a little way to the north, was the center of of a prosperous kingdom whose cultural flowering is evidenced by numerous Buddhist and Hindu statues. Considerably older even than these is the famous **Moon of Pejeng**, a gigantic bronze gong measuring 3 feet 7 inches in diameter (1.1 m) and just over 6 feet (1.86 m) long, which is believed to date as far back as the 3rd century B.C., that is to say the beginning of the Bronze Age in Indonesia. Its provenance is not clear. The Balinese insist that it fell from heaven, which would certainly explain the long crack in it. In style it is reminiscent of the Dong-son Culture of Indo-China, but the ancient Indonesians were also well-versed in the art of gong-making. Unfortunately, this gong, endowed with magic power and surrounded by legend, is kept on the top storey of a tower-like shrine in the royal temple of **Pura Penataran Sasih**. This means that its magnificent, finely engraved ornamentation – spirals, circles and an eight-pointed star – can only be admired through a pair of binoculars.

On the south side of Pejeng is the **Archaeological Museum**, with displays of sarcophagi, Stone Age axe-heads, bronze statues from the pre-Christian era and Chinese porcelain.

In the **Pura Kebo Edan**, the "Temple of the Wild Buffalo," stands the "Giant of Pejeng." This is a 13-foot (4 m) high statue, nearly 700 years old, representing the god of fertility, called Bhima by the Balinese, dancing on the head of a demon. The enormous penis of the deity and the two bulls kneeling at either side of him are characteristic of the ancient Indian cult of Shiva-Bhairava, which in Bali was enriched with tantric elements. The four round-headed nails in the Bhima's sex-organ, designed to increase the pleasure of his female partner, clearly show the sexual refinement of the tantric Hindus of the 14th century, who sought enlightenment through orgasm, and believed that by breaking taboos – such as drinking blood from a human skull, as demonstrated by the Raksasa standing in front of Bhima – they would be raised to new levels of ecstasy and heightened perception. Whether they also conducted human sacrifice remains a matter of speculation.

Equally dramatic forms of fertility symbolism are shown in the sculptures in the **Pura Pusering Jagat** ("Navel-of-the-World Temple"): four mustachioed demons swinging cudgels dance around a central *lingga* of Shiva. This temple, which dates from 1329, also contains a remarkable stone vase, 2 1/2 feet (75 cm) high, with a relief depicting the "The Stirring of the Ocean of Milk." The

Hindu gods wind the serpent of the world around the mountain of Mandara, which is held to be the axis of the world, set it spinning and thus obtain the elixir of life, *Amrita*, by a process of "churning."

THE UBUD REGION

Walking through a landscape of rich green rice-terraces between Ubud and Keliki; watching a procession of ducks solemnly following their duckherd, or peasants cosseting their champion fighting-cocks; enjoying a meal of grilled *sate ayam* at "Murni's Warung" in Campuan; visiting your favorite painter in Penestanan or Pengosekan; sipping tea in the Café Lotus at the Pura Saraswati; or witnessing a *Legong* dance on a warm night in Peliatan: all these activities and many more are possible in Ubud, which, in spite of the tourist boom of the last few years, is still an absolute "must" for anyone visiting Bali. Art-lovers can book into a *losmen* with the promising name of *Painter and Homestay;* and in little hotels in the middle of the rice-fields, romantics can still inhale the spice-laden air of a tropical paradise, which had already disappeared from Kuta twenty years ago.

It was the Ubud region which formed Bali's image as an island of artists. Many of the most famous painters, dancing-girls, musicians and wood-carvers originally came from the peasant villages around Ubud. Since time immemorial, fertile soil and an abundance of water for irrigation have provided the rice farmers of central Bali with good harvests. The agricultural surplus meant the farmers had enough leisure time to give their creativity free rein, while also guaranteeing the survival of the feudal court of the Rajas of Gianyar, who saw themselves as heirs to the lost Javanese empire of Majapahit, and were generous patrons of the arts. Around 1890, Cokorda Gede Sukawati of Ubud brought in craftsmen from all over Bali to work on temple and pa-

Right: A traditional Balinese subject painted in a modern manner.

lace decoration and persuaded them to settle in his village – with great success. But until the early 20th century, craftsmanship, painting and dance had a purely religious inspiration; statues and paintings only portrayed Hindu gods, and dances were only performed as part of temple festivals. That all changed in the 1920s, when the *Cokorda* (prince of the Ksatriya caste) Gede Raka Sukawati began inviting foreign artists to his residence in Ubud. This generated a creative climate, particularly in the years between the World Wars, when the Berlin-born painter and musician Walter Spies gave valuable encouragement to naive, naturalistic styles of painting as well as to native music and dance. Spies came to Ubud in 1927 after a stint as court conductor to the Sultan of Yogyakarta. His house, near the bridge over the Campuan river and above the Subak temple **Pura Gunung Lebah**, is today one of the area's more expensive hotels. Miguel and Rosa Covarrubias, two Mexican artists, visited Ubud in this period and immor-

talized its village culture in their classic book *Island of Bali*. The Dutch painter Rudolf Bonnet set up a studio in Ubud in 1931, and the village soon became known as the "in" place for art-loving Western travelers. The hospitable Walter Spies often acted as tour guide and arranged the sale of Balinese paintings. Backed by Prince Sukawati, he and Bonnet founded the artists' association *Pita Maha* in 1936 (revived in 1947 as *Ratna Warta*), which was joined by some 150 local artists, including such talented and versatile figures as I Gusti Lempad, who not only produced highly-prized ink drawings and masterly *Barong* masks, but also created the stone lotus-throne in Ubud's **Saraswati temple**.

After the war the former Dutch colonial soldier Han Snel arrived in Ubud, began painting, married a village girl called Sita and settled down. The couple run a restaurant near the lotus pond; and HanSnel's own gallery is worth a visit.

In 1956 another Dutch artist, Arie Smit, settled in the neighboring village of

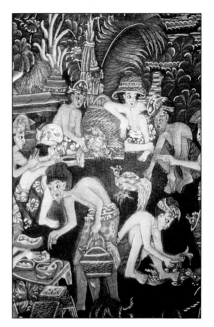

Penestanan, west of Ubud; his gifted Balinese pupils, known as the *Young Artists*, who developed a colorful, naive style of painting all their own, are now getting on in years, but their grandchildren are scarcely less productive than they used to be. Near the Campuan bridge lives an eccentric painter from the Philippines, Antonio Blanco, who married his favorite Balinese model and to this day continues to capture her on canvas.

Pengosekan, south of Ubud, is the home of gifted painters like Mokoh (who loves irreverent detail), Batuan (whose most famous work is *Turis dan Bali*), Kobot, Barat, Putra, Sana and Gatra. However, most of the inhabitants of Pengosekan are in the "wooden fruit business." The American furniture designer Linda Garland once encouraged the artists to carve and paint wooden frames for her pictures; soon, they were carving

and painting fruit, even whole banana-plants and four-poster beds – an occupation which has now become the backbone of the village economy.

Before buying a painting or wood-carving, try to get an overview of the different artistic schools, preferably by visiting a large gallery or museum. The **Agung Rai Gallery** in **Peliatan**, in the southeast of Ubud, offers a broad spectrum, while the new **ARMA** (Agung Rai Museum of Art) is the largest art museum in the region. Also in this area there are still painters who work in the traditional *Wayang* style, such as Made Kuanji, Ketut Madra and Nyoman Kuta. Two well-known and creative woodcarvers working here are Nyoman Togog and Wayan Pasti. And while you are in Peliatan, you should ask when the next dance performance will take place, since the district has a famous *Legong* group which has toured Europe and the U.S.A. No fewer than 15 *gamelan* orchestras take turns playing every evening in Peliatan and the neighboring village of **Teges.**

Above: "Let the cock-fight begin." Right: This descendant of Hanuman specializes in stealing religious offerings.

The **Puri Lukisan,** or "Palace of Pictures," which Prince Sukawati built in a small park in 1956, contains what its name suggests: exhibits spanning the full range of painting in this region from 1930 until 1978, the year in which Rudolf Bonnet, who was instrumental in setting up the museum, died. One can clearly trace the stylistic development from the classic *Wayang* painting, with its stylized silhouettes, right up to modern works which portray people with astonishing realism. The modest entrance fee seems sadly inadequate to cover professional conservation of the paintings and sculptures. In the building next door, a cooperative runs an exhibition of works for sale.

Opened in 1982, the **Museum Neka**, northeast of Ubud, beyond Campuan on the road to Kedewatan, presents works in better conditions. Here you can see not only work by the "old Europeans" such as Spies, Bonnet, Hofker and Smit, but also that of the Indonnesian avant-garde, including Ubud's own Lempad (d. 1978), Sujono and the very modern Affandi. If you have a gold credit card on you, you can choose from the best collection on the island. The **Neka Gallery**, close to the post office, is also a treasure-trove for art-lovers.

Walks in and around Ubud

All the large beach hotels offer excursions to Ubud as part of their palette of organized activities for their guests, and consequently the innumerable souvenir shops along the "Shopping Highway" between Peliatan and Campuan, and on the road to the **Monkey Forest**, believe they can get away with charging ridiculous prices. You'd be silly not to haggle: negotiation is the first duty of every tourist! In fifteen minutes you can reach the *Hutan Kerah* (Monkey Forest) from the center of Ubud. The children of Hanuman love to romp in the great banyan tree in front of the **Pura Dalem Agung Padang Tegal**. This temple to Durga, goddess of death, features a remarkable *Candi Kurung* gate, which is only opened

103

for sacrificial ceremonies. The monumental temple gate stands on the giant turtle Bedawang, which represents the underworld, guarded by seven terrifying, slack-breasted Rangdas – the two witches at either end appear to be in the act of devouring children.

From Ubud's Monkey Forest you can continue walking to the wood-carvers' village of **Nyuhkuning**, where you cross the river Wos, going west, then bear north through rice-fields, past **Klatikuning**, to the painters' village of **Penestanan**. A short, well-signposted path leads from there via Campuan back to Ubud. Another path goes through Penestanan to the **Yeh Ayung Gorge**, where luxury hotels are under construction, and on to the Monkey Forest of Sangeh.

Walkers who take the path northward from the Campuan temple (near the Kecak Inn) will encounter village culture

Above: The Candi gate to the shrine of Gunung Kawi. Right: At the sacred spring of Tirtha Empul.

as it was before the advent of tarmac roads and tourists. The path first winds along the picturesque rice-terraces in the steep-sided valley of the river Wos, then widens and leads through the villages of **Bangkiangsidem** and **Sebali**.

There, you can either cross the Wos eastwards and walk back to Ubud on a path through the fields, via **Batuyung** and **Sakti,** or you can stroll on as far as Keliki, and pick up the tarmac road eastward to **Tegalalang**, from where a *bemo* will take you back. En route it is worth stopping in **Petulu**, especially in the late afternoon. There is an interesting **bird sanctuary** here, in which thousands of white herons come to roost after a day's fishing.

North of Tegalalang are the two villages of **Pujung** and **Sebatu**, famous for their talented wood-carvers. If you are a good walker and set out before sunrise, you can, in a day, complete the 19-mile (30 km) walk from Campuan, via Keliki, Taro (coffee plantations) and Pisang right up to **Penelokan** (see p. 138), at the foot

of the Batur volcano. On the way you will experience rural Bali at first hand – though it's to be hoped you'll maintain some distance from the legions of roving village dogs!

Gunung Kawi and Tirtha Empul

Roughly halfway to Penelokan you come to the wood-carving village of **Tampaksiring**. About a mile (1.5 km) south of this is the shrine of Gunung Kawi, set idyllically in the gorge of the *Sungai* (river) Pakerisan. There are a total of ten *candis* in the Javanese style, standing in 23-foot (7 m) niches in the sheer rock walls on either side of the river. The giant Kebo Iwo must have been pretty busy: he is said to have hewn not only Goa Gajah but also these *candis* from the solid volcanic rock with his thumbnail. The shrine was probably built at the end of the 11th century, after the death and in honor of King Anak Wungsu. A group of four *candis* to the left of the steep staircase leading down from the car park are said to be in memory of the monarch's four favorite concubines. The *candis* on the opposite side of the river are dedicated to the king and his four chief wives, and the one on the left, slightly elevated, is dedicated to the deified Anak Wungsu. On the right, in front of this group of five *candis*, is a narrow gap leading to a Buddhist refuge which you can only enter barefoot. Its rock walls conceal niches for meditation, probably built by Buddhist monks some 900 years ago. At the foot of the staircase is a gate leading to a path which takes you southwest through rice fields for some half a mile (1 km) to the so-called "Tenth Grave." This is supposed to have been built for a Brahman who was one of Anak Wungsu's ministers, but the word "grave" is misleading, since the dead were burnt and their ashes subsequently scattered in a river – consigned, in other words, to the goddess Ganga in order to exert a favorable influence on the cycle of rebirth.

To the north of Tampaksiring the sacred river Pakerisan has its source. Not far from this beneficent spring, which the Balinese believe confers eternal youth, one of the Warmadewa rajas created a bathing-place in 960 A.D.; later, in the 11th century, King Airlangga had it adorned with statues and shrines. In all, 31 gargoyles feed the three basins of **Tirtha Empul**; the left-hand one is reserved for women and the middle one for men. The water in the small basin on the right is said to be of exceptional purity.

Tirtha is derived from the Sanskrit word *amrita*, which means something like "nectar of the gods" or "elixir of life." The myth of the holy bathing-place, which draws thousands of pilgrims every year, is bound up with the Hindu god Indra. Once, this Indian god-king was fighting in Bali against the demon king Maya Danuwa. The evil ruler treacherously poisoned the water of the river Petanu, from which Indra's warriors drank and then died. Indra saved them by driving his cudgel into the ground a little further to the east, thus creating the spring of Tirtha Empul and the river Pakerisan. The god-king sprinkled this holy water over his dead comrades and so brought them back to life. A gigantic block of black stone was later consecrated as a throne to Indra: it can be seen in the middle of the inner courtyard of the temple, in which there are also some 20 small shrines, each with a beautifully carved little door painted gold.

Holy water plays an important part in Hindu religious rites: the water of choice of Bali's Brahmans for their sacrificial and purification ceremonies is that from Tirtha Empul. On the other hand, water from the neighboring river Petanu was, until a few years ago, considered to be cursed, since the blood of the demon king, Maya Danuwa, had flowed into it after Indra finally killed him. Only after

elaborate sacrificial ceremonies was the water of the Petanu recently declared ritually pure (*suci*) – which was a blessing for local rice growers, because until then it had been taboo to use the water even for irrigation.

BANGLI

Gianyar's neighbor to the east is the predominantly agricultural regency of Bangli. With only 175,000 inhabitants, it is the second-smallest administrative district of Bali. The capital, of the same name, lies only 8 miles (13 km) northeast of Gianyar town, at the foot of the Batur massif, and thanks to its altitude of 1,650 feet (500 m), it has a pleasant climate. An inscription in the Pura Kehen dates Bangli's recorded history as far back as the 9th century A.D. In the 15th century, Bangli became a dependency of the kingdom of Gelgel. After gaining its independence in 1700, it reached the height of its power in the 19th century – paradoxically after signing a treaty subordinating it to Dutch colonial rule.

You can still live like a raja in Bangli today by staying at the historic **Puri Denpasar** (Jalan Merdeka), which has been converted into the palatial **Artha Sastra Inn**, and is run by descendants of the ruling family. Gilt carving, flowers, *bales* and sumptuous decor await the guest, who can even reserve the original bed (or so one is told) of the last Raja of Bangli, who died in 1960.

Every three days the sleepy provincial town is roused to hectic activity when peasant women from the surrounding area come streaming into the *pasar* (market square) to sell their peanuts, cloves, sweet potatoes, passion-fruit, maize, citrus fruits (*jeruk*), coffee and tobacco. Herbal remedies of all kinds (*jamu*) are also on sale; the nature-healers (*balian*) of the district are widely known for their practice of inducing trances, and there are many dark mutterings about black magic.

Right: A Balinese village just before an important temple festival.

On the northeast side of town, in a superb position on the slopes of Bukit Bangli, stands a temple which is possibly the most beautiful in Bali, and is certainly the second-largest on the island: the **Pura Kehen.** Founded in the 11th century and dedicated to Hyang Kehen, the god of the hearth, this became the state temple of the rajas of Bangli in the 18th century. The caste of the blacksmiths, the Pande, also come here to venerate Hyang Api, the god of fire.

A flight of 38 steps, flanked by nearly life-size *Wayang* figures, leads up to the sanctuary, which is laid out over eight terraces. In the first forecourt stands an ancient, spreading banyan tree, which conceals a *kulkul* tower in its branches. Beside it, above the *candi bentar* gateway, a carved *kala boma* face keeps away evil spirits. Passing through the middle courtyard, one reaches the *jeroan*, the holy of holies, whose walls are partly decorated with ancient Chinese porcelain plates. The *jeroan* is dominated by a *meru* with eleven *tumpangs*, or tiered roofs, which is dedicated to Hyang Kehen, one of the manifestations of Shiva. A *padmasana* (throne of the gods) for the trinity of Shiva, Brahma, and Vishnu, decorated with remarkable stone carvings, stands in the northeast corner of the inner courtyard. Its base is in the form of a turtle round which a snake is coiled: a symbol of the underworld. On the rear side of the stone throne are some magnificent sculptures; half the Hindu pantheon is assembled there, including Shiva and his son Ganesha; Durga; the goddess of death; Vishnu and his mount, Garuda; and the directional deities, as well as Prince Arjuna and other figures from the Sanskrit epic *Mahabharata.*

In the **Budaya Art Center** (not far from the Pura Kehen), you can see temple dancing and listen to *gamelan* music. As well as performances of *Kecak* and *Wayang,* you may occasionally be able to see unique local forms of dance, such as the *Baris Johor*, *Baris Dadap* or *Baris Tamiang,* which are reminiscent of archaic war dances.

CENTRAL BALI

You can easily reach most places in Central Bali from Denpasar – and often from each other – by means of *bemos*. If you only wish to visit Tanahlot, join an organized tour in Kuta, Sanur or Nusa Dua or catch a *bemo* from Denpasar heading for Tabanan and change in Kediri. If you are using bemos, start your return journey around 4 pm, because very few bemos operate after that time.

TANAHLOT
Accomodation / Restaurants

There are two moderately-priced bungalow complexes behind the market stalls. At the observation points around the temple there are rows and rows of *warungs* and other restaurants and bars. In high season, the place can get very crowded around sunset, when whole busloads of visitors arrive and spread themselves throughout the area.

UBUD and SURROUNDING AREA
Accommodation

(Prices always refer to double rooms)
LUXURY: **Amandari**, Sayan, P.O. Box 33,Ubud, tel. 975333, fax 975335, fantastic position above the Yeh Ayung river, from US$ 435. **Kupu Kupu Barong**, Kedewatan, tel. 975478, fax 975079, relatively far from Ubud, superb position above the gorge of the Yeh Ayung, excellent restaurant, no children under 12, from US$ 405.
MODERATE: **Ananda Cottages**, Campuan, near the Neka Museum, P.O. Box 205, Denpasar, tel. 975376, from US$ 42. **Cahaya Dewata**, Kedewatan, tel. 975495, lovely view of the Yeh Ayung, from US$ 73. **Juwita Inn**, Jl. Bisma, Tel, tel./fax 976956. Bungalows surrounded by a beautiful garden. **Oka Wati's Sunset Bungalows,** tel. 976386, central and quiet, from US$ 33. **Pringga Juwita Watergarden**, Jl. Bisma, Tel/fax 975734, borders on rice-fields, quiet, central location, rooms from US$ 55-70. **Sayan Terraces**, Sayan, nice view of the Yeh Ayung, from US$ 20. **Siddhartha**, Penestanan Kaja, tel. 975748, in the middle of rice-fields, from US$ 20. **Siti Bungalows**, P.O. Box 227, Denpasar, tel. 975699, central and yet cozy, behind the Lotus Café, from US$ 57. **Tjampuan**, Campuan, P.O.Box 15, Denpasar, tel. 975368, fax 975137, idyllic situation on the Cerik, walking distance from town center, from US$ 68. **Ubud Village,** Monkey Forest Road, tel. 975571, central location, from US$ 45.
BUDGET: There are a number of small **losmens** in and around Ubud, some of which charge less than 10,000 Rps. for a double room. The simplest thing is to hunt for lodgings on either side of the Monkey Forest Road. One quite respectable option here is the

Monkey Forest Hideaway, tel. 975354, with a view of the forest, from Rps. 20,000. There's additional budget accommodation beyond the big intersection on Jl. Suwata: the **Suci Inn** lets rooms for as little as Rps. 8,000.
In Peliatan, **Sari Bungalows** has rooms for only Rps. 10,000. In Penestanan, you should ask at the **Hotel Tjampuhan**. If you are seeking solitude, head for the **Pugig Homestay**, with accommodation from Rps. 10, 000 in a Balinese farmstead.

Restaurants

Just about every gourmet, whatever his preferences, will find something to his taste in Ubud. Top of the list for quality and high prices is the **Kupu Kupu Barong** hotel restaurant (Indonesian, Japanese und international). In Ubud itself, we can recommend the restaurant of the **Tjampuhan Hotel**, **Murni's Warung** (not a *warung* in the normal sense), the **Café Lotus** (pasta), **Oka Wati** and the **Nomad** (especially their steaks); all are in the middle price-range. There are good but cheap places on the Monkey Forest Road, like **Ibu Rai**, **Bendi's** or **Café Bali**.
Many travelers prefer to eat cheaply at the stalls in the night-market. In Peliatan, **Ibu Arsa's Warung** (near the big banyan tree) can be recommended to anyone who likes local Balinese food; unfortunately, it is right by a busy street. Ibu Arsa also knows all about dance performances and can get you tickets. Lovers of rich cakes will feel right at home in the **Café Wayan** ("Death by Chocolate") on Monkey Forest Road .

Shopping

The main street and Monkey Forest Road are lined with shops selling goods of all kinds. There is a covered bazaar in the town center. If you are staying in Ubud you should seek out the artists themselves, since the whole area is dedicated to the production of a wide range of handcraft items. Painters' studios are concentrated in Peliatan, Ubud and Penestanan. Wood-carvers work in Mas and Kemenuh, but also on the road that runs northward to Sebatu, from the east side of Ubud.
There's a *gamelan* instrument maker based in Blahbatuh. Silver jewelry is made in Celuk. The market in Sukawati offers the entire current range of available stock in dolls, sunshades, and basketwork in one easy-to-canvas location. However, the stall-holders are used to tourists and are not happy to be beaten down on price.

Evening Entertainment

Ubud is the best place to visit if you are looking for native culture. The shows that are put on here night after night have largely lost their sacred character, since dancing has become a source of money; however, religiousity has been replaced by a certain professional creativity. In a sense, Ubud could be called the Broadway of Bali. Individual *gamelan* players and dancers vie keenly for the visitor's favor; dance schools even instruct westerners in the intricacies of their art. The groups from Peliatan have taken a lead in this. The way they perform the *Kecak* surpasses even the dancers from Bona in its intensity and the harmony of their ensemble. The members of the excellent women's gamelan orchestra compose and perform their own solos, and girls join at an early age. One is struck by the earnest dedication of the dancers in these shows.

If you enjoy comic strips, make sure to see a *wayang kulit* shadow-puppet performance in the **Oka Kartini.** You can find out where a performance takes place, from the stall at the main intersection in the town center or from the hordes of young ticket-sellers roaming the area. Prices are around Rps. 7,000. When going to an out-of-town performance, such as the fire-dance at Bona, you should take advantage of the courtesy buses provided, rather than using your rental car, since returning late at night on the narrow roads can be quite dangerous.

Museums and Galleries

In addition to the commercial galleries and artists' studios, which are basically there to attract passing trade, there are several interesting collections of Balinese painting and western art inspired by Bali. The newest and biggest museum is the **Agung Rai Museum of Art** in Peliatan. At the center of town is the **Museum Puri Lukisan**, open daily from 8 am to 4 pm (admission: 1000 Rps.). This gives the best overview of all styles and periods. Also very good is the **Museum Neka**, north of Campuan, which is open daily from 8.30 am until 5 pm (admission: 500 Rps.). The **Neka Gallery** near the post office is principally a sales gallery, as are the **Agung Rai Gallery** in Peliatan and the **Agung Raka Gallery** at the northern end of the village of Mas.

A more intimate atmosphere can be found at **Antonio Blanco's Studio**, open nearly every day 9 am - 5 pm (admission: 500 Rps.). A private collection of the work of Han Snel can be seen at his own hotel, the **Siti Bungalows,** behind the Café Lotus.

Walking and Hiking

Ubud is an ideal starting point for walks and longer expeditions on foot. The following are two relatively easy walking tours:

Tour 1 : Ubud - Sangeh (one way, 7 1/2 - 9 miles, 12 - 15 km). Starting opposite the Hotel Tjampuhan, you climb the steep steps and keep going straight on

until you reach the paved north-south road at Sayan. (Before that, you may notice a little used tarred side-road that goes through Penestanan.) From the Sayan Terraces Hotel, follow a narrow path westwards, which leads into the gorge of the Yeh Ayung river. Cross the river by means of the swaying bamboo bridge. On the far bank, you have a choice of continuing northwards along the bank or heading south for a little way, then going westwards. If you go north, continue only as far as the village of Bongkasa, then turn west. A wide path through the forest and past rice-fields will bring you to Sangeh. For the return journey, you can take a bemo to Sayan via Lambing and Kengetan.

Tour 2: Ubud - Pejeng - Kelusu (there and back, about 9 miles/15 km). At the point where the main street of Ubud meets the road running north-south from Peliatan to Petulu, carry straight on eastwards and cross the Petanu river. In the middle of Pejeng, continue eastward to Kelusu.

Alternatively, head in a slightly more northerly direction and you come to the temple Pura Pengukur Ukuran and the river Pakrisan. Here, by the river, is a little-known but moderately spectacular archaeological treasure, **Goa Garbo**, an overgrown miniature version of Gunung Kawi. Make sure to bring a picnic.

For further tours and walks, it's helpful to buy a map on sale in Ubud, called **Bali Pathfinder.** It is admittedly not always very accurate but does help you get your bearings.

If you opt for a cycle tour, don't forget that there are some pretty steep hills, and be sure to avoid the very congested main Ubud - Peliatan - Teges road.

Useful Addresses

If you need any information, apply to the **Bina Wisata**, a small public office near the central crossroads.

The **post office** is on the south side of the main street, going east, set back a little from the road. It can be used as an address for poste restante mail, which should be addressed to *Kantor Pos, Ubud.*

The **telephone office** is outside the center, on the north-south Peliatan - Petulu road. You can send and receive faxes there (fax: 0062-361-975120).

Rental Vehicles

In Ubud, it is possible to hire jeeps, motorcycles and bicycles. However, in the high season there is often quite a long waiting list. There is a firm that rents out motorbikes and regular bicycles located right at the central intersection. Other rental firms have their offices near the main street, usually combined with a money exchange office and a public transport operation.

A RESERVE FOR
WILDLIFE AND WOODS

JEMBRANA
WEST BULELENG
WEST BALI NATIONAL PARK

JEMBRANA

Western Bali extends over two administrative districts: in the south, the regency of Jembrana; in the north, the western half of the regency of Buleleng. You can literally circle the whole area if you drive along the coast road from Gilimanuk on to Denpasar as far as Penggragoan, then head for the north coast, and from Seririt return to Gilimanuk along that coast.

The name Jembrana is derived from the Balinese *jimbar wana*, which means something like "great forest," and indeed more than half the 324 square miles (840 sq. km) of this district is thickly forested and forms part of the Bali Barat National Park. Under the Dutch, resettlement projects in the early part of the century brought Balinese villagers to this remote mountainous wilderness for the first time. With only 220,000 inhabitants, Jembrana is today still the most sparsely-populated region of Bali.

Gilimanuk

In Java there once lived a king who had a very badly-behaved son. In order to be

Previous pages: Separating the rice from the chaff. Left: On the south coast, east of Negara.

rid of him, the king took his wayward offspring far away to the east, to a point where the land became very narrow. There the king ordered the prince to keep on walking, and drew a line in the sand behind him; following this line, the waters of the Java Sea and the Indian Ocean flowed together, cutting off Bali, which was thenceforth an island of exile.

For backpackers arriving from Java, the ferry harbor of Gilimanuk is the gateway to Bali. This little seaport on the Bali Straits welcomes its visitors with a big **candi bentar**, or split gate, which is supposed to deny demons their entry to the holy island of Bali.

A loudspeaker on the mosque calling the faithful to prayer at regular intervals each day patently demonstrates that Islam long ago made the leap across the water to the Hindu island. In the **Rumah Makan Padang** restaurant, near the mosque, there's no pork on the menu, but you will find that followers of the Prophet in their voluntary Balinese exile have lost none of their culinary skill: the beef (*rendang*) is just as hot and spicy here as in Western Sumatra, where the chef comes from. If you spend a night in Gilimanuk, the night market (*pasar senen*) will give you a taste of the culinary skills of the Javanese and Balinese *Ibus* (*ibu* means "mother") at their cookshacks.

113

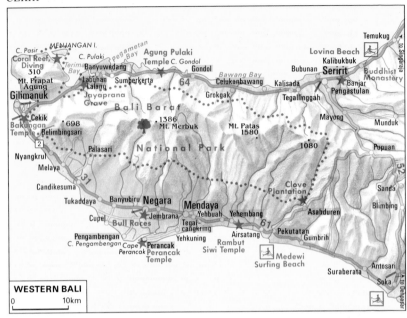

WESTERN BALI

0   10km

Little two-wheeled pony-carts, called *dokar*s, confer a Javanese atmosphere to the main street of Gilimanuk, lined with *warungs*. Every time a ferry arrives, the thoroughfare is crammed with over-loaded trucks, crowded long-distance buses, and hordes of foreign and Indonesian travellers.

Cekik

As the abovementioned legend of Bali's origin indicates, there was indeed a land bridge between Bali and Java during the great Ice Age; this is demonsstrated not only by the almost identical flora and fauna of the two islands. Objects excavated at Cekik, 2 miles (3 km) south of Gilimanuk, include stone axe-heads and pottery shards which reveal the existence of a Neolithic settlement, and point to Bali having been colonized at that time by people from Java.

Right: A representation of Christ in the Balinese manner.

The only monument in the area from a more recent period of Balinese history is the little temple of **Pura Bakungan** on the northeastern edge of the town of Cekik, which was built around 1450 A.D., at the time when two princes from the Kingdom of Gelgel were sent to West Bali to reclaim the wilderness for cultivation: this was how the states of Gilimanuk and Negara came into being. However, rivalry between the king's two sons soon led to a civil war, which effectively wiped out all the early successes in developing the region. This at least is the traditional explanation for the fact that so few Hindus settled in western Bali, inspite of the pressure of overpopulation in the middle of the island; a more convincing reason, however, is the lack of water for irrigation due to low rainfall, and the poor quality of the soil. However, this obviously did not deter seafarers and fishermen, and since the indigenous Balinese regard the sea with distinct suspicion, the west coast of Bali was settled in the 17th century by Bugis, who were

114

Moslem sailors from the Sunda Sea, especially from Java and Sulawesi (the Celebes Islands). In fact, exiles from the whole archipelago found a home here.

Cekik is home to the headquarters of the West Bali National Park (see p. 119); its information center provides literature and a small exhibition about forest ecology.

Belimbingsari and Palasari

After around 1930, Christian missionaries from the U.S.A. and the Netherlands worked among the members of *Sudra* under-caste in the Hindu villages of southern Bali – with the result that the newly-converted Christians were driven out of their villages, since they no longer fitted into the social hierarchy.

These religious refugees from the south made their home in forest clearings in the highlands of western Bali, 6 miles (10 km) southeast of Cekik. In 1939 the village of **Belimbingsari** was established, in which today some 2,000 Protestants (*kristen protestan*) live. Their church (*gereja*) has incorporated some traditional elements found in Balinese temples.

Thus the bell-tower looks like a *kulkul* tower and the church itself resembles a *bale*. Even the demon-repelling *candi bentar* has found its way into Christian church architecture, and the very cross of Jesus stands on a Brahmanic lotus throne. The tradition of temple dancing is also upheld, though with the difference that in Belimbingsari, according to Christian principles, Good defeats Evil, whereas Bali's Hindus seek the harmony which results from a balance between the forces of creation and of destruction.

Catholicism – "the competition," so to speak – has taken root further east: in **Palasari** (pop. 1,800) stands a Catholic church, built in 1960, which is the largest in all of Nusa Tenggara (Eastern Indonesia).

Negara

About 22 miles (35 km) southeast of Gilimanuk lies Negara, the capital of the Jembrana regency. The roads to it from the Java ferry in the west and Denpasar, 59 miles (95 km) away to the east, run through flat flood plains with vivid green rice-fields where little villages lie half-hidden under the coconut palms. The resettlement policy of the Indonesian government has transferred complete Javanese villages into this thinly-populated region, which hitherto has been spared from mass tourism.

At the most, tourist buses heading for southern Bali will stop in Negara for a tea break. The little market town has thus been able to retain its friendly, slightly provincial atmosphere. The main sights to see include the new white **mosque** and the **Heroes' Cemetery**, which recalls those who fell in the struggle for independence from the Dutch. Negara's tourist infrastructure focuses around the two main axes of Jalan Diponegoro and Jalan

115

Ngurah Rai: some simple hotels, *warungs*, restaurants, fruit-stalls, the Post Office and a gas station.

On the southern edge of Negara you can find the settlement of **Loloan Timur,** a *kampung* that's home to Moslem descendants of Buginese seafarers. Their rectangular dwellings, built on stilts, are quite atypical of Bali; whereas in Balinese peasant villages domestic life takes place at ground level, the living quarters of the maritime Bugis are on the first floor, to protect the occupants from exceptionally high tides.

A further 5 miles (8 km) southwest is the fishing port of **Pengambengan,** where motorized outrigger boats land their sardine catches. The fish are immediately processed in a canning factory; a crab-farming project has also been successful. So far, the beautiful beaches here have not been opened up to tourism.

Above: A water buffalo race in Negara.
Right: Awaiting the start with relish.

The chief attraction of the Jembrana region are the **water buffalo races** (*mekepung*) which take place every year in September and October, after the rice harvest. In these events, two teams of colorfully decorated water buffaloes, each pulling a sort of sulky with a driver, race around a 1 1/4 mile (2 km) course. There are two main teams: the buffaloes (*kerbau*) of the rice farmers living east of the Ijo Gading river compete with those of the villagers on the west bank. Trial runs take place on Sundays from April to October: in Bayubiru (3 miles / 5 km west of Negara) and in Dlodbrawah (1 1/4 miles / 2 km south of Tegalcangkring).

The buffalo has an important place in the fertility- and ancestor-cults of the ancient Malay tribes all over the Indonesian archipelago. The Toraja in Sulawesi kill buffaloes for their burial ceremonies; the Karo-Batak of northern Sumatra decorate the gables of their houses with buffalo horns, and in many aboriginal villages of Bali buffaloes are sacrificed to ensure the fertility of the rice fields.

116

For lovers of *gamelan* music, the Negara district offers something rather special: the *Gamelan Jegog*. The artistically carved and colorfully painted bamboo instruments of the *Jegog* orchestra are of a remarkable size and produce sounds which are so deep that you don't simply hear the vibrations, but actually feel them physically. In the *Jegog Mebarung* several groups of musicians compete for the favor of the listeners – visitors from outside can easily get the impression that volume is the only decisive factor. Scarcely less noisy is the music of the *Kendang Mebarung*, a rhythmic face-off between two musicians beating gigantic drums. *Kendang* drums can be as much as 8 feet (2.5 m) long with a diameter of 3 feet (1 m), and produce a deep sound so penetrating that at night it can be heard for miles. The musical domain of the women is the *Bumbung Gebyog*. The wives of the rice-farmers pound the ground with bamboo pipes of different lengths, producing sounds of varying pitches. The name *Bumbung* is onomato-poeic, and reproduces the sound of this orchestra rather well – the treading of the rice seems to have been the inspiration behind this particular form of *gamelan*.

Temples and Beaches
of the Southwest

In the 16th century the Sanskrit scholar and holy man Nirartha emigrated from East Java to Bali because Islam was gradually gaining the upper hand in his homeland. In Bali, he revived Hindu learning and faith, and he remains an important figure (see pp. 90, 95). Two sea temples in the Negara region, Pura Gede Perancak and Pura Rambut Siwi, recall his ministry:

The little white **Temple of Perancak** is seldom visited, as it is located 6 miles (10 km) southwest of **Mendoyo** beside a remote lagoon that is bordered by offshore coral reefs. The walls of the *Pura* are built of light-colored coral stone; the *meru* in the central court has only three palm-thatched tiers and is dedicated to

117

the Javanese holy man Nirartha, whom the Balinese call Pedanda Bau Rauh.

The most important temple on the southwest coast is without doubt **Rambut Siwi** (near **Yehembang**, 5 miles / 8 km east of Mendaya). Its name means, roughly, "Sacred Hair": Nirartha is said to have cut off his own hair and left it as an object of worship in a shrine of the Pura Rambut Siwi in 1546. The notion that hair possesses magic powers is an element of the Indian cult of Shiva; a turban of hair is the distinguishing characteristic of Shiva as the supreme yogi. You approach the temple by steps leading down to a beach of black sand at the foot of a sheer cliff. Seen from the sea, the temple buildings of mellow brick and stone seem even more impressive, especially the Pura Luhur complex, shaded by frangipani trees.

Surfers from Australia have discovered the black sand beach of **Medewi**,

Above: The last expanse of wilderness in western Bali.

about 2 miles (3 km) west of Pekutatan, beside the mouth of a river. A few little *losmens* have already been set up to meet the needs of the surf-riders.

Just 12 miles (20 km) further westward, Lalang Linggah attracts bathers with its palm-fringed beach.

If you have always wondered where the Indonesian national cigarette, *Kretek*, gets its inimitable flavor, you should make the trip north to the village of **Asahduren**, 9 1/2 miles (15 km) away, where clove plants cover the hillsides as far as the eye can see. The cloves harvested here are taken to a factory in Java and mixed with sugar and tobacco to make the cigarettes whose aroma is as typical of Indonesia as incense is of the Vatican. At **Pekutatan**, a beautiful road branches off to lead through the mountains to Asahduren with its clove and vanilla plantations; passing picturesque rice-terraces to **Pupuan** (coffee plantations), it continues through Pengastulan and finally on to Seririt on the north coast of the island.

WEST BULELENG

A coastal road runs from Singaraja through the busy market town of **Seririt**, and on westward towards Gilimanuk. Bali's relatively dry north coast is sparsely populated; the roads are lined with kapok trees, coconut palms, fields of maize, and – something you might not expect to see in the tropics – vineyards! The grapes are pressed to make *anggur*, a heavy, liqueur-like red wine, which sick people drink to restore their strength.

Little fishing boats with bamboo outriggers and brightly colored sails have their home port in the small harbor of **Celukanbawang.** Further west, on the Bay of **Gondol**, a gorgeous white shell-sand beach is an inviting place to stop for a swim. At Cape Gondol there is a breeding center for sea turtles.

A cluster of stalls selling lemonade and take-out food marks the turnoff to **Pura Agung Pulaki**. This ritually significant temple, devoted to the religious reformer Nirartha, has recently been renovated and given a new gateway and shrines. Its beautiful position on the clifftop, with a view over the sea, the beach and the volcanoes of Java, is also enjoyed by a horde of wild monkeys, who, while not as uncouth as their cousins in Sangeh, should still be regarded with mistrust.

A perfect base for the nearby diving paradise around Menjangan Island is **Pemuteran** (with mid-price to luxury hotels), which has its own bay with a few stands of coral.

Local doctors send people with skin complaints to the **Air Panas of Banyuwedang,** a hot sulphur spring not far from Sumberkerta.

West Bali National Park and Menjangan Island

Just too late to save the Balinese tiger, which had already been hunted to extinction in the 1930s, a wildlife reserve was established in western Bali in 1941. The original intention was to preserve the rare Balinese white starling (Indonesian name: *jalak putih*; zoological name: *Leucopsar rothschildi*) and the Balinese wild cattle (*banteng*) from extinction. In the 1980s, the area was enlarged to create the **Taman Nasional Bali Barat**. Javanese wild buffalo (*Bos javanicus*), Muntjak deer, leopard, civet, wild boar, monkeys, snakes – including some highly poisonous varieties – and many species of birds now inhabit the reserve.

The national park covers about 300 square miles (765 sq. km), of which 200 square miles (500 sq. km) is forest. Evergreeen rain-forest flourishes on the well-watered southern slopes of the central highlands up to an altitude of 5,000 feet (1,500 m); on the dryer northern slopes are less dense, deciduous monsoon forests and palm savannah. A marine reserve in the northwest of the park, extending over some 15,000 acres (6,000 ha), includes mangrove swamps and coral reefs full of fish off the coast of the **Prapat Agung peninsula** and **Menjangan Island**, as well as bird sanctuaries on the small islands in Gilimanuk Bay. Park authorities keep careful control over the forest; they keep an especially watchful eye on wood-clearing by farmers from the villages bordering the park. The boundaries of the park were redefined in 1984, and coconut and eucalyptus plantations within those boundaries are being returned to a wilderness state – a sensible but distinctly unpopular measure. Fishing and coral collecting are banned along the park's coasts. The ultimate goal here is the introduction of a "gentle" form of nature tourism, geared to individual outdoorsmen rather than jeeploads of safari travelers awaiting a programmed introduction to local wildlife. In the tropical jungle, it is a matter of luck whether or not you see wild animals because, unlike those in the East African bush, they are not forced to seek out well-known water-

holes at certain hours of the day.

The information center is at the **Park Headquarters** in Cekik. Here, as well as in **Labuhan Lahang** on Terima Bay or in Denpasar, you can obtain a visitor's permit, which costs nothing but is compulsory, and be assigned the obligatory official guide. Anyone planning to trek and spend the night in the national park must take a sleeping bag, mosquito-net, water and provisions. Boots with sturdy soles and good traction are a great aid in walking on the slippery earth. Food is cooked on camp-fires and one sleeps in very basic huts. If you want to be more comfortable, you can rent a *losmen* in Labuhan Lahang, Gilimanuk or Negara and make expeditions into the mountains.

Trekking in the Taman Nasional is still something of a novelty. However, word is getting around that the island **Pulau Menjangan** is the most fascinating place in Bali for diving and snorkeling. In La-

buhan Lalang there is an office of the park authority which rents out little outboard motorboats for trips to "Deer Island." For Menjangan is indeed a refuge of the Java deer, and also of the protected Bali starling. However, the rangers advise against walking in this area because of the pois-onous snakes. Fortunately the undisturbed beaches of this paradise island are reptile-free. You only need a pair of goggles to enter a completely new cosmos: just 5 feet (1.5 m) below the surface, the tropical underwater world is populated with an unbelievable variety of brightly-colored fish romping among the petrified branches of white coral. Strange as it may sound, you should always wear a shirt in the water, because the UV rays of the tropical sun can do terrible things to a naked back – and one loses all sense of time, so bewitched is one by the undersea magic. Snorkeling equipment can be rented in Labuhan Lalang; while you can pick up scuba-diving gear in the hotels of Pemuteran.

If you have plenty of time, you can walk right round the peninsula of Prapat Agung in a longish day (15.5 miles / 25 km) and snorkel undisturbed among the coral reefs.

A little way inland from Terima Bay is a tomb which is highly revered both by Balinese Hindus and syncretic Javanese Moslems: the **Makam Jayaprana.** A steep climb over several terraces brings you to the temple, which rewards your exertion with a superb view across the Bali Strait to the Merapi volcano in Java.

A tragic love story is connected with the temple: the orphan Jayaprana, who rose to become the favorite of his raja, took the extraordinarily beautiful fruit-seller, Leyonsari, as his wife. Unfortunately she also caught the eye of the old raja, who sent Jayaprana into the mountains and had him murdered. When Leyonsari saw the murder in a dream, she killed herself rather than submit to the unwelcome embraces of the king.

Above: The fascinating underwater world off the coast of Menjangan Island.

WESTERN BALI

Large parts of Western Bali are sparsely populated and unknown to tourists. Buses and *bemos* run regularly on the main roads (Gilimanuk-Denpasar, Gilimanuk-Singaraja, Singaraja-Denpasar). The best way to explore Western Bali is by car or motorcycle.

GILIMANUK
Accommodation

Gili Sari, **Kartika Candra** (both from Rps. 10,000), **Surya** and **Lestari** on Jl. Raya, which runs down to the harbor, offer very simple accommodation. The same is true of the **Putra Sesana,** right by the bus terminal.

Ferries to Java

As many as 16 ferries a day run between Gilimanuk and Ketapang in Java. The crossing takes about half an hour. Prices: adults Rps. 750, motorcycles Rps. 2,400, cars around Rps. 9,000, according to size.

CEKIK
Accommodation

The **headquarters of the West Bali National Park** is located in Cekik. Anyone who wants to trek in the National Park can pick up a permit and information pack here, or at an office in Denpasar: PHPA, Jl. Suwung 40, P.O. Box 320.

NEGARA
Accommodation / Restaurants

BUDGET: **Cahaya Matahari**, 1/2 mile/1 km east of the town, breakfast only, no main meals. **Hotel Ana**, Jl. Ngurah Rai 75, very basic, rooms from Rps. 5,000. **Hotel Ijo Gading**, Jl. Nakula 5, from Rps. 10,000; **Losmen Taman Sari**, Jl. Nakula 18, with restaurant, rooms from Rps. 9,000. **Hotel Wirapada**, Jl. Ngurah Rai 107, with restaurant, rooms from Rps. 12,500. You can also eat simply and well at the **Rumah Makan Puas** on Jl. Ngurah Rai.

YEHEMBANG
Accommodation / Restaurants

On the main Negara-Tabanan road, about 4 mi/6 km beyond Yehembang, a road branches off S leading to a long, remote beach of black lava sand. In the village, a *losmen* offers simple overnight accommodation; there's a small restaurant close by. It's in Yehembang that the well-known painter Putu Windya Anaya runs the *Sangar-Nirartha* painting school.

MEDEWI
Accommodation

Hotel Nirwana, on the beach, rooms from Rps. 15,000; **Medewi Beach Cottages**, on the beach, new, luxurious bungalows, rooms from Rps. 65,000. There is also a simple **losmen** on the main street,

rooms from Rps. 10,000. The beach here is very popular with surfers.

LALANG LINGGAH
Accommodation

Balian Beach Club, amid coconut palms, lovely view of Yeh Balian river; rooms from Rps. 15,000.

SERIRIT
Accommodation

Hotel Singarasari, by the *bemo* terminal, rooms from Rps. 10,000.

CELUKANBAWANG
Accommodation

The **Hotel Drupadi Indah**, with restaurant, is the only place you can stay in Celukbawang.

PEMUTERAN
Accommodation

LUXURY: **Mata Hari Beach Resort**, tel. 0362/92312, fax 92313, swimming pool, diving excursions, catamaran sailing, mountain bikes, motorboats, windsurfing, tennis. *MODERATE:* **Tamran Sari**, reserve in Denpasar, tel. 0361/288096, fax 289285, spacious complex, some bungalows with sea view. **Pondok Sari Beach Bungalows**, tel/fax 0362/92337, right on the beach.

TERIMA BAY
Accommodation

Margarana Accomodations, with restaurant, rooms from Rps. 15,000.

LABUHAN LALANG
Accommodation

Labuhan Lalang only has a few simple tourist bungalows near the beach, with rooms from Rps. 7,500.
Excursions

At the tourist bungalows in Labuhan Lalang you can hire a boat to Menjangan Island (about 1/2 hr). Prices per person per hour: 7,500 Rps; a guide costs another Rps. 5,000. The island of Menjangan is the gateway to a fascinating underwater world, providing wonderful opportunities for divers. Since Labuhan Lalang lies within the West Bali National Park, there is a charge of Rps. 1,000 to go on to the beach. **Scuba-diving tours** can be organized from the resorts of Kuta, Sanur, Nusa Dua or Lovina Beach; you have to bring your own equipment with you (or rent it in Permuteran's hotels). You can rent snorkels and goggles in Labuhan Lalang. **A walk** of about 10 hours will take you right round the Prapat Agung penisula. You will see macaque monkeys cavorting in the mangroves. There are small huts or refuges along the route. Bring your own food and water.

VOLCANOES, TEMPLES AND BEACHES OF BLACK SAND

SINGARAJA
LOVINA BEACH
EAST BULELENG
LAKE BRATAN
BATUR VOLCANO

SINGARAJA

Singaraja, on the north coast of Bali, is the administrative capital of the regency of Buleleng, which extends from the Prapat Agung peninisula in the West Bali National Park as far as Cape Ngis in the east. The coastal region is protected from rain by the "screen" of the great volcanoes of the interior and therefore – in comparison with the south – has a considerably drier and hotter climate. On the plains the farmers of northern Bali grow not only rice, by the irrigated and non-irrigated methods, but also maize and grapes. At higher altitudes they cultivate fruit, coffee and cloves. They also raise pigs, buffalo and cattle for the market.

In the 17th century, the domain of the Raja of Buleleng, Ki Gusti Panji Sakti, extended as far as eastern Java. The name Singaraja means "Lion King"and recalls that terrible ruler of the feudal age, under whose aegis Balinese slaves were shipped over to Java in exchange for gold and opium. The trade was extremely profitable; Singaraja blossomed into a wealthy royal capital.

Previous pages: The meru of the Pura Ulun Danu in Batur, with the sacred mountain Gunung Agung behind. Left: Balinese man with "destar," traditional festival headgear.

As the Dutch were already establishing themselves in this region by 1849, European influence had a much deeper and more lasting effect here than in the south, until Indonesian independence a century later, . Consequently, the rigid caste system and the rajas, supposed to be allied with the Hindu gods, lost much of their power. The local feudal rulers were turned into Dutch colonial administrators, fettered by regulations. In 1882, Singaraja was granted the status of capital of the colony of Bali, and gained further importance through its flourishing port. But after World War II, measures introduced by the new national government deprived the Dutch-influenced capital of its importance: the port was transferred westward to Celukanbawang; the government offices were moved down to Denpasar; and an international airport was opened in the south of the island. The development of beach resorts in Sanur, Kuta and Nusa Dua led to the further downgrading of the former colonial capital.

At the **Old Port**, dilapidated warehouses are the only reminder of Dutch colonial prosperity in the days when this harbor was the commercial hub for all of eastern Indonesia and (until 1940) the first place where tourists arriving in Bali touched land. Since the main export cen-

125

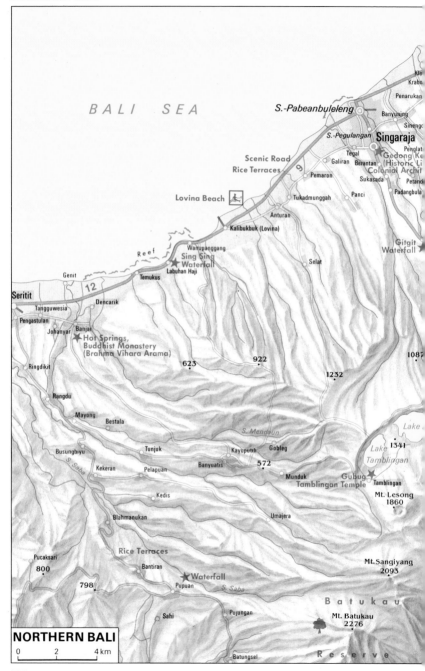

BALI SEA

S.-Pabeanbuleleng

Klo
Krabo
Penarukan
Banyuning
Sinengo
S.-Pegulangan
Singaraja
Tegal
Penglat
Galiran Berantan
Gedong Ke
(Historic Li
Colonial Archit
Scenic Road
Rice Terraces
Pemaron
Sukasada
Petand
Padangbula
Tukadmunggah
Panci
Lovina Beach
Anturan
Kalibukbuk (Lovina)
Gitgit
Waterfall
Reef
Warupanggang
Sing Sing
Waterfall
Selat
Genit
Labuhan Haji
Temukus
12
Seritit
Tangguwesia
Dencarik
Pengastulan
Johanyar Banjar
Hot Springs,
Buddhist Monastery
(Brahma Vihara Arama)
623
922
1087
Ringdikit
1232
Rangdu
Mayong Bestala
S. Mendaun
Lake
Busungbiyu
Tunjuk
Kayuputih
Gobleg
1341
Lake
Tamblingan
Kekeran Pelapuan
Banyuatis
572
S. Saba
Munduk
Gubug
Tamblingan
Kedis
Tamblingan Temple
Mt. Lesong
1860
Blahmanukan
Umajera
Rice Terraces
Pucaksari
800
Bantiran
Mt. Sangiyang
2093
798
Waterfall
Pupuan
S. Saba
Batukau
Sahi
Pujungan
Mt. Batukau
2276
NORTHERN BALI
Reserve
0   2   4 km
Batungsel

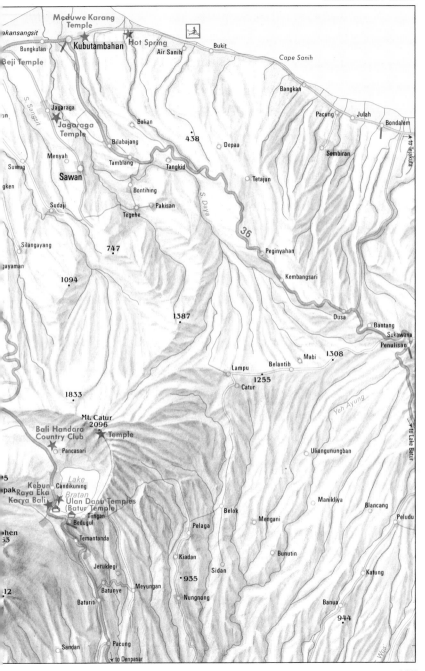

akansangsit

Meduwe Karang
Temple

Bungkulan

Kubutambahan

Hot Spring

Air Sanih

Bukit

Cape Sanih

Beji Temple

S. Sangsit

Jagaraga

Jagaraga
Temple

Balian

438

Depaa

Bangkan

Pacung

Julah

Bondalem

to Tejakula

un

Menyah

Tamblang

Tangkid

Sembiran

Suwug

Sawan

Bontihing

Tetajun

gken

Sudaji

Pakisan

Tegehe

Silangayang

747

S. Daya

36

Peginyahan

jayaman

1094

Kembangsari

1387

Dusa

Bantang

Sukawana

Penulisan

Mabi

1308

Lampu

Belantih

1255

1833

Catur

Yeh Ayung

to Lake Batur

Mt. Catur
2096

Bali Handara
Country Club

Temple

Pancasari

Uliangunungban

5

pak

Kebun
Raya Eka
Karya Bali

Lake
Bratan

Candikuning

Manikliya

Blancang

Peludu

Ulan Danu Temples
(Batur Temple)

Tingan

Belok

Mengani

hen

Bedugul

Pelaga

33

Temantanda

Kiadan

Bunutin

Jeruklegi

Sidan

Katung

12

Batunye

Meyungan

935

Baturiti

Nungnung

Banua

944

Sandan

Pacung

to Denpasar

W.os

ter for cattle, coffee, spices, and maize was moved to Celukanbawang – after the original anchorage at the mouth of the River Buleleng silted up – the only boats trafficking here are the little outriggers of local fishermen. In the Sukarno era, a statue to a famous freedom fighter, called the **Yuddha Mandalatama**, was erected by the harbor. In style and form it is reminiscent of the heroic mode of Socialist Realism which has influenced so many monuments in the emerging nations of the Third World.

The Dutch colonists' prosperity drew Chinese traders and artisans to Singaraja; their industry and business acumen helped them become the city's economic elite. In the **Chinese Temple** by the Buleleng Bridge, Confucian merchants and their families pay homage to their ancestors. A colorful relief above the temple entrance illustrates the "Legend of the Eight Immortals." The **Chinese Cemetery**, which has some tombs of very unusual design, is near Lingga Beach on the western edge of the city.

Long before the voyages of Vasco da Gama, Arab seafarers already had the spice-routes across the Indian Ocean firmly under their control. When the Moroccan traveler Ibn Battuta visited Sumatra in 1340, he encountered an already well-established Islamic sultanate. The long-standing Moslem community in Singaraja can also be traced back to Arab, Javanese and Buginese origins. Their Friday mosque is located to the south of the harbor on Jalan Imam Bonjol; you can spot it from a long way off thanks to its zinc-covered dome. The **Masjid Agung,** or Great Mosque, dates from the 19th century. To the east of it lies the market quarter, or **Pasar Anyar**. At night, many people also visit the **Pasar Banyusari**, by the bus station of the same name, at the western end of Jalan Ahmed Yani.

On Jalan Veteran on the southern edge of town is a building which, until the

Japanese invasion of February 1942, was the residence of the Dutch governors – who no doubt enjoyed the change from the cold, damp climate of their homeland. Until the 1930s, they managed, for tactical reasons, to protect Balinese Hindus from the missionary zeal of their Christian countrymen. At sunset, the **Colonial Residence** offers a fine view of the Old Port and the sea. Not far from this building, which today houses the administrative seat of the Regent (*bupati*) of Buleleng, stands the emblem of the city, the statue of the winged lion **Singambaraja**, which dominates the intersection of Jalan Ngurah Rai and Jalan Veteran.

A "must" for bibliophiles is the **Gedong Kertya Historical Library** (only open in the mornings), situated a little further east along Jalan Veteran. Here you can see more than 3,000 ancient manuscripts written on the leaves of *lontar* palms. There is also a collection of *prasastis*, which are copper plates inscribed with the edicts of the rajas, dating from the 14th century. In part of the former Rajas' Palace, the **Puri Kawan**, immediately behind the libraray, you can now see sarongs being woven.

On high ground by the Jalan Gajah Mada stands the **Temple of Shiva**, the Pura Dalem of Singaraja. The steps leading up to the inner courtyard are flanked by terrifying reliefs of the witch Rangda. And Durga, the female embodiment of Shiva's destructive energy, watches over the nearby cremation site. Maintaining the balance between creation and destruction, death and birth is the underlying theme of Balinese Hinduism.

In the village of **Bratan**, about 1 1/4 miles (2 km) further south, you can watch silversmiths at work. Some 6 miles (10 km) southward at **Gitgit**, a path leads off the main road to a 30-foot (10 m) high waterfall (*air terjun*) on the upper reaches of the river Buleleng; these cascades are at their most impressive during the monsoon season.

Lovina Beach

In 1970 the last Raja of Buleleng, Anak Agung Panji, built the first hotel on the 4 1/2 mile (7 km) gray-black beach of Lovina, which runs from Pemaron past Kalibukbuk to Temukus. Word of Bali's new hangout spread rapidly among the backpacking fraternity: it was a quiet, palm-fringed, low-budget beach resort with beautiful underwater coral reefs offshore. Today, it's true, the sunsets are just as impressive as ever, but apart from that quite a lot has changed. In the 1980s, simple *losmens*, cheap compared to those in Kuta, sprang up like mushrooms; now, there are more than 40 modest bungalow hotels. At night, heavily-laden trucks rumble along the Singaraja - Gilimanuk - Java highway, which runs parallel to the beach. In spite of this, Lovina Beach is still a quieter and more restful place than Kuta or Legian. You will not find any culinary sensations in the numerous little restaurants, but at least the fish is good and fresh. For variety, you can get authentic Chinese cooking at the **Aditya Restaurant**. There is still a lack of accommodation in the higher price-range, but plans are in hand to remedy this.

In the early morning the sea water is clear, even close to the beach; otherwise you can get a fishing-boat to take you out to the snorkelling areas on the coral reefs. There, around dawn, you will see dozens of dolphins playing among the outrigger boats with which they have become familiar.

In the early afternoon, the heat tends to reduce beach activity to a somnolent minumum, so it makes a nice change to take an excursion to the village of **Banjar**, 8 miles (13 km) from Lovina (you can get a moped taxi in Dencarik for the last 2 miles/3 km of mountainous terrain). On a hill above this Hindu village stands the Buddhist monastery of **Brahma Vihara Arama**, founded in 1958, and worth visiting for more than

129

just its beautiful view over rice terraces and down to the sea. Stone watchmen guard the staircase leading up to it, and a lotus pond adorns its outer courtyard. The main hall of the white-walled Vihara is decorated with reliefs showing scenes from the life of the Buddha, from his birth until his ascent into Parinirvana. A *stupa* presents symbolic representations of the elements and the stages of enlightenment according to Buddha's teachings. In the next hall stands a gilded figure of Buddha, flanked by two statues of Avalokiteshvara, the savior in Mahayana Buddhism, who lives on today in Japanese Zen and certain other religions. However, the yellow-garbed monks who live in the monastery follow the rather puritanical meditation regime of Theravada Buddhism, which is widespread in Sri Lanka, Burma and Thailand. Visitors who are interested can take part in a two-week course in meditation.

The **hot springs** (*air panas*) near Banjar have been recently revovated and are a popular bathing-place for the Balinese. A hot sulphur spring gushes out at a temperature of 100°F (38°C) from the stone heads of eight sacred snakes and into three tiered basins. Recently installed changing rooms, showers, a restaurant and a *losmen* add considerably to the comfort and enjoyment of bathers.

The Temples of Eastern Buleleng

A particularly fine example of the almost Baroque temple architecture of northern Bali can be found at **Sangsit,** 4 1/2 miles (7 km) east of Singaraja. The **Pura Beji** of Sangsit is a *subak* temple for the local farmers, who for generations have been organized into irrigation associations. A closed *gedong* or shrine is dedicated to the rice-goddess, Dewi Sri, who is responsible for the fertility of the fields. Phallic *linggas* symbolize the pro-

Above: The day's catch is landed on the beach near Lovina. Right: A serpent's head spews water at the thermal spring in Banjar.

creative power of the god Shiva. The temple has become famous for its extravagant reliefs and highly detailed sculptures, which, in contrast to the dark volcanic stone of southern temples, are carved from pink sandstone. The wide temple gate of the Pura Beji is covered with arabesques, heads of demons and Garudas, and crowned by so-called *kayonans*, symbols of the Tree of the World and the Mountain of the World, which have become familiar through the shadow-puppet plays.

About 3 miles (5 km) southeast of Sangsit lies the village of **Jagaraga**, whose **Pura Dalem** is worth a visit to see its unusual reliefs: two rather corpulent Dutchmen are sitting in a Model-T Ford that has been reproduced in loving detail. They are being stopped by a Balinese who is threatening them with a peculiar-looking revolver. The richly ornamented statues of the bloodthirsty witch Rangda indicate that the temple is dedicated to the goddess Durga.

About 2 miles (3 km) further south is the village of **Sawan**, lying picturesquely among *sawah* fields. Here, smiths still practice the traditional art of making bronze gongs.

Back on the coast road, the next stop is **Kubutambahan**. In the **Pura Meduwe Karang** (3/4 mile/1 km east of the fork to the Batur volcano) farmers bring offerings to the sun-god Surya, the "Lord of the Fields," and to Mother Earth (*ibu pertiwi*), to ask them to grant fertility to the fields which they are unable to irrigate. There is a famous relief in the third courtyard, the Holy of Holies, to the left of the stone plinth which supports the shrines. At first glance the figure it depicts seems to be a Balinese, since the straight-backed cyclist is wearing a sarong printed with a floral pattern and some Indonesian-looking headgear. But in fact, it is a Dutch ethnologist named Nieuwenkamp, whose long nose – the typical mark of a Westerner to Southeast Asian

eyes – remains clearly visible, having survived restoration following an earthquake. Nieuwenkamp explored the island by bicycle in 1904, and one can imagine the excitement which his appearance must have caused in the villages. In the Balinese interpretation, the back wheel of the bicycle becomes a lotus-flower, the chain is left out as being superfluous, but instead a rat and a dog have been placed under the chain-guard, which itself bears a marked resemblance to a circular saw.

Continuing along the coast road, shaded by avenues of trees, you arrive, 11 miles (18 km) east of Singaraja, at the pools of cool spring water of **Air Sanih,** by a quiet beach of black sand. This is a wonderful place to relax, frequented mainly by Indonesian tourists; its beautiful gardens even surround a hotel and restaurant.

The Bali-Aga village of **Sembiran**, high up in the hills (19 miles/30 km from Singaraja) is not necessarily worth a visit, because – unlike Tenganan in eastern Bali – the villagers no longer keep up

their pre-Hindu traditions. On the contrary, they are obviously anxious to be regarded as perfectly normal Balinese; they even see the very name "Bali-Aga" as discriminatory. Nowadays they cremate their dead and no longer, as they once did, leave them in nearby megalithic hilltemples to be eaten by birds. Nevertheless, the tortuous mountain road to Sembiran certainly offers a superb panorama over orange groves and fields of maize to the sea.

Tejakula, 22 miles (36 km) from Singaraja, is a sleepy village with a distinctly Chinese stamp. In the banjar, Pande silversmiths make personal ornaments and ritual objects. A **horse bath** recalls the feudal era, when the raja's mounts used to be washed there. Nowadays, however, even the common people are allowed to bathe in it.

Above: The Meru of the Pura Ulun Danu stands in the middle of Lake Bratan.

LAKE BRATAN

If you are tired of burning your feet on the scorching black sands of the north coast, you can go and cool off in **Lake Bratan** in the nearby volcanic mountains. To get there, you have a choice of two roads. The fastest route into the mountains is the well-maintained Singaraja - Bedugul road (19 miles/30 km). But since, as the Buddhists say, the road is itself the destination, we would recommend a longer route which, although making for more difficult driving, goes through much more attractive landscape: via **Pengastulan**, **Rangdu** and **Banyuatis** to **Munduk** in the highlands, and then steeply up to the twin lakes of Tamblingan and Buyan. The two lakes were one until separated by an earthquake in the 19th century; they lie on the thickly jungle-covered north slopes of Gunung Lesong (6,100 feet/1,860 m) and Gunung Tapak (6,250 feet/1,905 m). From the village of **Tamblingan** a road leads up to **Lake Tamblingan** (4,260 feet/1,300 m),

– a forgotten oasis of silence. A few farmers have planted fields of maize and built huts on the shore of the lake; they are genuinely pleased to see visitors, provided these have mastered a few words of Bahasa Indonesia. Here and there, you can see fishermen crossing the lake in dug-out canoes. On the southern shore, the **Pura Gubug Tamblingan** stands among the reeds, recognizable by its new *merus*. This temple is dedicated to the ancestors of the rajas of Buleleng and Tabanan.

A road which was not paved until the 1980s runs high above the north shore of **Lake Buyan** and continues westward until it joins the main Singaraja - Denpasar road, about 37 miles (60 km) away. Soon, **Lake Bratan** appears to the south, lying picturesquely in an extinct volcanic crater. On the western shore, the **Pura Ulun Danu** indicates the religious significance the lake has for the Balinese. The lake-temple complex, which includes two islets, is where sacrifices are made to the water-goddess Dewi Danu (the three-tiered *meru*), as well as to Shiva (the seven-tired *meru)* and Vishnu (the eleven-tiered *meru*). Even the Buddha is honored with a pagoda temple containing five meditating Dhyani Buddhas, to the left of the split *candi bentar* gate; Balinese Hindus consider Gautama Buddha to be one of the many manifestations of Vishnu, the preserver of cosmic continuity.

The cool mountain climate, with temperatures as low as 52°F (11°C) at this 4,000-foot (1200 m) altitude, is particularly attractive to the foreigners who live and work in Bali. They come to relax in the elegant **Handara Country Club**, which has a good restaurant and an 18-hole golf-course, and is also open to ordinary mortals. In the middle of sacred Lake Bratan there is a water-ski jumping-ramp belonging to the **Hotel Bedugul**. This hotel, popular with Indonesian tourists, also offers parasailing. Moderately-priced bungalows (e.g. "Lila Graha") can be found in the village of **Candikuning**. There is also a colorful flower market there, where peasant women offer ornamental tropical plants, including many rare species of orchid. The broad bowl of the crater with its fertile soil and ample rainfall provides ideal conditions for growing fruit and vegetables: strawberries, passion-fruit, pineapples and apples all thrive amazingly here. Garden enthusiasts take delight in a 320-acre (130 ha) botanical garden, the **Kebun Raya Eka Karya Bali**, where you can see more than 600 types of tree and some 400 different species of orchid.

If you have brought hiking boots with stout soles and good traction, and are prepared to set out at sunrise, you can brave the ascent of **Gunung Catur** (6,875 feet/2,096 m), whose summit is crowned by a temple, the **Pura Pucak**, dedicated to Shiva. It is advisable to take a guide on this trek, which starts at the Hotel Bedugul and initially follows a path through the fields to village of **Tihingan**. From here, a path leads uphill through constantly changing rain-forest, where you have to climb over fallen trees. Soon the going becomes so steep that you, as an *orang putih* ("white man"), wonder how the locals, wearing only slippers, can make any headway in the loamy red soil, made sticky and slippery by the rain. You haul yourself up the slope, from one palm-vine to the next, until after a good six hours, you reach the tree-clad summit and the Pura Pucak temple. Having negotiated the descent in series of skids and slides, there is an alternative route, branching westward, high above the north shore of Lake Bratan, to Candikuning and from there along the lake shore back to Bedugul.

AROUND THE BATUR VOLCANO

The name **Penelokan** (35 miles/57 km from Singaraja and 19 miles/30 km from

Ubud) means "beautiful view," and the place lives up to this promise – although the famous view is often distorted by souvenir-sellers, touts, volcano-guides and boatmen. If you can ignore these, Penelokan, 4,750 feet (1450 m) in height, does indeed offer the best view over the Batur region: far below, in a gigantic volcanic crater, lies long, narrow Lake Batur, flanked by the still-active Batur volcano (5,630 feet/1,717 m) to the west and Gunung Abang (7,060 feet/2,153m) to the east.

Following the volcanic eruptions of 1917 and 1926, which cost thousands of lives, the inhabitants of the threatened village of Batur chose to move their settlement and its lake temple from the lake shore to the edge of the crater. Thus was born the **Pura Ulun Danu Batur**, an extensive complex comprising nine major temples on the ridge beside the road to

Above: A winged monster in the Pura Ulun Danu Batur. Right: Morning mist over the new town of Batur on the edge of the crater.

Kintamani. The lake goddess Dewi Danu (a Sanskrit word which is related etymologically to the European river names Danube and Don) is worshipped with offerings, even by rice farmers from the south of Bali, since Lake Batur feeds many of the springs which emerge some distance away in the regencies of Bangli and Gianyar.

Every three days, in **Kintamani** (altitude 4,900 feet/1,500 m), there is a bustling fruit and vegetable market; the cool climate may make sun-saturated beach tourists shiver, but it is ideal for horticulture. Kintamani also "produces" dogs in very large numbers; their presence is especially notable – or rather, audible – at night. The view is not as magnificent as that from Penelokan, but to compensate for this, the people of Kintamani generally seem rather more friendly.

Less than 4 miles (6 km) further north, in Sukawana, not far from **Penulisan**, a small road leads off to the mountain temple of **Pura Tegeh Koripan**, which is not only the highest temple in Bali, but also one of the most important. It may well also be the oldest, since you will not find any *merus* here. A seemingly interminable flight of steps leads up to a height of 5,725 feet (1,745 m), but it is well worth the climb: in the morning you can see as far as Java and, the other way, to Lombok. Unfortunately, after midday a cold damp fog often blows in.

In the highest group of temples, the **Pura Panarajon**, you will find numerous stone phallic symbols (*lingga*), more than 1,000 years old, and mounted on plinths which are said to represent the female sex-organ (*yoni*): they symbolize the Hindu god Shiva and his female energy-principle, Shakti. In Tantric imagery, this expresses both the worship of sexual energy and creative force and the uniting of opposites in an abstract sense. There is a row of vine-covered, much-weathered sculptures of the god Vishnu and his consort Lakshmi, and of Shiva

and Parvati – not forgetting their elephant-headed son Ganesha. You can also see a stone portrayal of a couple who are presumed to be King Udayana and his wife Mahendradatta (11th century A.D.). The statue of Brahma, Creator of the World, shows an East Javanese influence, and can be recognized by its four faces looking to the four points of the compass – statues like these are found at many crossroads on the island. It is possible that before the Pura Tegeh Koripan assumed its function as royal temple of Pejeng, it was a megalithic sacrificial site, since to this day unidentifiable stone fragments are still to be found near the temple.

Ascent to Gunung Batur

Seeing the sunrise over the Batur volcano is an unforgettable highlight of any trip to Bali. The best base-camp for this mountain tour is the little village of **Toya Bungkah** (also known as Tirtha) on the shore of Lake Batur, which has restaurants and simple *losmens*. You reach it by a winding road which runs from Penelokan down into the wide crater. Beside the lake, the nights are milder than on the edge of the crater. And in Toya Bungkah you can also revive your tired joints in the hot sulphurous water of an **air panas** at the lakeside.

For the climb up Gunung Batur you need a flashlight, sweater, water and sturdy footwear with good traction, since the upper slopes are covered with slippery lava sand. It is best to start out before 4 am; you can climb the first 2,000 feet (600 m) in two to three hours. The shortest path begins in Purajati; the ascent from Toya Bungkah takes rather longer. To be on the safe side, you should hire a guide at the hotel. When you reach the rim of the crater you have a wonderful view over the whole surrounding area; for Gunung Batur is in fact a volcano within a volcano: it rises out of a larger crater bowl, which was created millions of years ago by an explosion of gases which blew the top off the huge

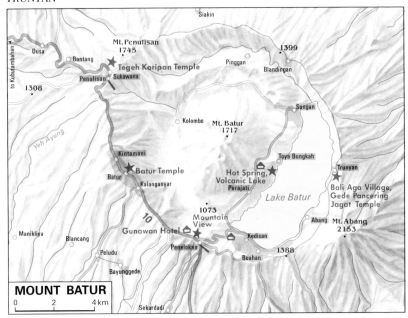

MOUNT BATUR

0   2   4 km

original volcano. In the bowl or *caldera* thus created, "little" Mount Batur was formed, and is still growing: plumes of yellow sulphurous steam rise into the air and to the southwest stretches a broad black lava-field which was created relatively recently, between 1965 and 1974. At sunrise, if visibility is good, you can see another volcano, Gunung Rinjani, on the island of Lombok to the east, while to the west you can make out the volcanoes of Java.

Trunyan

Lake Batur is about 1 1/2 miles (2.5 km) wide, 4 1/2 miles (7 km) long and 230 feet (70 m) deep. Because the lake provides water and therefore fertility for the rice-fields of the south, every year the *subaks* (irrigation associations) from the Ubud region come and sacrifice a water

Right: Beyond Lake Batur lies the Bali-Aga village of Trunyan.

136

buffalo here. The ancient Balinese villages which lie along the lake's shore are known as the "Stars of the Lake": Kedisan, Buahan, Abang, Trunyan and Songan. The only one of these which still has no road access is the Bali-Aga village of Trunyan; visitors thus have the choice of hiking there or arriving by boat. You can hire a motorboat in Toya Bungkah; the trip takes less than an hour. If you have already hired a skipper in Penelokan, he will probably put you ashore in the fishing and farming village of **Kedisan**, which boasts not only *losmens* and hot food stalls but also a jetty with a ticket office. If you have had enough of boats when you get to Trunyan, you can walk back to Kedisan via Abang in a little less than two hours.

There is no doubt that the "main sights" in Trunyan are of ethnographic rather than art historical interest. The ancient Balinese villagers do not cremate the bodies of their relatives, but lay them out under a spreading sacred banyan tree, to be eaten by the birds and animals of

the jungle; as a result, there are plenty of skulls and bleached bones lying around. Although foreigners may find it rather disconcerting, this ancient Mongolian and ancient Malay manner of dispatching the dead is still customary today among the Parsees of India and the tantric-influenced Buddhists of Tibet. The notion behind it is that the birds carry the dead souls up to heaven and thus favorably influence the cycle of rebirth.

Beside the cemetery stands the **Pura Gede Pancering Jagat** (literally: Temple at the Navel of the World). Its principal shrine houses the 13-foot (4 m) statue of the god Da Tonte, who embodies the creative and destructive forces of nature – and indeed the people of Trunyan, living in the middle of a volcanic *caldera*, have good reason to know all about natural forces. Only once a year, at the full moon in October, is the statue of Jagarat, which resembles a megalithic *menhir,* displayed to the faithful.

The fertility cult of Da Tonte/Jagarat is reminiscent of the ancient Indian cult of Shiva, and it is true that the Bali-Agas of Trunyan came into contact with Hinduism as early as the 10th century A.D. However, due to the remoteness and inaccessibility of their village, they remained unaffected by the further spread of Hinduism in Bali under the rajas.

Even today, the villagers are anxious to preserve their Bali-Aga traditions and cling to their isolation. Any villager who wishes to marry a partner from outside the village, for example, has to leave Trunyan altogether. Thus, anything foreign and unfamiliar is held to be of little value in the eyes of the villagers. Sometimes the tourist visitor is made very aware of this attitude. It is therefore a good idea to bring a guide from the hotel with you on this excursion.

Trunyan has always been a poor community, since the steepness of the volcanic slopes makes agriculture extremely difficult. As a result of this poverty, the sight of persistent, even oppressive beggars is quite common, unlike in the rest of Bali.

SINGARAJA
Accommodation

As all accommodation in Singaraja is rather modest, most people drive 6 miles (10 km) further on to Lovina Beach. Nevertheless, the following can be recommended: **Duta Karya**, Jl. Jen Achmad Yani 59, from Rps. 10,000; **Garuda**, Jl. Jen Achmad Yani 76, tel. 41191, from Rps. 9,000; **Saka Bindu**, Jl. Jen Achmad Yani 104, and **Gelar Sari**, Jl. Jen Achmad Yani 87, near the bus station, both from Rps. 7,000; **Sentral**, Jl. Jen Achmad Yani 48, from Rps. 9,000; **Singaraja**, Jl. Veteran 1, former residence of the Dutch colonial governor; **Tresna Homestay**, Jl. Gajah Mada, tel. 21816, from Rps. 8,000.

Restaurants

Gandhi, set back a little from Jl. Jen Achmad Yani in a little marketplace, is not particularly cheap, but reckoned to be the best Chinese restaurant in town. **Segar II**, opposite, is challenging Gandhi for the top spot. **Kartika**, not far away, also serves Indonesian food.

Useful Addresses

The **post office** is located at the T-junction of Jl. Jen Achmad Yani and Jl. Imam Bonjol.

The **telephone and telegraph office** is a little further south in a side street off Jl. Diponegoro.

There are two **bus stations**: one in the west on the road leading out to Lovina Beach, Jl. Jen Achmad Yani (for buses to Denpasar und Gilimanuk) and one in the east on the road going out to Sangsit (for buses to Kintamani and Amlapura). Bus fares: to Lovina Beach, 600 Rps.; to Gilimanuk, 2,500 Rps.; Denpasar, 2,500 Rps.; Kintamani, 1,800 Rps.; Amlapura, 3,000 Rps. Near each of the bus stations there is a **gas (petrol) station.**

There is a **hospital** on Jl. Diponegoro.

Evening Entertainment

In Singaraja in the evening, one either strolls around the bombastic Independence Monument and enjoys the sunset, or one goes to the cinema to see schmaltzy romances Indonesian-style or Kung-Fu thrillers. The **cinema** is on the far side of the river, east of the monument.

LOVINA BEACH
Accommodation

Lovina Beach is the name of the stretch of black sand, nearly 6 miles (10 km) long, which offers plenty of accommodation. The tourist center is **Kalibukbuk**. Out of season it is easy to find good, cheap accommodation; but at Christmastime and in August, especially on weekends, there is a serious shortage of rooms. There are still no luxury hotels.

But here is a small selection of hotels and bungalows (from east to west, as far as the big radio mast): **Baruna Hotel**, tel. 41745, fax 41252, right beside the sea, with swimming pool, from US$ 20-60. **Permai Beach Cottages**, tel. 41471, among rice-fields, not directly on the beach, from Rps. 15,000. **Jati Reef Bungalows**, tel. 41952; the reef in the sea right in front of this facility, is said to be the most beautiful on this stretch of coast, from Rps. 15,000. **Bali Taman Beach**, tel. 41126, fax: 41840, US$ 27-55. **Homestay Agung**, with bathrooms downstairs and bedrooms upstairs, restaurant on the premises, from Rps. 10,000. **Celuk Agung Cottages**, tel. 41039, with swimming pool and tennis courts, not directly on the sea, from US$ 29-64. **Lila Cita**, simple, right on the sea, from Rps. 15,000. **Adi Hotel**, other side of the main road, some distance from the sea, from Rps. 14,000. **Kali Bukbuk Hotel**, with restaurant, right by the sea, from Rps. 15,000. **Rumah Kita Cottages**, tel. 21660, 3 large houses (2-6 people each) in attractive garden, from Rps. 35,000.

Hotels and bungalows beyond the big radio mast: **Palma Beach Hotel**, tel. 41775, fax 41659, the the one and only luxury-class hotel, US$ 75-194. **Rambutan**, tel./fax 41388, on the road to the beach, attractive rooms, from Rps. 30,000. **Puri Bali Bungalows**, nearer the beach, from Rps. 15,000. **Rini**, on the beach, very clean, from Rps. 15,000. Along the main road there are a number of very cheap lodgings, such as **Wisata Jaya Hotel**, from Rps. 10,000; **Nirwana Cottages**, tel. 41288, spread over a large area by the beach, restaurant with view of the sea, from Rps. 15,000, two-storey bungalows from Rps. 50,000; **Angsoka Cottages**, tel. 41841, fax 41023, good value considering closeness to beach, from Rps. 15,000, but more expensive rooms available; **Aditya Hotel**, Tel. 41059, fax 41342, one of the most luxurious places, right by the sea, with swimming pool and shops, from US$ 23-52; **Ady Rama Beach Hotel**, tel. 41759, with restaurant and pool, right by the sea, simple rooms, US$ 25-50; **Parma Hotel**, nice location by the sea, from Rps. 10,000; **Toto Homestay**, good location, simple rooms, from Rps. 7,000; **Samudra Hotel**, tel. 41751, some distance from the sea, from Rps. 30,000. Further west there are a few more small, cheap establishments, including **Krisna Beach Inn**, tel. 41141, from Rps. 8,000.

Restaurants

The two-storey **Nirwana Pub** was long the gastronomic and social hub of Kalibukbuk. It is now generally thought to be overpriced, but is still a good place to go for a drink at sundown. The **Badai**, nearly opposite, is good and relatively cheap. The decor is very basic, but that does not seem to worry its many patrons. Going towards the beach you will find two reasonably-priced restaurants: the **Bali Bintang** and the **Kakatua**. **Khi Khi**, on the main street, is praised for its fish dishes. But the restaurants further out of town are also worth visiting. For lovers of seafood, **Banyualit**, on the beach going towards Singaraja, can be recommended. In the other direction, **Marta's Warung** and **Johni's** are very popular. Many restaurants advertise special evening buffets, but these do not always live up to their promise.

Useful Addresses

In Kalibukbuk there is a **Tourist Bureau**, open daily except Sun, 8 am - 8 pm.
There is no **post office**; some shops, however, offer a **"postal service."** And you can make **telephone calls** from the Aditya Bungalows.

Activities

No sooner have you arrived than you are deluged with offers to make the boat trip to see the **dolphins**. This begins at daybreak and costs Rps. 10,000 per person, unless you negotiate a group rate. The price usually includes one or two stops for snorkelling on the reef. A boat trip to the reef alone, for snorkelling, costs Rps. 5,000 an hour. Lovina Beach is also a good base for **scuba-diving**. West of the center of Kalibukbuk on the main road to the mosque is the diving sports agency **Spice Dive**. It offers the best opportunity for diving on the reef off Lovina Beach; they also organize diving expeditions to the island of **Pulau Menjangan** in the national park. These cost around US$ 60 per person.
On August 16th and on the day after Galungan, **buffalo races** are held in Kaliasem.

BEDUGUL
Accommodation / Restaurants

LUXURY: **Bali Handara Country Club**, beautiful view of the lake, tennis courts and an 18-hole golf course, from US$ 60. Prices in the very good restaurant begin at US$ 12.
MODERATE: **Bedugul Hotel**, tel. 26593, within the Taman Rekreasi Bedugul Zone at the southern end of the lake, from Rps. 25,000; the restaurant attached is a bit overpriced and has a rather dull menu. **Bukit Permai**, tel. 0362/23662, US$ 22-25; **Lila Graha**, old colonial building forms part of the hotel, prices start at Rps. 30,000. **Ashram Bungalows**, tel. 22439, right by the lake, prices start at Rps. 18,000.
BUDGET: **Hadi Raharjo**, very simple, in the main street, from Rps. 10,000. **Losmen Mawa Indah**, on the road to the Botanical Garden, from Rps. 12,000.

Activities

In **Bedugul**, motorboat trips (at Rps. 35,000 per boat per hour), waterskiing and paragliding are on offer. In order to enjoy the delights of the scenery to the full, trips in rented paddle-boats (Rps. 6,000 for 4 hours) are absolutely ideal.

LAKE BATUR
Accommodation / Restaurants

KINTAMANI: There are some *losmens* right on the main street, such as the modest **Superman's**, from Rps. 12,000, and the comfortable **Losmen Miranda**, from Rps. 6,000.
Approximately 550 yards (500 m) from the road into the crater itself is the **Puri Astin Inn**, from Rps. 12,000. From the new rooms you have a magnificent view of the sunrise. The hotel has its own restaurant.
PENELOKAN: Losmen Gunawan, superb view over the lake, with restaurant, from Rps. 15,000. **Lakeview Homestay**, tel. 23464, the cheap rooms are extremely cramped, but there is a magnificent view, with restaurant, from Rps. 15,000.
KEDISAN: Segara Bungalows, out towards Toya Bungkah, simple, from Rps. 8,000. **Segara Homestay**, near the center of town, from Rps. 8,000. **Surya Homestay**, in the direction of Toya Bungkah, with restaurant, from Rps. 8,000.
BUAHAN: Baruna Cottages, new, with restaurant, very quiet, from Rps. 8,000.
TOYA BUNGKAH: Alina, bathing-grottoes are a feature, from Rps. 8,000. **Amerta Homestay**, near the hot springs, from Rps. 8,000. **Awangga Bungalows**, the cheapest accommodation available, from Rps. 5,000. **Balai Seni Toya Bungkah**, located higher up, held to be the best accommodation in the town, has a small but interesting library, from Rps. 15,000. **Under the Volcano Homestay**, popular, has its own restaurant, from Rps. 8,000. In addition, there is further reasonably-priced accommodation and several new bungalow-resorts.

Excursions

Mountain tour of Gunung Batur: You can ask for a guide at your accommodation. If you need advice about tours, talk to the knowledgeable Jero Wijaya at Awangga Bungalows. The usual ascent starts in Toya Bungkah and takes 2-3 hours. Provided the visibility is good, you don't need a guide for this tour. You should aim to reach the summit by sunrise, or at the latest by 10 am, because after that the summit often disappears in cloud. Towards the end, the climb gets very steep, and slippery underfoot.
Boat trip to Trunyan: The price of a ticket includes visits to Trunyan, the cemetery outside the village and the hot springs in Toya Bungkah. Tickets (ca. Rps. 35,000) at the office on the jetty at Kedisan.

BALI SEA

JAVA

Singaraja

Gilimanuk

Banyu-
wangi

Western
Bali

Penga-
stulan

Northern
Bali

Negara

Central
Bali

Eastern
Bali

Karan-
gasem

BALI

Ubud

Klung-
kung

Denpasar

Sanur

Kuta

Southern
Bali

NUSA
PENIDA

INDIAN OCEAN

UNDER THE VOLCANO

KLUNGKUNG

SOUTH-EAST COAST

TEMPLE OF BESAKIH

AMLAPURA

Looming over eastern Bali is the volcano of Gunung Agung, which in a devastating eruption in 1963 buried three-quarters of the region under streams of red-hot magma and a rain of ash, and left more than 80,000 Balinese homeless. Because so much farmland had been irreparably devastated, the Indonesian government resettled many of the victims in Sulawesi. Since then, there has been a successful program of reforestation in Bali, and the natural ecology is slowly reestablishing itself.

Eastern Bali, consisting of the regencies of Klungkung and Karangasem, has many cultural and scenic attractions to offer: Klungkung town, the former capital of the rajas, with its active artisan traditions; the black sand beach of Kusamba and the bat caves of Goa Lawah; the beach resort of Candi Dasa and the Bali-Aga village of Tenganan; the mother-temple of Besakih in the shadow of the island's highest volcano (10,305 feet/3,142 m); the royal baths of Tirthagangga in the middle of a superb landscape of rice-terraces; and, last but not least, the lonely mountain temple on the Seraya massif, at the eastern tip of Bali.

Previous pages: The coast near Candi Dasa. Left: Rice-fields near Tirthagangga.

KLUNGKUNG (SEMARAPURA)

The administrative district of Klungkung, which includes the islands of Nusa Penida and Lembongan, is today admittedly the smallest of the island's eight *kabupaten* or regencies; but its influence has left a lasting mark on the whole of Bali. For after the collapse of the Majapahit empire in Java, Klungkung became the religious, cultural, political and intellectual center of the Hindu elite in the island. At that time the raja, who was known as *Dewa Agung* ("Great Divine One"), ruled from Gelgel, a few miles south of Klungkung. In the mid-16th century his domain extended from eastern Java over Bali, Lombok and Sumbawa as far as southern Sulawesi (Celebes Islands). In 1685, the capital was transferred to Klungkung, which, following the fragmentation of the Gelgel dynasty, was no longer Bali's most poweful city, but nevertheless remained the seat of the supreme court of justice and guardian of the Hindu tradition.

The main street of Klungkung, **Jalan Diponegoro,** is a hot, noisy shopping-street, lined with antique, souvenir, and video shops. A remarkable number of shops are owned by Chinese, since Klungkung is the main center for trade between Lombok and eastern Java. It is

143

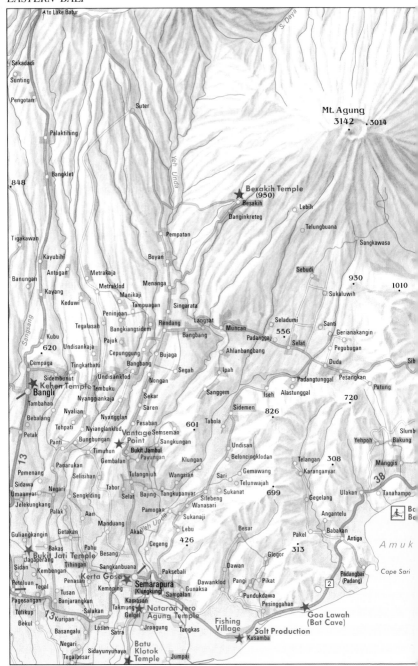

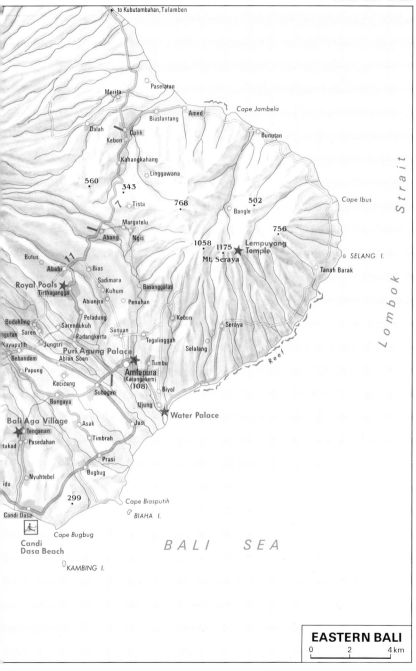

to Kubutambahan, Tulamben

Paselatan

Merita

Cape Jambela

Biaslantang
Amed

Dalah
Culik
Kebon
Bunutan

Kahangkahang

Linggawana

560
343

Tista
768
502
Cape Ibus

Bangle

Margatelu
756

Abang Ngis
1058
1175
Lempuyang
Temple

Mt. Seraya
SELANG I.

Butus
Tanah Barak

Ababi
Bias

Sadimara
Royal Pools
Tirthagangga
Kuhum
Basanggalas

Abianjro
Penahan

Budakling
Peladung
Kebon

ngutan Saren
Sarendukuh
Seraya

Kayuputih Jungsri
Padangkerta
Susuan

Bebandem
Puri Agung Palace
Tegalinggah

Abian Soan
Selalang

Papung
Tumbu

Kecicang
Amlapura
(Karangasem)
(108)
Biyol

Bungaya
Subagan

Ujung

Bali Aga Village
Asak
Jasi
Water Palace

tukad
Tenganan
Pasedahan
Timbrah

Prasi

Nyuhtebel
Bugbug

idu
299

Candi Dasa
Cape Biasputih

BIAHA I.

Candi
Dasa Beach
Cape Bugbug

BALI   SEA

KAMBING I.

Strait

Lombok

Reef

EASTERN BALI

0   2   4 km

145

well worth paying a visit to the busy **market** on the southeast side of Jalan Diponegoro.

Its is difficult to believe that as recently as 1950 the venerable Supreme Court of Bali still convened in the **Kerta Gosa** law courts. The rectangular *bale* which housed the courts stands, slightly elevated, immediately behind the entrance to the **Taman Gili**, the "island garden" that belonged to the rajas' palace, which was destroyed by the Dutch in 1908. It is impossible to miss, since it is right by the main intersection in Klungung. The *bale* where the law courts met is famous for its *wayang* style paintings, which portray not only the joys of heaven, but also the agonies of hell, with some very vivid scenes of torture. With help from the Dutch, the paintings were restored in 1930; in 1960, the roof of the hall was renewed and the paintings reproduced on

Above: The Bale Kambang in the island garden of Klungkung. Right: A Wayang painting in the Kerta Gosa.

asbestos sheets. The latest general overhaul was carried out in 1984 – unfortunately using chemical paints in places, which do not produce the same subtleties of color as the original natural paints.

The ceiling paintings, which are divided into nine rows of pictures, tell the story of *Bhima Suarga*, or Bhima's Descent into Hell – one of the *Mahabharata* legends about the five Pandava brothers, which particularly focuses on proper respect for one's father. While out hunting, Bhima's father, Pandu, brought down a deer, which, as ill-luck would have it, was one of the manifestations (*avatar*) of a Brahman. As punishment, Pandu and his second wife, Madri, had to boil in the cooking-pot of the death-god Yama. To redeem his father, Bhima forced his way into the hell of sinners; in the paintings, you can recognize him by his dark skin, moustache, jewel-encrusted club and black-and-white checked sarong. In the third row of pictures, he sees dreadful tortures: genitals are being burned off, women who have had abortions are being thrown to the crocodiles; mothers who do not want to breast-feed are being forced to suckle caterpillars; criminals are being hacked to pieces with knives or trampled by elephants; the demons of Yama are sawing into the skulls of sinners who do not honor their parents or ancestors; homosexuals and sodomites are devoured by pigs. In contrast to all this, the top row of pictures show the joys of heaven, open to the upright and the godly. After many setbacks – including being killed twice by his own father – Bhima succeeds in lay-ing the bones of his parents properly to rest. With the help of Shiva, he finally comes to the holy water (*tirtha*) with which he can perform the cremation according to the prescribed Hindu rites, and thus release the soul of his father.

The **Bale Kambang** ("Floating Pavilion") is a rectangular, open-sided hall which stands like an island in the lotuspond right beside the Hall of Justice. Its colorful, highly-detailed ceiling-paintings by Balinese artists, last restored in 1983, show scenes from the *Sutasoma* legends. The bottom row of pictures depicts Balinese astrology, and the one above tells a childen's fairy-story called *Pan Brayut.* In the third row there is the beginning of the story of Sang Sutasoma, a Tantric Buddhist holy man who symbolizes care and the renunciation of violence. In the course of his wanderings he converts the murderous elephant Gajah and the serpent-king Naga to Buddhism. When Sutasoma encounters a tigress about to devour her young for lack of food, he offers himself in their place – for Sutasoma personifies altruism and the victory over the strongest of all human instincts, the desire for self-preservation.

On the west side of the Taman Gili stands the **Pemadal Agung.** This gate, decorated with reliefs in which you can recognize Dutch figures, is the only part of the rajas' palace, Pura Semara, to have survived; the rest of it burned down during the colonial war of 1908.

Artists' Villages around Gelgel

In the village of **Tihingan,** 2 miles (3 km) west of Klungkung, you can watch smiths at work using old techniques to cast bronze gongs and metal instruments for *gamelan* orchestras. In the artists' village of **Kamasan,** the ancient Balinese tradition of painting in the *wayang* style is still practiced. The village is 2 1/2 miles (4 km) southeast of Klungkung, near the former rajas' capital of Gelgel. The original 18th-century paintings in the Kerta Gosa, as well as their recent restoration, were the work of the artists of Kamasan, who still mainly use natural colors. The village children learn the artistic skills of their forefathers in the painting school of the renowned artist Nyoman Mandra. In the 14th century, the ancestors of the gold- and silversmiths of the Banjar Pande Mas district crafted the crown jewels of the rajas of Gelgel.

East of Kamasan, in the village of **Tangkas**, the time-honored musical tradition of the *Gong Luang* is kept alive.

A place that has always held a particular magic for the Balinese is the village of **Jumpai**, further towards the sea, and famous for its *Barong* dance troupe. In the temple of **Pura Batu**, on the quiet beach of **Klotok**, processions of the faithful make sacrificial offerings to the gods of the sea on their way to the mother-temple of Besakih.

There is little in **Gelgel** (2 1/2 miles or 4 km south of Klungkung) to show that it was the headquarters of the most powerful raja dynasty on Bali between the 14th and 17th centuries, a dynasty from which all the island's aristocracy is descended. The dilapidated **Pura Nataran Jero Agung,** the ancestral temple of the rajas of Gelgel, marks the former site of the palace, which was abandoned in 1700. On religious holidays, members of the ruling castes of Bali gather in the **Pura Dasar** to worship some extremely weathered stone "statues" sitting on a throne

Above: School's out – fun on the beach at Padangbai.

of honor – but no amount of imagination can help discern what these are supposed to represent. With its nine- and eleven-tiered *merus*, the Pura Dasar has a ritual significance, since it forms the counterpart to the great mountain temple of Besakih. The split *candi bentar* gate at the entrance is interesting, since its inner surfaces, which would normally be smooth, are decorated with carved snakes.

The nearby **mosque** is one of the oldest on the island; it is said to date from the 14th century, having been built by a raja of Gelgel as a refuge for unsuccessful Moslem missionaries from Java.

THE SOUTHEAST COAST

With the exception of Candi Dasa, Bali's southeast coast has seen little tourist development. The route from Klungkung eastward into the old rajadom of Karangasem brings one first to **Sampalan**, where valuable silk *ikats* and gold-embroidered *songkets* are woven. The next stop is the fishing village of **Ku-**

samba. On its black sand beach, workers in simple straw hats build rectangular pans in the sand, where they leave seawater to evaporate – a primitive method of extracting salt which brings them only a small income. The brightly painted outrigger boats (*jukungs*) of the local fishermen are also very primitive, but in skilled hands quite seaworthy. The *prahus* are a bit bigger, with outboard motors as well as sails, but in the treacherous currents neither of these craft are exactly safe. They serve as ferries to the island of Nusa Penida, which can be seen in the distance; boats also go there from Padangbai and Sanur.

The easternmost tourist attraction in the Klungkung regency is the bat cave of **Goa Lawah**. Thousands of bats have made their home in the cavern which leads deep into the cliff, and right back – so the Balinese believe – as far as Besakih, 12 miles (20 km) inland. The air is filled with the shrill squeaking of these creatures and with the acrid smell of their droppings. By the cave entrance stands the **Pura Goa,** one of the royal temples of the rajas of Klungkung. The group of buildings contains, among other things, a throne for the mythical serpent-king of the underworld, Basukih, who is said to inhabit the cave. The cave's actual residents are thought to be pythons, which feed off the little vampire bats.

In a picturesque bay, its blue waters ringed by palm-covered hills, lies the little port of **Padangbai**, which comes alive for a short time each day when the car ferry from Lombok arrives. Sometimes, even an international cruise-liner will drop anchor in the bay. The fishermen of Padangbai are mainly Moslem; their big outriggers, or *prahus*, are painted in vivid colors, and have bows of a very unusual design, resembling the gaping jaws of a crocodile. Although there is an inviting stretch of white sandy beach, only a few *losmens* have so far been built for the use of tourists.

Scuba divers will find a fascinating submarine world on the coral reef off nearby **Pulau Kambing** ("Goat Island") – but may have to share it with a few cruising sharks.

On the wide, crescent-shaped Amuk Bay lies the beautiful, very peaceful and sandy **Balina Beach**. Almost the only accommodation you can find here are the **Balina Beach Bungalows,** which are in the medium price range and cater principally to scuba divers. Equipment, boat-excursions and even diving instruction are available. In the morning, you can take pleasant walks to the traditional villages of the hinterland, for example through Manggis and Ngis to Tenganan (four hours) or up into the mountains to Putung (three and a half hours).

Foreign investors in Bali's newest beach resort, **Candi Dasa**, wanted to convert it from its erstwhile status as an idyllic haven of tranquillity, known only to a few, into a tourist fun-fair a la Kuta. The name Candi Dasa means "Ten Temples," but perhaps not enough praying was done during the construction boom of the 1980s. For since the offshore coral reef was removed, the vengeful gods of the sea have brought heavy surf to deprive the owners of *losmens,* restaurants, discos and gift shops of their most important asset: the beach. This strip of sand is now so narrow that only at low tide can it be called a beach at all.

The bungalow-hotels were built much too close to the sea, and attempts are now being made to protect them from the breakers with thick, reinforced concrete walls – but it is doubtful whether this will succeed. Erosion by the surf continues unabated, and the once-famous little blue lagoon at the eastern end of Candi Dasa is turning an increasingly unattractive brownish-green color. In spite of this, *losmens* and shops continue to spring up like mushrooms all along the 2-mile (3 km) long "development axis" of paved highway.

Tenganan, 2 miles (3 km) north of Candi Dasa, is one of the most exhaustively researched villages in Southeast Asia. Scientists in every field, starting with ethnologists, have examined all aspects of the Bali-Aga (aboriginal Balinese) of Tenganan, even down to the genetic details of their blood-groups. Imagine how it would be if a group of Tenganese were to visit a European city, such as Basel, and take blood samples from the original inhabitants, or observe their Mardi Gras celebrations and draw farfetched conclusions about cannibalism among the ancestors of the Swiss from the Hindu Kush...

The village of Tenganan is surrounded by a wall and can only be entered through a narrow gateway. It is laid out on the ancient Malay pattern: the houses stand at an angle to the unusually wide "high street," in the middle of which are the in-

dividual rice-storehouses, shrines and *bales*. Outsiders are not allowed to enter the meeting-halls built on stone platforms and used by youth groups and clan associations, and especially not the 50-yard long Bale Agung where the village council (*krama desa*) holds its meetings. The 300 or so inhabitants of Tenganan believe themselves to be the chosen people of the god Indra, and set themselves rigorously apart from the outside world. With property of more than 2, 500 acres (1000 ha), they are so prosperous that they can give all their time entirely to leisure pursuits and the upkeep of their traditional customs. Their fields are cultivated by tenant farmers, including people banished from the village for having transgressed the complicated rules of cohabitation and ritual purity. Sacred stones play a major role in the belief system of the Tenganese, inspired by ancient India, and relatively unaffected by the spread of Hinduism and the influence of Java in the Majapahit era. At the upper end of the village square stands a Megalithic throne

Above: Sceptical observers of the temple festivities in Timbrah. Right: The simple merus of the "mother-temple" of Besakih.

of the gods. Unlike the rest of Hindu Bali, the dead of Tenganan are not cremated, but buried.

The *ikat* fabrics of the village are both famous and expensive. The traditional *Kamben Geringsing* is woven by women in the double-*ikat* technique, which takes months of work; some of the patterns are said to have been designed by the god Indra himself. It is a religious obligation to wear a temple-sash of *Geringsing* at all important ceremonies, such as name-giving or marriage, *rejang* dancing or the playing of *Gong-Selonding* music.

BESAKIH: THE MOTHER OF ALL TEMPLES

An absolute must on any trip to Bali is a respectful visit to the temple of Besakih on the southwest slope of Gunung Agung, the fateful mountain of the eastern Balinese. Modest clothing should be worn, for the god Agung is quick to anger, and punishes the frivolous with red-hot streams of lava.

If you are driving to Besakih through Klungkung, you can stop in **Bukit Jambul** in the neighboring regency of Karangasem, from where there is a magnificent view over emerald-green rice-terraces – best of all from the **Panorama Restaurant**. However, since Gunung Agung and Besakih are hidden in cloud by about midday, you should postpone gastronomic pleasures until after you have visited the temple.

About 5 miles (8 km) further up the mountain, in **Rendang**, a lively fruit market is held every three days. Durians and salaks are the specialities. In the village a research station has been established where vulcanologists monitor the seismic activity of Agung.

The mother of all *puras*, the holy Besakih, stands in an imposing position some 3,000 feet (950 m) up on the southwest slope of Agung – halfway to heaven, so to speak. But the gods certainly make you sweat for it: climbing the steep path in the warm sun, past rows of soft-drink shops, you may wish you'd started out earlier. Visitors, male or female, who are showing too much leg must borrow a sarong and put it on to avoid profaning the holiest place in Bali.

The Pura Besakih was probably founded in the 8th century as a shivaitic shrine, and in the 11th century it served as a Buddhist place of worship. After an earthquake in 1917 the buildings were fully restored; and in 1963 the lavastreams from the eruption of Agung spared the sacred shrines of Besakih – which, to the Hindus of Bali, seemed nothing short of a miracle. The extensive temple grounds, which contain more than 50 *merus*, are oriented along their central axis towards the summit of Gunung Agung. The Balinese believe that the volcano of Agung is the *Mahameru*, the mountain of the gods and throne of the Sanghyang Widhi Wasa, who, in a contest for mastery of heaven, turned himself into a column of eternal fire – a kind of super-*lingga* – and thus trumped his rivals, Brahma and Vishnu. When he descends to earth as Shiva, he resides in Besakih, in the central complex of the **Pura Pentaran Agung**.

A broad staircase, flanked by figures from the *Mahabharata*, including the five Pandava brothers, leads up to the Paduraksa Gate, which only Hindus may enter. Non-Hindus can walk around the outer walls of the Pura Penataran Agung, and get a glimpse into the interior. The ritual center of the temple is the lotus throne in the first courtyard, only accessible to Hindus. The three chief gods, Shiva (center), Brahma (right) and Vishnu (left), seat themselves here when they visit the world of mortals on the holy day of *Turun Kabeh*.

It used to be a privilege reserved for the royal families of Bali to worship their deified ancestors in the individual Pura Padharman shrines. Nowadays, peasant

Right: The sacred mountain of Bali, Gunung Agung, seen from Lombok.

pilgrims also come here to make offerings to the rice-goddess Dewi Sri in the Pura Banua for the continued fertility of their rice-fields, and to take consecrated water (*tirtha*) home with them. The craftsman caste of smiths have their own temple in a rectangular building on the west side of the Pura Agung. There you can often see processions of wives of the gamelan-, gong- and swordmakers' castes carrying high piles of imaginatively-decorated sacrificial offerings balanced on their heads.

About 100 yards northwest of the Pura Agung stands the much smaller **Pura Batu Madeg**, dedicated to Vishnu. Some 25 yards east of the temple of Agung is the **Pura Kiduling Kreteg,** the temple to the god Brahma, with a row of tiered *merus*. You may not find any nectar of the gods (*amrita*), but soft drinks are on sale on some higher ground in the northeast corner of the Pura Agung, from where there is also a fine view of Besakih, the Agung volcano and the coast.

Temple Festivals

When the full moon shines in the month of Kedasa, the fourth in the Balinese calendar, Besakih becomes an arena for impressive processions. On the day when the gods visit the Pura Besakih, tens of thousands of Balinese come here to celebrate the festival of *Batara Turun Kabeh*. This is simultaneous with the *Odalan* festival, the anniversary of the founding of the temple, which according to the Hindu calendar is celebrated every 210 days. The new year festival of *Galungan* is also celebrated here and lasts about ten days.

The great *Eka Dasa Rudra* only takes place every hundred years – the last one was in 1979. Back in 1963, there was a plan to move the date of the festival forward to coincide with a visit by President Sukarno, but the Agung volcano put an end to that: the dramatic eruption was

seen as a bad omen and a punishment for having monkeyed about with the divinely ordained calendar. In 1965, there was terrible butchery when devout Hindus unleashed their hate against the godless Communists, whom they blamed for the whole disaster. Finally, in 1979, the *Eka Dasa Rudra* ceremony for the appeasement of the angry Shiva and the ten other chief Balinese deities was held on schedule, without incident and with the support of the Indonesian government. President Sukarno, although himself a Moslem, was guest of honor. No cost or effort was spared: no fewer than 77 animals were brought for sacrifice, including a tiger, an eagle and a crocodile, as well as domestic animals and even insects. The sacrificial ceremony took place in Besakih on March 27th, 1979, and thus was the harmony between gods and men restored.

Every ten years – the last time in 1989 – the *Panca Walikrama* is held in Besakih; this sacrificial festival serves to purify the souls of Hindus.

Climbing Gunung Agung

It is true that there is a path leading up to the 10,305-foot (3,142 m) summit of Gunung Agung, but this is no gentle mountain walk: to do it, you need to set off shortly after midnight, not just in order to reach the top ridge by sunrise, but so that you can be down again before sunset! The climb involves some 7,200 feet (2,200 m) of vertical ascent, and takes five or six hours. There is a nasty surprise towards the end: a very steep lava-field that is really tough going. Before that, the path winds through jungle and brushwood, in which – particularly on the lower slopes – it is easy to lose your bearings, and it's therefore a good idea to hire a local guide. These are usually physically fit students, who will even carry your backpack. You should bring with you several liters of water, provisions, a flashlight with spare batteries, and warm clothes, since it is easy to underestimate the icy wind at that altitude. Once you arrive at the top, you can

look down on to the floor of the Agung crater, 300 feet (100 m) lower than the summit ridge, and measuring about 500 yards in diameter across the top. The view across the whole of eastern Bali as far as the sea is nothing short of overwhelming.

From Besakih to Amlapura

Away from the mainstream of tourist traffic, a little road leads eastwards from Rendang through the superb landscape of the southern foothills of the Agung massif. Particularly impressive are the rice-terraces around **Muncan**. In the little village of **Padanggaji**, the old tradition of the *Gambuh* dance has been preserved.

In **Selat**, a mountain track branches off towards Gunung Agung, leading through the village of **Sebudi** and ending about 4 1/2 miles (7 km) further on. From here,

Above: The view from Gunung Agung over southeastern Bali. Right: A Lontar scribe at work in Tenganan.

you have to continue up the mountain on foot. In the area around Selat, traces of the volcanic eruption of 1963 can still be clearly seen; a few hardy plants and cultivated fruit trees only sparsely cover the solidified streams of dark lava. It will be a long time before *sawah*, or rice-paddies, flourish here again, as they did before the catastrophe.

East of Selat, you can make a little side trip southwards to the farming village of **Iseh**. It was here, in the 1930s, that Berlin-born artist Walter Spies, father of the modern Balinese school of painting, bought a hut and called it home. He immortalized the magical views it commanded in his paintings *Iseh in the Morning Light* and *Sawah Lanscape with Agung*.

From **Sidemen**, a weavers' village about a mile (2 km) down the valley, on the road to Klungkung, there is a panoramic view out over the rice-terraces, reaching as far as the coast. Here *ikat* and valuable *songket* fabrics are hand-woven in tradtional patterns, using silk and gold and silver thread. You can stay overnight in stylish accommodation with a private family in Sidemen.

Back on the hilly road between Rendang and Amlapura, you should make another detour to the little village of **Putung** for some superb views. From the tea-terrace of the **Putung Bungalows** your gaze sweeps over a deep, narrow valley, whose steep slopes are terraced with rice-paddies, down as far as Amuk Bay on the southeast coast. A pleasant walk takes you in just three hours from Putung through Yehpoh and Bakung downhill to the almost medieval-looking village of **Manggis**. Here you will find probably the classiest "homestay" on the island – a good opportunity to get a first-hand experience of the way Balinese farmers really live.

Plantations with thousands of prickly salak palms, a bit further eastwards, are a sign that you are approaching the village of **Sibetan**. The main harvest season for these delicious but tough-skinned fruit lasts from December right into the summer. Continuing through Bebandem, Bungaya and Subagan, you finally reach Amlapura, capital town of the regency of Karangasem.

AMLAPURA

This sleepy regional capital was given the new name of Amlapura as a symbol of a fresh beginning after the devastating eruption of Agung in 1963, which affected this region particularly badly. For centuries before, the town had been called Karangasem – the same as the old rajadom, and today's administrative district in eastern Bali.

The Raja of Karangasem was an important man to the Dutch colonial regime, because, ever since the successful Balinese conquest of neighboring Lombok in 1678, he had ruled that island, as well, through viceroys from his own family. The Dutch cleverly exploited family

quarrels and, after military intervention in 1849, appointed a Karangasem prince of the Lombok line who was collaborating with them to govern Lombok and eastern Bali. Dating from this period are some of the Sasak villages around Amlapura, as well as the traditon of *Cekepung* music, a kind of vocal *gamelan* in which the singers perform alternate verses in the Balinese and Sasak languages.

Officially, the feudal age came to an end in Bali after the World War II, with the independence of Indonesia. However, a prince of the royal house acted as *Bupati,* or regent, of Karangasem, until as recently as 1979.

Altogether there are four historic royal residences in Amlapura. However, the only one open to the public is the **Puri Agung Kanginan**, north of the market square. It was built as a palace for the Raja Anak Agung Gede Jelantik, who held court there from 1902 until 1935 – though subject to Dutch administration. More than 100 members of the royal family still live within its walls.

The palace consists of several court-yards with *bales* and ponds fringed with trees and shrubs. A gate gives entrance to an outer court of the palace which is like a little garden with a beautiful old lychee tree in the middle. Through a second to-wered gateway, guarded by two stone lions, you enter the second courtyard, dominated by the **Maskerdam**: a recep-tion hall for important guests, with gilded wooden towers that were carved by Chinese craftsmen. You can look through its windows to get an idea of the rooms inside. In the last of these stand chairs in a baroque style; these were a gift which the Dutch queen, Wilhelmina, presented to her oriental subjects in 1910. The Bale London (not open to view) contains pieces of antique furniture bearing the royal coat-of-arms of England.

The former **water palace of Ujung**, 2 1/2 miles (4 km) south of Amlapura, was

almost completely destroyed in the erup-tion of Mount Agung in 1963.

It is certainly worth visiting, and per-haps staying a few days at the **royal baths of Tirthagangga** ("holy water of the goddess Gangga"), 3 3/4 miles (6 km) northwest of Amlapura. You can have a fine time splashing about in its pools, set in an enchanting landscape amid the rice-fields at the foot of Mount Agung. The village children also enjoy the cool, fresh water that gushes out from demon-faced gargoyles. For those who want to stay overnight and experience the real Bali, there are several small *losmens* to choose from. As you walk through the surround-ing countryside, you can see every stage of rice-growing in the waterlogged *sawah*, or rice paddies. Here, the tradito-nal Balinese types of rice have not yet been driven out by the high-yielding but more disease-prone and fertilizer-hungry varieties brought in by the so-called "green revolution."

From Tirthagangga, you can also take a pleasant walk along the path that first

Above: The picturesque remains of the water palace of Ujung. Right: One of the ponds in Tirthagangga.

runs northward to **Ababi** and then bends south to the goldsmiths' village of **Budakling**, in which there lives a small community of Mahayana Buddhists.

It is a steep climb – but worth the effort – up to the crater-rim of the volcanic Seraya massif (3,850 feet/1,175 m), whose northern slopes are crowned by the seldom-visited little **Pura Luhur Lempuyang** temple. As you climb, ever more magnificent views open out before you. The best place to start this day's walk is **Ngis** or **Basangalas** (reached via Abang). The Lempuyang temple is one of the six chief temples of Bali. At the New Year's festival of *Galungan* it is the scene of a great religious ceremony.

If, from Tirthagangga, you take the road northeast to Singaraja, it is worth turning off at the village of **Culik** and detouring past the peanut fields (*kacang*) to the Moslem fishing village of **Amed** with a quiet beach for swimming and snorkeling (simple *losmens* available). A little road leads from Amed around the Seraya massif and back along the coast to Amla-

pura, but it is winding, in poor condition, and therefore very time-consuming. Ever since the volcanic eruption of 1963, this easternmost tip of Bali has been largely depopulated; only a few fishermen, saltpanners and coral-gatherers still eke out a meager existence along the black shores.

If you carry on from Culik towards the north coast, past kapok plantations, you come to **Cape Muntik** and the village of **Tulamben**, whose waters are frequently visited by divers on day trips from Balina and Sanur. On the ocean floor about a mile (1.5 km) offshore lies the wreck of the *S.S. Liberty,* an American merchant ship torpedoed in 1942 by Japanese forces based on the island. Snorkelers will also be amazed by the number and variety of fish off this stretch of coast. In contrast, the hinterland is dry and studded with cactus, although it has a certain rugged attraction. However, as you continue driving north along the picturesque coast road, Bali once again shows her most beautiful face – a face that has up to now scarcely been scarred by tourism.

KLUNGKUNG
Accommodation / Restaurants

Ramayana Palace Hotel, east of the town center, relatively quiet, slightly set back from the main street, simple rooms, with restaurant and garden, from Rps. 12,000. **Losmen Wishnu**, Jl. Gunung Rinjani, centrally located, near the bus station, ask for a room on an upper floor.

The best places to eat are the Chinese restaurant **Bali Indah**, on the main street, or at nearby **Sumber Rasa**, south of the main street.

SOUTHEAST COAST
PADANGBAI
Accommodation

The best bets for accommodation are on the beach, east of the pier:

Rai Beach Inn, 2-storey bungalows built like rice-storehouses, from Rps. 25,000.
Sedani Kerthi Beach Bungalows, similar to the above, from Rps. 15,000.
Padangbai Beach Inn, with a view over the bay, from Rps. 8,000.
Topi Inn, furthest to the east, from Rps. 10.000.
Pantai Ayu Guesthouse, nice rooms, clean, with good views, on a hill at the edge of the village, from Rps. 15,000. In town, but away from the main street, you can spend the night in a farmstead: **Homestay Dharma**, very clean, from Rps. 8,000.

Restaurants

Topi Inn, on the beach, offers the best ambiance and good fish. Among the *warungs* on the beach, **Pantai Ayu** is especially worth a mention because of the friendly service, but the others are worth a try. People waiting for the ferry often sit in the **Warung Sederhana**, because it is the best place from which to see when the ferry ticket office opens.

Ferries to Lombok

As long as no ferries are cancelled, there are twelve departures per day to Labuhan Lembar on Lombok. Ferries depart every two hours, from 2 am to 12 pm. Depending on the weather, the crossing takes about 4 hours.

Fare per person (depending on which class): VIP class (with air conditioning): Rps. 9,000 for adults and Rps. 5,000 for children; economy class: Rps. 4,800 for adults and Rps. 2,500 for children; motorcycle: Rps. 6,000; car: Rps. 32,000; jeep: Rps. 40,000.

BALINA BEACH (BUWITAN)
Accommodation / Restaurants

Pondok Pantai Balina, tel. 41002, fax 41001, large complex on the beach, with restaurant, US$

48-120. **Puri Buitan**, tel. 41021, between US$ 35-75. **Amankila**, tel. 41333, fax 41555, luxury bungalows on a beautiful hillside site, from US$ 435.

Scuba Diving and Snorkeling

From the Balina Beach Bungalows, diving-trips are organized along the coast as well as to Nusa Penida and Pulau Menjangan. Cost: US$ 30-65, depending on duration and destination. Snorkeling trips begin at US$ 10.

CANDI DASA
Accommodation

There is an ample choice of accommodation in all price categories.

LUXURY: **Candi Beach Cottages**, tel. 41234, fax 41111, situated outside the town, to the west; swimming pool, tennis courts; on the beach, which is less built up than in Candi, from US$ 100-120. **Rama Hotel**, tel. 41684, closer to Candi Dasa, spacious complex by the beach – which is just a narrow strip here – from US$ 70. **Taman Air** (water garden), tel. 41540, fax 41164, inland from the center of town, with small fish-ponds, from US$ 75. **Puri Bagus Villa**, tel. 41131, fax 41290, under palm trees east of Candi Dasa, from US$ 85.

MODERATE: **Candi Dasa Beach Bungalows Two**, tel. 41126, fax 41537, three-storey hotel, in the center of town, on the seaward side, from US$ 78-180. **Pondok Bamboo Seaside Cottages**, tel. 41534, in town center, by the sea, with restaurant, from Rps. 27,500. **Puri Oka**, on the beach, east of the lagoon, with swimmingpool, from Rps. 35,000.

BUDGET: among the cheapest, but still pleasant, establishments are the bungalows on the sea, west of the road-junction to Tenganan, e.g. **Pelangi** and **Taruna Homestay**, from Rps. 8,000. Also very reasonable are some of the places near the lagoon, such as the **Rama Bungalows**, tel./fax 41778, and **Sidhu Brata Bungalows**, tel. 41825, from Rps. 15,000.

Restaurants

Many of the hotels by the sea have their own restaurants. Among the best are the **Pandan** and the **Pondok Bamboo**. On the landward side of the main road, **TJ's** has a little pond and is quite idyllic. There is a platform built out into the water, on which you sit on cushions, in the Balinese manner, and eat your meal on the floor. Mexican food is supposed to be one of the attractions here, but in fact this is generally limited to guacamole und tacos.

The **Kubu Bali Restaurant**, with its open kitchen, is spectacular and particularly popular. The cooks, bathed in sweat, juggle with their pans, and now and then a sheet of flame shoots six feet in the air. Good

Chinese and Indonesian food is served here. Some of the tables are placed round a secluded little pond.

Activities

The reef directly in front of Candi Dasa is no longer particularly suitable for **snorkelling**. Fishermen take snorkellers out in their *prahus* to the little off-shore islands.

The **Candi Dasa Bookstore** organizes a snorkeling tour by *bemo* to three different points along the coast towards Padangbai. The best place is on the blue lagoon. Rough cost per person, depending on numbers, from Rps. 12,000.

There is really nothing that one could call an exciting **night life**. Occasionally, dance groups are brought in from outside to put on a show, usually in conjunction with a buffet dinner. Posters advertising these events are put up everywhere.

Candi Dasa is also a good base for **walking tours** of the area. One small expedition is to climb the heights behind the town. This is worthwhile chiefly for the beautiful view over the lagoon and the beach. One pleasant day-long walk – bring your own food – is the round trip via Tenganan (you go through the town and up to the end of the adjoining valley) – Macang (here you can buy tea and peanuts in a *warung*) – Ngis – and back to Tenganan. On this walk you pass through inhabited rain-forest and over curving rice-terraces, reaching one summit after another which command wonderful views of the coast, Nusa Penida island and villages like Ngis, nestled in the jungle. Essential requirements include a strong sense of direction, good physical condition and sturdy footwear.

Useful Addresses

There is no **post office,** but several shops sell stamps. The Permuntel **telephone office** is in the middle of the town near the top end of Pondok Bamboo. Several money exchange offices also cash travelers checks at acceptable rates.

At the **Pandawa Tour Information Center** (near Pondok Bamboo) you can book coach tours or rent jeeps, motorcycles, scuba-diving and snorkeling equipment. In addition, there are several smaller rental agencies.

Climbing Gunung Agung

Anyone who wants to climb the mountain without a guide is best advised to pick the route that starts near **Sebudi**, southeast of Besakih. Drive up the steep, potholed road until the paved surface ends; at the parking lot, you have to leave your car and walk. Only very heavy-duty overland vehicles can, in dry weather, drive on a bit further, as far as a temple that is being built. The path starts climbing beyond the

temple. In daylight you cannot miss it, since it climbs straight up the mountainside, turning neither to right nor left. The climb can take up to 6 hours, assuming you are carrying equipment for a possible overnight camp in one of the few, only passably comfortable, clefts in the rock. You should only undertake the climb if the weather is forecast to be fine for several days ahead, since the sole reward you get for your considerable exertion is the view over the green contours of the island. In addition to being in excellent physical condition, you'll need to have sturdy hiking boots and warm, waterproof clothing in case the weather changes. And don't forget to take plenty of drinking water!

AMLAPURA
Accommodation / Restaurants

Hardly anyone spends the night in Amlapura, since Tirthagangga is so near. As you enter the town, near the monument on the left, there are two *losmens*: **Lahar Mas**, at the edge of the rice-fields, from Rps. 10,000; **Homestay Sidha Karya**, nearer to the town center, from Rps. 8,000. Some way out of town, going towards Rendang, there is also the **Kembang Ramaja**, tel. 221565.

For meals, the best place to go is **Lenny's**, on Jl. Gajah Mada (the continuation of the road leading to the Raja's Palace), or else to the *warungs* at the bus station.

TIRTHAGANGGA
Accommodation / Restaurants

Tirtha Ayu Homestay, in the grounds of the Water Palace, has a restaurant above the pool; use of the pool included, from Rps. 25,000. **Losmen Dhangin Taman Inn**, near the water palace, with garden and restaurant, from Rps. 12,000. **Kusuma Jaya Inn**, situated above the town with a view over the rice-fields, rooms extremely simple, from Rps. 18,000. **Rijasa Homestay**, on the side of the street facing the palace, simple but pleasant rooms, from Rps. 7,000.

In front of the palace there are some simple *warungs*. At the **Taman Sari**, you can choose your fish fresh from the pool.

TULAMBEN
Accommodation

Gandu Maya Bungalows, located very close to the wreck (100 yards), are much-frequented by divers and diving schools, from Rps. 15,000. **Paradise Palm Beach Bungalows**, nice spot with garden and fish restaurant, from Rps. 30,000. **Mimpi Resort**, luxury site, booking through "Mimpi Jimbaran Resort," tel. 0361/701070, fax 701074, US$ 50-175.

HISTORY AND CULTURE OF LOMBOK

While the first settlers on Bali may have arrived on foot – since Bali was once linked to Java as part of the continental shelf – seaworthy craft would always have been required to reach Lombok. The depth of the Lombok strait makes it unlikely that there could ever have been any land link between Lombok and the land mass of the Asian continent. For a long time, it was assumed that the first settlers crossed the straits some time between 50,000 and 30,000 years ago. However, some archaeological finds on the island of Flores, which have not yet been precisely dated, may go back as far as 100,000 years; it is therefore conceivable that people could have been living on Lombok as long ago as this. Yet the earliest archaeological discoveries on Lombok itself date only from the Iron Age. On the mountain of Gunung Piring in southern Lombok, shallow graves have been discovered with bronze bracelets, iron tools and earthenware vessels buried alongside human remains. Traces of a megalithic culture are also detectable. On the south coast near Sepi, a 4 1/2 foot (1.5 m) high menhir is still worshipped as the *Batu Pujaan* (stone of worship). It is said to be 3,000 years old.

Recorded history also has relatively little to say about Lombok: it appears to be mentioned for the first time in the 14th-century chronicle *Nagarakertagama,* the richest source of information about the East Javanese empire of Majapahit, which records Lombok as a tribute-paying dependency. Otherwise, authority was in the hands of local rulers, one or another of whom from time to time set himself up as a prince over a larger region. In the east, particularly, a kingdom called *Selaparang* was able to establish itself and hold sway for a time, temporarily lending its name to the whole island. The present name of Lombok is presumably derived from the chili plant of the same name, and was given to the island by traders. The native Sasak call the island *Bumi Gora*, which means "dry farmland."

As the East Javanese Majapahit empire rose to become a major power in Southeast Asia (after around 1294), the first Hindu influences reached the island. As on Bali, some of the population wished to remain apart from this new culture and religion and withdrew to other, less accessible and more mountainous parts of the island. It is not clear whether these native inhabitants were the "Budas" (also described as "mountain people" or "Sasak living apart from the others") mentioned by a German expedition to the Sunda straits in 1911. Just as little is known about the origins of the name "Budas" – it may go back even earlier to the Buddhist gurus and thus indicate a link with the Indianized kingdoms of central Java and Sumatra. The influence of the Javanese variety of Islam was joined, after the 17th century, by the more orthodox form of Islam practised by the Bugis and Makassars of Sulawesi.

Politically, western Lombok came under the informal influence of the Balinese rulers of Gelgel, which had emerged as a new center of Hindu power after the downfall of the Majapahit empire in 1527. The Raja's palace at Selaparang was destroyed in 1678 by Balinese invaders, though they were initially unable to subjugate the eastern part of the island. The irrigation system of western Lombok was improved under Balinese rule, so that the region around Mataram flourished economically.

Previous pages: Summit and crater-bowl of Gunung Rinjani. Fishing in the old harbor of Ampenan. Left: Going down to the river.

165

After 1740, western Lombok was governed by the Karangasem dynasty. In the ensuing period, quarrels between the Balinese feudal overlords meant that the Sasak aristocracy was able to win new freedoms. Meanwhile, in the east of the island, Moslem Makassars from southern Sulawesi were from time to time able to gain a foothold.

In 1843, the Balinese Raja of Mataram, a descendant of the lords of Karangasem, signed a treaty of protection with Holland which expressly excluded the subjugation or even the occupation of the island by the Dutch. Thus secured, and with the support of the Sasaks in his own territories, the Raja of Mataram proceeded himself to subjugate the east of the island in 1849 and force the peasant farmers there into serfdom. Revolts against the new feudal lords broke out in 1855, 1871

Above: Learning lessons beneath depictions of historic deeds in the former Raja's Palace at Cakranegara. Right: A village in the poor southeastern region of Lombok.

166

and 1891, but were ruthlessly suppressed.

When the Sasak rebelled again in 1894, the Dutch used it as an excuse to intervene and to colonize Lombok. The first Dutch advance resulted in heavy Dutch losses, because Mataram's raja had modern weapons at his disposal; but a second invasion was more successful (from the Dutch point of view). After a bitter struggle, many members of the Balinese aristocracy ended their lives through honorably ritual suicide, or *puputan*. The raja's palace was burned down and its rich treasure-chamber plundered. Miraculously, the sole copy of the 14th-century *Nagarakertagama* somehow survived.

The new rulers proved themselves the equals of their predecessors, at least as far as the exploitation of the island was concerned, and the Sasak, who had turned to the Dutch for help, once again found themselves at the mercy of a harsh regime. The native population were forced to labor on the construction of roads and dykes, and under an administrative system enforced by local potentates, were compelled to pay high taxes. It is true that the agricultural yield increased thanks to the improvements in infrastructure, but the growth in population together with a drastic increase in the levy imposed on harvests – from 50 percent under the Balinese rajas up to 80 percent – led to food shortages for the thereto self-sufficient population. Their plight was aggravated by the Japanese occupation of the island in World War II. Two years after Indonesia achieved independence, in 1951, Lombok was combined with Sumbawa to form the province of Nusa Tenggara Barat. Still, the island has yet to recover fully from the effects of colonization. In years when the weather is unfavorable and harvests are poor, thousands die of starvation even now. Particularly vulnerable are those living in the dry southeast of the island.

LOMBOK SOCIETY

The Sasak people, of Malay origin, comprise the majority of Lombok's population. Apart from a few coastal villages that have been settled by Buginese fishermen, they inhabit all the land to the east of the area around Mataram that was formerly under Balinese influence. Most of them rely on agriculture as their chief source of income, yet only about half of them own their own arable land.

The land belongs either to the large hereditary landowning Sasak aristocracy or to the Indonesian government; the latter leases it to peasant farmers. The landless peasants lack capital and so do not make a very good job of farming the land that they have leased. Others simply hire themselves out as seasonal agricultural workers. However, the frequently recurring periods of drought, and problems over land-tenancy, make it impossible to eke out a living, and they have no choice but continually to seek supplementary sources of income. Even landowning farmers are not immune to this fate, since about 70 percent of them own less than 2 1/2 acres (1 ha) of land, and 40 percent own just over one acre (0.5 ha).

To keep starvation at bay, some of them cut firewood in the forests, even in the nature reserve on Gunung Rinjani, and sell it at the market. Many of them have to move from the country into the three-town capital of Ampenan-Mataram-Cakranegara and seek work in the few factories and artisan workshops that have been set up there. A number of them try their luck as hawkers along the beaches of Senggigi.

Living in the west of Lombok are about 85,000 Balinese, who form an important political and cultural minority. Many of the island's religious customs, even those in other areas of Lombok, stem from them. Some of them were quick to react to the possibilities afforded by the still-fledgling tourist industry, and have successfully specialized in providing cheap accommodation and mid-price hotels for independent travelers.

167

The conditions of land tenure in Balinese western Lombok are the same as in the rest of the island, except that here it is the Balinese aristocracy which forms the top stratum of big landowners. In many of the village communities a traditional feudal form of cooperation has been preserved, whereby in times of need the landowners are obliged to provide special assistance to their tenants and bondmen. However, as the land gradually loses its ancient mythical significance and becomes a commodity, so these traditional feudal bonds between master and serf are also becoming looser.

Urban life, on the other hand, thrives in the capital in the west of the island, a conglomerate that grew out of the three once-separate villages of Ampenan, Matram and Cakranegara. More than ten percent of Lombok's population already lives here. Apart from the Sasak and the Ba-

linese, there are two other conspicuous ethnic minorities: the Chinese and the Arabs. Most of the latter live in a quarter called the *Kampung Arab* in the old port of Ampenan and generally pursue middle-class occupations, while the Chinese basically control the food and restaurant sector and the rapidly expanding number of small businesses. Particularly in Ampenan and Cakranegara, the number and variety of Chinese shops is striking.

The wealth of these descendants of former coolies, who were originally brought to the island as cheap labor by the Dutch, is now a thorn in the sides of many Indonesians. In 1965, when everyone suspected of being a Communist was ruthlessly persecuted, many Chinese fell victim to these pogroms, and numerous small communities in eastern Lombok were almost completely wiped out. Even today, there are official regulations in force which impose strict limits on the separate cultural activities of the Chinese minority.

Above: A mosque in central Lombok. Right: Religious and national elements mingle at many festivals.

THE RELIGIONS OF LOMBOK

In contrast to Bali, the majority of Lombok's inhabitants are Moslem. In the west of the island, Balinese Hindus live peacefully alongside more or less orthodox Moslems and Chinese Buddhists, Confucians or Taoists, whose faiths are not recognized by the state. A symbol of this coexistence is the temple of Lingsar, where people of different faiths and creeds worship together.

Lombok further differs from other Indonesian islands in that it has its own form of Islam, found here and nowhere else: the *Wetu-Telu* religion. This is a hybrid religion which, beneath a veneer of partially observed Moslem precepts, clings to old animistic beliefs and has even incorporated Hindu rituals. As this religion is not recognized by the state, there are only approximate figures of the number of its adherents, estimated at around 30,000; the numbers are made all the more uncertain by the steady flow of converts to orthodox Islam. The main

centers of this Sasak faith are in Bayan and the region around Tanjung in the north, as well as Sade and Rambitan in the south.

There are two main written sources which feed the streams of the Islamic faith: the Koran, which is the holy word as revealed by Allah to the Prophet Mohammed, and the Hadith, a collection of sayings and deeds attributed to Mohammed. From these are derived the basic principles of the practice of the Moslem faith, or the "five pillars of Islam": 1. Belief in Allah as the only God, and in Mohammed as his last prophet; 2. prayer five times daily; 3. observance of the laws of fasting in the month of Ramadan; 4. giving alms to the needy, and 5. the pilgrimage to Mecca.

The followers of the Wetu-Telu religion only partially adhere to these dictates. They certainly recognize the Koran as Holy Writ, but less from a desire to do God's will than from their belief that the Koran is something invested with magic power. Accordingly, their copies of the

169

Koran, like the Balinese *lontar* writings, spend most of the time locked up in a small chest beneath the roof of the mosque, and are only read out on a very few high holidays. Allah is invoked not five times, but only three times a day; the religion's name (*telu* = three) seems to derive from the recurrence of the number three. An orthodox Moslem might also take exception to the Wetu-Telu prayers, because they might sound to him more like the recitation of a mantra than a reminder of the supreme power of God.

Followers of Wetu-Telu even observe Ramadan in a different way: instead of fasting during daylight hours for a month, they only abstain from material pleasures for three days. The injunction to be charitable and give alms is followed by making offerings of rice, in Balinese style. And in lieu of the great pilgrimage to Mecca, believers seek out sites holy to Islam on Lombok or Java. In accordance

with their animistic traditions, they visit the graves of their ancestors and make offerings to them. The Rinjani is also a sacred mountain for them; they make pilgrimages there on nights of the full moon, to spend three days by the lake and at the hot springs, which they believe will confer upon them magical powers.

Wetu-Telu worshippers, whose faith orthodox Moslems regard as an imperfect form of Islam, have always been the target of revivalist Islamic movements – for better or worse. So it was that in the purges of 1965, when they were paradoxically suspected of being atheists, they suffered terrible persecution, and to to this day refer to it as "the year of danger to life."

Orthodoxy has found many new followers, especially as the result of a fundamentalist revival that began in Sesong in the east of Lombok. One of the orthodox believers' most effective recruitment techniques was generously to distribute food supplies in times of widespread drought and hunger.

Above: A young mother finds shade beneath a banana plant.

FESTIVALS AND CEREMONIES

Whereas in many parts of Bali the people are proud and pleased to welcome respectful outsiders as spectators at their festivities, foreign visitors at Lombok's religious celebrations are still a rare and unaccustomed sight. Thus, villagers tend to have an ambivalent reaction to tourists. On the one hand, the visitors are something of a sensation; but on the other; the villagers wonder rather anxiously what these foreigners with their constantly flashing camera equipment are actually doing in the middle of the ceremonies. Then again, the law of hospitality demands that they should protect the visitor from the brazen curiosity of the local children. And yet there is a danger that strangers can cause real annoyance when the commotion inevitably caused by their unaccustomed intrusion on the scene frightens the water buffalo, causing them to stampede out of the village pond and flee in wild confusion across the parched rice-fields. In short, it is more difficult for the tourist to participate in the "real" life of Lombok than it is in Bali, and requires the utmost restraint and sensitivity.

In terms of the number of festivals it holds, Lombok is distinctly behind Bali, although there's a wider range of different ceremonies here as a result of the many different religions. Too, the ceremonies here can't offer anything to compare with the professional skill of the Balinese dancers from Ubud. On Lombok, ceremonies have retained their original, rustic, if slightly amateur flavor.

West Lombok's calendar of religious festivals basically recognizes all Balinese celebrations because the Balinese minority clings doggedly to its traditions, which are nurtured devoutly by each temple community. However, these festivals often have different names from those used on Bali, and no variations of them have yet developed as tourist attractions, as they have on Bali. Especially

wort mentioning is the annual *Pujawali* festival in honor of the god Batara in the Kalasa Temple at Narmada. At the same time crowds of devout Hindus make the pilgrimage to the seat of the god on Gunung Rinjani, and during a ceremony called *Pekelan* they offer him golden objects such as drinking goblets, which are cast into the crater lake. The date of this festival is determined by the *Saka* year and takes place at the time of the full moon in the fifth month, which corresponds to July or August in the Gregorian calendar.

In March or April, a festival of thanksgiving for the harvest is held at the shrine on Gunung Pengson, in the course of which a water buffalo is sacrificed. Every year during the full moon in June, one of the most splendid of Balinese temple ceremonies is held at the Pura Meru temple in Cakranegara.

The Balinese Hindus and the Sasak followers of the Wetu-Telu religion celebrate another festival together in the double temple of Lingsar. Also called *Pujawali*, it begins in the late afternoon before the night of the full moon towards the end of November or early December. The festivities climax in a rice battle between the two groups, Hindus and Wetu-Telus: cooked rice is packed tightly into banana-leaves which function as a kind of artillery shell. Outsiders, and especially tourists, are considered fair game. The "battle" is not without an element of danger, because stones sometimes "accidentally" find their way into the ammunition (just as they do in snowball fights back home). The festivities conclude with cock-fights, which are officially sanctioned only on this occasion, and the sacrifice of water buffaloes, goats or hens.

The calendar of Wetu-Telu festivals partly follows along the lines of the Balinese celebrations surrounding the principal milestones in a person's life, and partly reflects the high feast-days of the

Moslems. Here, as on Bali, the rituals following the birth of a child include the burial of the four "brothers and sisters" born at the same time – placenta, afterbirth, amniotic fluids and blood – in a coconut-shell container by the front entrance of the house; and there is also a ceremony to accompany the child's first haircut after 105 days. From the Moslems comes the custom of circumcising boys between the ages of twelve and fifteen, after which they are carried round the village on a decorated trolley in the shape of a lion. The expressions on the faces of the elaborately bandaged boys speak volumes. At the same age, the girls have their teeth filed, according to the Balinese custom. Once they have menstruated for the first time, they are carried through the village on wooden horses, so that everyone will know that they are now of marriageable age.

Above: Girls of marriageable age are carried through the village. Right: Musicians on their way to the festival near Senaru.

172

Many Sasak communities have special traditions enabling teenagers who are ready for marriage to get to know each other. One of these is the *Nyale* festival, which takes place in Kuta once a year between February and April. The whole night is spent catching glowing *nyale*-worms, which swim in these waters by the thousands; cooking them; and eating them together. In families of higher castes, there are opportunities for getting to know your future partner in a domestic setting. If there is more than one suitor for a girl's hand, her family invites them all over and gives them a chance to win her over with their charms, ranging from compliments to poems they've written themselves. However, touching, to say nothing of kissing, is very much frowned upon. If a girl publicly accepts a gift from a potential bridegroom, she is permitted or even obliged to marry him.

As a rule, marriages take place by arrangement between the families concerned, or between their cousins. As on Bali, kidnapping the bride is another option, particularly if the abductor is a suitor which the bride, rather than her family, has chosen. If this does happen, however, the families have to agree on a price for the bride before the couple can return to the village.

The official state holidays, such as the Indonesian national holiday on August 17th, are fixed according to the international (Gregorian) calendar, and are celebrated with as much extravagance on Lombok as everywhere else. In addition, there are a number of Moslem festivals: the most important, the *Hari Raya* ("great day") lasts for at least two days and ends the month of fasting of Ramadan. This is a time for visiting relatives and, so it seems, making up for time lost during the fasting period by cramming as much fun into a short period as possible. Huge feasts give ample opportunity for carousing. Tourists travelling during this period must be prepared for high prices and crowded public transportation.

HINTS ON ETIQUETTE

Much of what is true for Bali also applies in Lombok. But in addition there are one or two peculiarities that one should note when dealing with the Moslem population. These people, even though they may not be orthodox in their observances, nevertheless think in basically religious terms, and therefore one should take account of this in one's own behavior. For instance, Moslems have to obey their dietary laws, which forbid them to eat pork or drink alcohol. A particularly awkward time is the fasting month of Ramadan. Moslems have to get up before dawn in order to take a final meal and say the morning prayer before the sun rises. This means that as the day wears on, they often become nervous and irritable. In these circumstances you should treat them with consideration. You should not, for instance, eat or smoke in their immediate company. If you are travelling in

the east of the island at this time of year, you should equip yourself in the evening with food for a picnic the next day, since many shops are closed during the day.

As far as clothing is concerned, one should perhaps be more fully covered than is necessary in Bali, even in supposedly isolated areas. On the beach women should wear at least a one-piece swimsuit and preferably cover up with a tee-shirt or sarong enveloping the whole body. Men should also avoid wearing anything too casual and revealing.

If you're travelling as a "confirmed" single person, it is advisable, and, more importantly, courteous, not to argue against marriage or children when in conversation with local people. Outspoken views of this kind will, in a traditional society like Lombok's, only meet with incomprehension: children and marriage are established, essential elements of the social structure. The same applies to any confession of an atheistic philosophy – however much it may be founded on ethical and humanistic principles.

AUSTERE BEAUTY

WESTERN LOMBOK
SENGGIGI AND THE GILIS
GUNUNG RINJANI
EASTERN LOMBOK
SOUTHERN LOMBOK

WESTERN LOMBOK

If you're crossing from Bali to Lombok by boat, you can either take the ferry from Padangbai, which takes between four and five hours depending on the sea conditions, or the hydrofoil from the port of Benoa, which takes approximately two hours. On the way, you'll pass the fishermen's outriggers with their typical triangular sails. You may also catch sight of dolphins swimming near the ferry. On Lombok, the ferry docks at a pier in a sheltered bay in the harbor of Labuhan Lembar; the little town itself is just over half a mile (1 km) further inland. From here you can take a bus or a *bemo* to the three-town capital of Ampenan-Mataram-Cakranegara, a journey of about an hour. Most people prefer to continue their journey immediately to Senggigi, which will take another half-hour or so by *bemo*. There you will find a well-developed (and continually expanding) tourist infrastructure, offering accommodation in all price categories. As long as you are not sleeping next to a building-site, this is the one place on Lombok

Previous pages: In the markets you will find colorful arrays of tropical vegetables and fruit for sale. Left: Deserted beaches north of Senggigi.

which comes closest to offering everything one could wish for in a South Sea paradise. At the height of the season, in August, accommodation is admittedly hard to come by. If you are arriving in Lombok by plane, you land at the airport of Selaparang on the northern edge of the town of Mataram, from where you can get a *bemo* into the town center. If you are heading for Senggigi, you should go west to the *bemo* station on the northern edge of Ampenan. From there, you can reach your destination in less than half an hour.

Ampenan

Ampenan is the oldest and most authentic of the three towns in western Lombok which have grown together to form the capital. The rusty pillars of the jetty are a reminder that this was once a port; today, fishermen sit on them and cast out their lines. The warehouses behind the beach are gradually decaying, while the shoreline is adorned with a bright fleet of fishing boats, lying on the sand in the sun.

The heart of the town lies around the Jangkok river. The people here are a mixture of Sasak, Balinese, Javanese, Arab and Chinese. Those living beside the river are predominantly immigrants from

177

B A L I

Labuhan
Carik

Lokorangan

Papak

Gondang ★ Waterfall
Gangga

GILI
MENO
GILI
AIR
Tanjung Krakas
Sira
GILI
TRAWANGAN ★ Temple Selelos
Bangsal Tembabar
Cape
Ketinan Pemenang
714
2210

Segara
Anak
G.

Rinjani

Mangsit 969
Senggigi Tourist Gunung
Baun Pusuk Punikan
Resort 1490 Reserve
Batu Bolong Sidemen
Batu Layar
Meninting Lendang
Bajur Endut Sesaot
Selaparang Airport Temple Peseng
Lingsar ★ Temple Aik
Ampenan Suranadi Bukak
MATARAM Cakra- Sweta Pancordau
negara ★ Narmada Wadja-
Pagutan Bengkel Mantang geseng
Bajur Summer Pringgarata Kopang
Prampuan Rumak Palace
Kedin Bonjeruk Su
Koranji Gunung Kuripan Ubung
Bangsal Pengsong Puyung Janapriya
Temple Gerung
385 Sukarara Praya Bele
Traditional
Weaving Batunyale
Batujai Penjanggik
Cape Terang GILI Pandanan Penunjak
Bebera GILI Bay NANGGU Labuhan /Potteries Mujar
POH Lembar Kawe
Cape GILI
Pandanan Poh GEDE 716 Mangkung Pegambur Sengkol
Bangko Pelangan Ketapang Marketplace
Bangko Taun Sekotong Jelateng
Surfing BATUGENDENG Patu Sade/ Awang
476 Jangke 153 Rembitan
Trad. Aan
Sepi Village Tan
Belongas Sepi Silung Aan
Bay Pengantap Blanak Kuta
Pegantap Mawun Tourist Grupuk
Cape Bay Are Resort Desert
Cape Sara Goling Point
Pangga Cape
Tampa

I N D I A N

Ferry Bali - Lombok

LOMBOK

0   5   10   15 km

Java and Sulawesi. From the bridge which links Ampenan with Mataram, you can see beds of *klangkung* (water spinach), as well as a now-defunct "River Kwai"-type bridge, of a sort frequently found on the west coast. Close by the harbor is the maze of small streets which make up the **Arab quarter**, the size of which has been considerably reduced by the sale of a piece of land to an oil firm.

The Chinese presence is evident from the many Chinese shops and a number of restaurants. On the northern edge of town is the large **Chinese cemetery**, which is still in use. It is said that wealthy Chinese have their most valuable possessions buried along with them, even including motorcycles. Their place of worship is the small, colorfully restored **Chinese temple** on Jalan Yos Sudarso (also known as Jalan Pabean).

Right next to the Chinese cemetery in the north of town, on the beach, is a Balinese temple, **Pura Segara**. It only comes to life at times of temple festivals; in fact, the scenery here is more striking than the temple itself.

Apart from a few cheap places to stay, Ampenan can boast a large market (by the *bemo* station), a cinema (*bioskop*), a Catholic hospital, and a number of antique shops. You can obtain useful information about climbing Mount Rinjani from the **Wisma Triguna** on Jalan Koperasi.

Mataram

Mataram is the capital of Nusa Tenggara Barat, a regency which includes the neighboring island of Sumbawa as well as Lombok. As befits its role, the town is filled with imposing modern government buildings, banks, and business headquarters, and the streets are alive with government officials and local administrators, unifomed schoolchildren and students.

Running from west to east through the three-town conurbation is a broad boule-

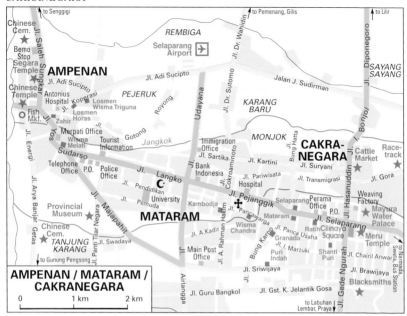

AMPENAN / MATARAM / CAKRANEGARA

0   1 km   2 km

vard which changes its name several times along its course. The little horse-drawn carriages (*dokar* or *cidomo*) are not permitted on this thoroughfare. Located along the border between Ampenan and Mataram are the Tourist Office, post office, police station, telegraph office and the office of Merpati Airlines.

Apart from wandering around the streets and alleyways of Mataram, it's worth making a visit to the **Provincial Museum of Nusa Tenggara Barat**. Along with basic illustrated charts and models explaining the geography, geology, culture and history of Lombok, exhibits (some labelled in English) include textiles, domestic utensils, amulets, krises, weapons and masks. To reach the museum, go to the intersection where the tourist office is located, then turn south onto Jalan Panji Tilar Negara; after a few hundred yards (0.5 km), you'll see the museum on your right.

Right: Horse-drawn dokars play up the rustic atmosphere of Cakranegara.

Cakranegara

Adjoining the handsome, but rather sterile town of Mataram is Cakranegara, which is quite a contrast, being more primitive and exceptionally busy. The rush-hour traffic here is worse than anywhere else on the island. Endless rows of shops and workshops line the streets; there's even a supermarket, on Cilinaya Square. Here, too, efficient and industrious Chinese businesspeople continue to play an important role in the town's economic life.

The center of Cakra, as people like to call the town, is the intersection of the main street, Jalan Selaparang, and Jalan Hasanuddin, which further south becomes Jalan Gede Ngurah. Located here, also, is the town's lively market, the Pasar of Cakranegara.

About four blocks further south is the blacksmiths' quarter. The smiths can be seen working at open furnaces, which are kept blazing with bamboo bellows. They make mainly agricultural imple-

ments, and their raw material is often scrap metal from old cars.

Cakra has the Balinese settlers to thank for its two most important sights: a palace and a temple. The **Pura Meru** – the largest temple of its kind in Lombok – can be recognized from a distance by its three soaring towers (*merus*) which have given the temple its name. Built in 1720 near the market area, the temple is dedicated to the Hindu trinity of gods, Shiva, Vishnu and Brahma. The temple's founder, Anak Agung Made Karang of Singosari, intended it to foster peace and unity among the quarrelsome Balinese feudal lords of Lombok.

The temple, which sadly has rather fallen into disrepair, has three courtyards. In the first, a wooden *kulkul*, or drum, calls the faithful to temple ceremonies. In the second courtyard, two raised platforms serve as altars for offerings to the gods. The innermost court has one large shrine and thirty-three small ones.

The *meru* with eleven roofs is dedicated to Shiva, that with nine roofs to Vishnu, and the seven-roofed pagoda to Brahma.

Opposite, on the other side of Jalan Selaparang, stands the **Mayura Water Palace**, or at any rate as much of it as the Dutch left standing. It was built in 1744, and until the conquest of Lombok in 1894 it served as the residence of the Balinese Karangasem dynasty and their court. Its centerpiece today is a large lotus-pool, in the middle of which stands an open-sided hall, reached across a little walled causeway. This apparently floating pavilion (*bale kambang*) was a courthouse for matters relating to the raja's empire, as well as a place of assembly for Hindu princes. In 1894, the palace's extensive grounds were an arena for two fierce battles, from which the Dutch emerged victorious. Today, they provide a tranquil refuge from the stress of city life. Amidst the green lawns and trees, fighting-cocks crow in bamboo cages. The palace also has its own temple.

One block away, on a side street, there's a **weaving factory**, which is open

to visitors. This is worth a look, especially in the morning, which is the only time when most of the looms are in use. As well as the weaving itself, you can see how the cloth is colored: either dyed beforehand, or painted by hand after it's woven. Much of what is manufactured here is exported to Bali.

If you walk north along Jalan Hasanuddin you soon come to the **livestock market**. Before you reach it, you can turn right into Jalan Gora, which takes you the short distance to the **race-track**. Horse races are held here on Sundays and holidays, and the jockeys taking part must be *under* twelve years of age. Falls are not uncommon, so the young riders wear crash-helmets and sometimes motorcycle goggles as well. In order to make the competition fair, the faster horses are handicapped. Betting is part of the fun, as

Above: In a weaving-factory in Cakrane-gara. Right: Sacrificial offerings for the double temple of Lingsar.

are the bitter tears shed by the losers who have not come up to the expectations of the supporters from their home village.

Sweta

Just outside the gates of Cakra lies Sweta, the crossroads for overland traffic and the home of Lombok's largest market. Buses, minibuses, *bemos*, *dokars* and trucks leave from the bus station in every direction. If you want to get a comfortable seat, do not wait until the market closes around 4 pm. But the market is certainly worth a visit, simply for the fact that is gives you a chance to see everything the island produces in one place, in colorful abundance.

As well as every conceivable kind of fruit and vegetable – including many you may never have seen before – the market sells dried fish, spices, tobacco, household goods, raffia and rattan articles, fabrics and even reproduction antiques.

An earthy, peasant atmosphere predominates; only occasionally will you

see the incongruous figure of a smartly-dressed housewife from Mataram among the customers. The throngs of people, the heat and the sheer abundance of everything can be oppressive. In the half-shade of the covered bazaar, and also outside, there are numerous *warungs*, tempting you to stop off for a drink and a tasty snack.

Narmada

A visit to Narmada, only 7 1/2 miles (12 km) east of Cakranegara, is a more relaxing experience. If you're coming from one of the resorts along the west coast rather than the three-city capital, you can detour around the heavily-trafficked city center along the airport road (Jalan Adi Sucipto). Make sure to bring a respectable bathing suit with you. Centerpiece of the visit is the former **Summer Palace** of the Balinese rajas in the center of Narmada, named after a sacred river in India. The terraced site with an artificial lake at the foot of the hill is sup-

posed to symbolize the sacred mountain of Lombok, with its crater lake – although admittedly it's a rather approximate reconstruction. The Raja of Mataram ordered it built in 1805, because he had reached an age when he could no longer climb up the Gunung Rinjani to make offerings. From that time on he made his offerings in the **Pura Kalasa**, which was part of the palace and where the solemn *Pujawali* ceremony is still held every year. Rumor has it, however, that the old raja had another reason for building the palace: he would invite young girls to swim in the lake and select the loveliest of them to be his mistress.

It was the Dutch who were responsible for the enormous irrigation pipes to the rear of the palace grounds. These were part of an island-wide infrastructure program designed to enable the tax-paying owners and tenants of agricultural land to achieve higher yields. Colonial administrators hoped that, in the long run, this would result in a significant improvement in their tax revenues.

The rather neglected park-like grounds are used on weekends as a recreation area by enormous crowds of local visitors. One can ride around the lake in rather kitschy large boats shaped like swans. There is also a swimming pool with cool, clear water.

Suranadi

A few miles northeast of Narmada, in the midst of an idyllic landscape, is one of the most ancient and sacred temples of Balinese Lombok, and the oldest: the **temple of the sacred springs of Suranadi**. The bathing-places of the shrine are decorated with ornate reliefs, and the pool is the home of sacred eels which can be coaxed ou from their hiding-places with the lure of hard-boiled eggs. The water itself is ice-cold.

Not far from the temple is the **Suranadi Hotel**, where back in the 1930s Dutch colonial officials were entertained in style. The water in the hotel swimming pool is continually replaced so that it is always refreshingly cool (64°F/18°C). The hotel has recently been enlarged with two bungalow-style buildings and is an ideal base for restful walking holidays. The hilly countryside in these parts alternates between rice-fields and jungle. Quite close to the hotel is a small area of protected forest, where some of the trees are labelled for educational purposes. There are many species of birds and butterflies here, and monkeys romp through the trees.

Worth an excursion is the wood-cutters' village of **Sesaot**, 3 miles (5 km) away. From the village's main street, you can turn off and cross a bridge to reach the river, ideal for picnics and swimming – although the water, which comes directly from the Rinjani massif, is very cold. In the village there is a simple *wa-*

Right: In the Balinese Pura Gaduh, part of the double temple of Lingsar.

rung on the main street. If you have a car and wish to return by a different route, you can swing through the hinterlands on minor roads that wind their way through the landscape, past small isolated market towns and along the extensive network of irrigation canals, before bringing you back to the main roads that cross the island.

Lingsar

If you head west from Suranadi, you will come, after a few miles, to the **double temple of Lingsar**, which was built in 1714 on the orders of the Raja of Lombok, I Gusti Wayan Tegeh, a member of the Balinese Karangasem dynasty. The site consists of the Balinese Hindu temple, **Pura Gaduh**, on the north side, which is linked by a flight of seventeen steps down to the Wetu-Telu temple of **Kemaliq Lingsar**. The number of steps is intended to symbolize the seventeenth day of the month of Ramadan, the day on which the Koran was presented to mankind. The construction of this temple is thought to have been a gesture of tolerance on the part of the raja, who wanted to gain the allegiance of his non-Hindu subjects.

There are four holy shrines in the Hindu temple. The two outer ones face the two sacred mountains of Bali and Lombok, Gunung Agung and Gunung Rinjani. The central double shrine embodies the twofold link between Bali and Lombok and is a symbol of their spiritual unity. The left-hand section of the shrine is dedicated to the mighty Gaduh (representing Lombok); the right-hand part is to the deified son of Ayu Nyoman Winten, the Raja's daughter (standing for Bali). Another shrine here is richly encrusted with stones, a phenomenon hearkening back to ancient animistic traditions.

In the Wetu-Telu part of the temple there is a tiled pool dedicated to the god

Vishnu and inhabited by sacred eels. A small statue shows the god mounted on his winged steed, Garuda. This is another small reminder of the way Balinese mythology and the Wetu-Telu culture are interwoven. Separate bathing-places for men and women and a larger pond complete the temple complex.

Followers of other religions worship their god, or gods, here as well, something demonstrated by the mirrors in the temple donated by Chinese merchants. Even Christians and strictly orthodox Moslems come here to offer up their prayers. The latter are also called Wetu Lima, on account of the five principal commandments of Islam (*lima* means " five").

Anyone wanting to drive from here direct to the west coast should take the narrow country road that joins the airport road not far from Cakra. The road takes you past open cattle-pens; with a bit of luck, you can see water-buffaloes in the irrigation canals having their backs neatly shaved.

SENGGIGI AND THE "GILIS"

Senggigi is a good place to catch your breath and get your bearings after the journey over from Bali. It is also an ideal base from which to explore western Lombok. There is a lot of new construction going on in Senggigi, especially around the main street. This may spoil your aesthetic enjoyment a little as you stroll around, but the buildings that have been completed so far show evidence of considerable sensitivity on the part of the developers.

It is easy to see why Senggigi has become so popular with tourists. There are long, white sand beaches, punctuated by palm-covered promontories reaching out into broad sweeping bays; stretches of offshore reef just waiting to be explored by snorkelers; and almost every evening a gorgeous picture-book sunset that floods the sky with red behind the sharply-etched silhouette of Gunung Agung on Bali, across the straits of Lombok.

Luxurious hotel complexes have started to replace some of the more basic accommodation, and the trend is definitely in the direction of up-market tourism. Even the nightlife has livened up a good deal. In the ever-popular **Pondok Senggigi** the band sometimes begins testing the amplification for the evening open-air concert in the early afternoon. But if you are looking for peace and quiet you will find it in the extensive hotel complexes by the beach. There, too, you're protected from the continual onslaught of the vendors who parade up and down the beach. Even in many of the more popular restaurants you have to exercise caution, otherwise one of these roving salesmen may step in and, with persistent sales pitches, glib tongue and swift hand, turn your pleasant meal into a heavy business lunch.

If you want a bit of exercise, you can take pleasant short walks up and down

Above: The temple of Batu Bolong, south of Senggigi.

the beach in either direction. If you're up for a longish walk, however, you'll find you have to keep detouring from the beach onto the coast road. Some half a mile (1 km) to the south is a small Hindu temple built on a rocky promontory. The temple derives its name, **Batu Bolong**, from a crack in the rock here, washed by the sea (*bolong* = hole, *batu* = stone). The temple is oriented towards Bali's sacred mountain, Gunung Agung. Legend has it that virgins were sacrificed here by being thrown to the sharks. There are certainly still sharks to be seen cruising expectantly round the rocks.

A bit more than a mile (2 km) further on, you come to an important Wetu-Telu shrine, **Batu Layar**. A small building here houses the tomb of a holy man, and behind it is a Moslem cemetery.

Because of its many curves and changes in elevation, the beautiful road north of Senggigi can be especially fun for motorcyclists. From the top of each little hill, you get a wonderful view of palm-groves beside the sea, deeply indented bays, and little half-hidden settlements. From the road, you can also look across to the trio of little islands lying off the coast of Lombok: Gili Air, Gili Meno and Gili Trawangan.

The Islands off the Northwest Coast

From Senggigi, there are two ways to reach the islands off the northwest coast: either directly with an outrigger boat (*sampan*), or by driving along the highway to the little harbor at Bangsal and taking a boat from there. Each method has something to recommend it. Travelling straight there by sampan – which you can do not only from the main beach at Senggigi, but also from other bays such as Mangsit, further north – you can enjoy the sea at close quarters, see many beautiful bays on the way, and have much less bother with luggage.

If you're going overland to Bangsal, you can opt for the inland route as an alternative to the coast road (or as a way to vary your trip, if you don't want to go back the way you came). This route involves going from Senggigi back towards Ampenan. At **Meninting**, the first major intersection, turn east and continue as far as the small market town of Landang Bajur (Gunung Sari, also known for its production of bamboo furniture), where you pick up the main road going north. Driving along this road, you'll soon pass through **Sidemen** with its small groups of modern residential buildings and a recently-constructed mosque. Sidemen is also known for its delicious red palm sugar, which is made by boiling down palm juice; it is usually sold at markets in the form of cylindrical chunks.

Shortly after leaving Sidemen, the road ascends in a series of tight bends to the **Pusuk Pass**; at its summit, there's a simple café with a magnificent panorama of the jungle and the islands. Here, you may encounter your first Javanese monkeys, who gather at frequent points along the twisting road down into the valley in the hope of retrieving tidbits from passers-by. However, you should not get too close to them, particularly the old patriarchs, who are fiercely territorial and may let interlopers know it. Whether driving in your own or a rented car, it's wise to take the precaution of honking your horn as you round the bends – not for the sake of the monkeys, but to warn oncoming traffic. Leaving the forest behind, the road passes through small villages lying in the midst of rice paddies. Finally, at **Pemenang**, you reach the turning for **Bangsal** "harbor." Once there, you can either take the regular ferry service or hire a fishing boat; it's less hassle to book the trip at the local ticket office and spare yourself haggling with the boat owners. The press of over-eager would-be porters and pushy T-shirt vendors can get quite annoying.

If you want to spend the night on one of the islands in the high season (July/August), make sure to arrive before midday; otherwise, you run the risk of being forced to sleep on the beach.

Gili Air

Gili Air, or "water island," which lies closest to Lombok, is the smallest and the most densely populated of the three islands. The majority of the 1,000 inhabitants live at the southern end of the island, facing the Lombok mainland. Most of the tourist accommodations are located here, as well as a diving shop. Apart from income derived from the still-fledgling tourist industry, the locals earn their living from fishing, from the produce of their coconut palms and from raising cattle and goats on a modest scale.

The palm-clad isle has a rural charm; it's ideal for leisurely walks. The coast consists of one long pale sand beach running right round the island. Although fishermen using dynamite have destroyed the coral reef in many places,

there are still some beautiful spots. In general, the best places for snorkeling are in the south (west of the landing-stage, in the southeast and the northeast; by contrast, the west coast, apart from a bit in the northwest, is hardly worth bothering about. Scuba divers like to go by boat to the north, near an underwater freshwater spring bubbling out of the sea floor.

Gili Meno

The middle island of the group, Gili Meno, is slightly larger than Gili Air, but has only one-third of the population (about 400). The island's most distinctive – and rather unusual – geographical feature is a salt-water lake in the west, which is used for the extraction of sea-salt. More interesting for tourists are the groves of palms and the island's hotel, which boasts its own water-treatment plant, as there is no fresh water on Gili

Above: Proper care and feeding of your water buffalo includes a good shave.

Meno. The other *losmens* have to obtain their water from the mainland. Make sure, therefore, to bring some kind of disinfectant or sterilisation tablets for the water you use to clean your teeth.This is the most peaceful of the islands, not least because there's hitherto been little accommodation available. The east, north and northwest coasts are the best for snorkeling.

Gili Trawangan

The largest island is Gili Trawangan, whose population of some 700 people is a mixture of immigrant Bugis and indigenous Sasak. A hundred years ago, the Raja of Lombok selected this island as a penal colony for 350 Sasak rebels. During World War II, the Japanese built a coastal battery on the hill in the south of the island with three big gun emplacements, the remains of which can still be seen today. The hill is worth climbing anyway for the wonderful views of sunrise and sunset which it affords; Bali in the west and Gunung Rinjani in the east provide magnificent backdrops. Once an insider tip jealously guarded by snorkelers, Gili Trangawan has developed into a charming base for travelers, with a range of amentities. Most of the available accommodation is still simple, in little houses on stilts; water for the *mandi* (bath) has to be pumped in from goodness knows where. There is no electricity on the island; thus, unless you are staying in a complex with a working generator, you can enjoy savoring the tropical night by candlelight or an old kerosene lamp. (Don't forget to bring oil of cloves to ward off mosquitoes.) At the height of the season, the numerous trendy local places (Rudy's Pub is especially "in" at the moment) compete for the favors of their low-budget guests, offering them free samples of Indonesian food (when they have fought their way to the buffet), accompanied by lively music.

The snorkeling is good along the whole of the east coast, but care should be taken not to swim too far from the reef, because the current becomes very strong further out. As a rule, however, you can let it carry you gently along the whole reef and enjoy the wide variety of species of tropical fish – a good guide to these is essential. For scuba-divers there is a shop which offers spectacular diving trips. Giant rays, sea turtles, sharks and giant clams are among the creatures you can regularly "bag."

NORTHERN LOMBOK AND GUNUNG RINJANI

The road along the north coast leads to a high point of the island, in more senses than one: Gunung Rinjani, Lombok's sacred mountain and highest elevation. The importance of this massif and its rain forests for Lombok's ecology was recognized by the Dutch when they came here, and so they placed the mountain, the second-highest in Indonesia (after the range

of 15,000 foot/5,000 m mountains of West Irian, New Guinea) under special protection. The protected area today covers more than 230 square miles (600 sq. km), in which foresting is subject to official restrictions in order to preserve the mountain's function as a reservoir of rain water. You can judge the success of these measures at first hand by touring the area yourself.

Along the North Coast

Between Pemenang and Desa Anyar, the coast road goes past rice paddies, coconut plantations and villages on river estuaries that have branched out into lagoons. In the rivers, you can sometimes see floating gardens of water spinach (*kangkung*); the men of the village washing their horses; or the women their laundry. The further northeast you go, the more frequent the sight of dry pastureland where one or two dusty water buffalo graze and the earth glows red-brown through its sparse covering of vegetation. The beaches are of black volcanic sand. The distances between settlements increase, and the dwellings become poorer. However, you can detour to the coast at frequent intervals along the way.

Shortly after **Pemenang**, where the road branches off to Bangsal and the ferry to the three "Gilis," you come to a track down to the coast at **Sira**, where a white sandy beach and wonderful snorkeling waters await you. A tourist hotel is being planned.

More than a mile (2 km) before you get to **Tanjung**, to the west (above the bay where one can snorkel), stands a **Balinese temple**, which is a good point for taking photos of the picturesque sunsets with Bali in the background. Beyond Tanjung, in **Krakas**, you can go out to sea with the fishermen to a fresh-water spring which bubbles up from the ocean floor, where they collect water for the village. You can also dive along the reef.

Gondang offers a different kind of attraction. A signpost in the village points the way to a **waterfall**. On a cross-country motorcycle you can get up to within 500 yards of it, having first forded a knee-deep stream; the climb up on foot will take a good hour from the road.

Leaving behind **Desa Anyar**, a modern village inhabited by people who have been resettled from Java, the road south to Gunung Rinjani will soon bring you to Wetu-Telu territory. Today, **Bayan** is the stronghold of this faith; according to legend, it was also the first early Islamic community on Lombok. A road leads from here up to **Senaru**. A view opens out across a fertile valley; soon after this you reach a row of *losmens*, shops and restaurants which have settled on the mountainside to the east of the road. Here, in **Batu Kok**, you can stock up on

Above: The boys of Gondang play Tarzan at the waterfall. Right: The hot springs of Rinjani emerge from a cleft in the crater bowl beneath Segara Anak.

provisions for the climb up to Rinjani, hire guides and porters, and rent a room for the nights before and after the expedition. Once a grand and infrequent undertaking, the ascent of Rinjani is now an everyday occurence. On nights of the full moon in the dry season many people – from local pilgrims to tourists – can be seen making the trek up the mountain. If you are spending the night before the ascent in Batu Kok, below Senaru, you should make a point of walking to the waterfall at **Sendang Gila**. You can see it as soon as you reach the last restaurant, in an exposed position east of the road.

The Ascent of Rinjani

The classic ascent begins and ends in Senaru. You should allow for two overnight stops on the mountain; if you want to go further than the crater lake and the hot springs and climb the peak itself, you'll need three nights. The path is easy to find, but it is steep and difficult. Anyone considering the climb should take

into account his or her own stamina and capabilities, and give serious thought to hiring a guide and porters; in any event it is definitely not advisable to set off alone.

At first, the path follows the marked route up to a village at the edge of the forest at a height of 2,000 feet (600 m), and from here plunges into the rain-forest where the felling of trees has created clearings. (The timings that follow are for serious walkers with light baggage. The native porters are in such great physical shape that they can easily keep up while carrying loads of 45 lbs/20 kg.) After what is for the most part a steep climb of between one and two hours through increasingly dense forest, one reaches the so-called Position II (Pos II) which is distinguished by a somewhat lopsided *bale*. If you have to, you can spend the night here. There is a watering-place about 200 yards away that sometimes has water. You may already need your rain gear at this stage; at this altitude, even in the dry season, and particularly in the afternoons, mist clings to the tree-tops, or a tropical

downpour will soak walkers already bathed in sweat.

Initially this presents no problems, because temperatures are still high, but after another 1 1/2 to 2 hours you get to Pos III, at an altitude of 6,900 feet (2,100 m) and you begin to notice the cold. Awaiting you here is a simple hut on stilts which you can use as an overnight stop, although at the height of the season it's nowhere near large enough to accommodate everyone who comes along. Anyone arriving after 2 pm should stop at this point, because the next campsite is at the lake or the hot springs, another 4 hours further on, and setting up camp in the pitch-dark and fog is an unattractive proposition. However, Pos III is not particularly inviting, as many walkers dump their trash here and the watering-place does not always look very appealing.

Shortly after leaving Pos III, you reach the tree line, and the path again gets very steep; but the view across to Bali is compensation for your efforts. After two or three hours, you reach the lip of the crater

at 8,500 feet (2,600 m), and the amazing view of the crater lake, with the volcano in the lake and the summit beyond it, more than repays you for your hard work – assuming, of course, you arrive early enough in the afternoon that the peak and lake are not obscured by cloud. The descent to the lake, which is at an altitude of 6,550 feet (2,000 m), is very steep in many places and takes about two hours. The best place to make camp is either at the level of the lake, near where it flows over the edge, or a little further down by the hot springs. The local authorities have stocked the lake with carp (*ikan karper*) and a species called *tilapiae* (local name: *mujair*), which are often kept in fish-farms and make excellent eating. Judging by the keen local anglers that one sees, the lake is well-stocked.

Crescent-shaped lake **Segara Anak** is about 800 feet (250 m) deep. The crater

Above: View across Lake Segara Anak towards Gunung Baru. Right:Young people from Sembalun Bumbung.

forms an oval 3 1/2 miles long and 5 miles wide (6 km by 8 km). The small volcano in the lake, known as **Gunung Baru** ("new mountain"), is about 500 feet (150 m) high and is believed to have gotten taller in the last 30 years. Despite reports to the contrary, the volcano was definitely there as long as 80 years ago, because there are photos from that time which show clearly a fumarole, or vent, emitting smoke and ash. Rinjani's last major eruption was in 1901, so it's still seen as highly active. Its summit is 12,220 feet (3,726 m) high. The **White Springs** (*kokok putih*) below the cleft of the crater are sulphurous and the water emerges from the rock at temperatures of more than 160°F (70°C). The islanders come to the springs to cure skin disorders and to seek physical and spiritual healing. Regularly each afternoon, mist and clouds descend and drift across the lake through the cleft, so that the temperature drops rapidly and it gets cold and wet. At this point, many walkers are reluctant to leave the steaming hot natural baths.

Very few people go on to undertake the strenuous ascent to the summit of Rinjani. It is only worth attempting when the weather is particularly fine, and if you can manage to be at the top before the clouds come rolling in and the strong wind threatens to blow you down into the lake. To see the sun rise over Sumbawa from the peak is a memorable experience. But it is not without its perils. This is because you have to set off from the lake by midnight at the latest, and really struggle up in the moonlight. The question: "Why on earth am I doing this?" will spring to your lips more than once before you have reached the summit – or given up the enterprise. Before setting out, you should give some thought to the fact that night climbing really can be dangerous.

The Plateau of Sembalun

If you drive on further east from Bayan, you reach a crossroads at **Kali Putih** ("white river"). Here, one road turns south into the mountains and winds steeply up to the Sembalun plateau, passing through stretches of virgin rainforest with occasional banyan trees. In this apparently isolated high valley, it's something of a surprise to come upon two large villages, which are said, furthermore, to be among the wealthiest on the island. In **Sembalun Lawang**, there is a market with one *warung* and a modest lodging-house which you see as you enter the village. The twin village of **Sembalun Bumbung** lies on the far side of a fertile plain which is intensively cultivated and produces onions, shallots and garlic; hence the wealth. This pocket of civilization and fertility, so high in the mountains, is a beautiful sight that keeps changing in aspect throughout the day. Sembalun Bumbung also offers modest accommodation.

Running to the south, the paved road, still relatively new, scales the eastern flank of the Rinjani massif by means of a pass through forests inhabited by black long-tailed monkeys, past waterfalls, hot strpings, and cinnamon plantations. After passing through **Pesugulan**, the East-West route through the mountains con-ludes in Aik Mel.

EASTERN LOMBOK

Eastern Lombok is undeveloped as a tourist destination; many people see it merely as a region to be passed through on the way to Sumbawa and Flores. Yet its varied landscape has enough to offer that it's an attractive destination in itself. There are beaches of both white and black sand in the northeast; rain forests, rice paddies and open heathland in the foothills of the Rinjani; and between the settlements on the narrow strip of coastal plain, there are expanses of flat wilder-ness which appear almost surreal.

If you want to explore eastern Lom-bok, there are several good bases to choose from. The best way to reach the north coast is from Batu Kok (between Bayan and Senaru, north of the Rinjani massif) – as long as none of the bridges were washed away in the last rainy sea-son. If you are looking for more variety, make for Tetebatu, on the south side of the Rinjani massif. Apart from Batu Kok, it offers the best accommodation (includ-ing simple but clean little cabins); it is conveniently close to the east coast; and walkers have a choice of refreshing ex-cursions right on their doorstep. Alterna-tively, you can base yourself right on the coast at Labuhan Lombok.

The Northeast

Although *bemos* operate between Bayan and Labuhan Lombok, it is prefer-able, if you can, to make your own way there in an all-terrain vehicle. The dis-tance along the north coast, starting from Batu Kok or even from Sembalun, can easily be covered in a day, including

Right: In eastern Lombok, the Buginese fishermen build their houses on stilts.

stops by the sea to swim, have a meal or take pictures.

After Bayan, the road doubles back again into the interior of the island before reaching the coast at Medas. Near the verdant paradise of **Obel-Obel** you can swim off the black sand beaches. After this, the road leads once more into the in-terior, through ever-changing landscapes made all the more variable by river-beds which dry up in summer but fill up and flow torrentially in the rainy season. De-posits of debris and boulders, damaged roads and broken bridges bear eloquent witness to their force. One such wrecked bridge is likely to be encountered near Obel-Obel.

Near **Belanting**, just after a steep, blind S-curve, you'll come upon a simple restaurant where you can also fill up your gas tank.

In **Labuhan Pandan**, you can nego-tiate with the fishermen to take you out in their boats to the offshore islands. The at-traction of these uninhabited isles lies in their beautiful sand beaches and the good opportunites they offer for snorkeling. On **Gili Sulat** there are mangrove swamps. You have to bring your own provisions and water.

Beyond Labuhan Pandan, opposite the little island of **Gili Pentangan** (Lampu), there is a beach where two *losmens* with bungalows wait for tourists.

From here on, fertile oases alternate with patches of barren, stony land. Shortly before Labuhan Lombok, you pass a small grove of tall trees – the last remaining, isolated stand of giant tropical hardwood trees outside the Rinjani con-servation area.

From Labuhan Lombok to Tetebatu

Labuhan Lombok, on the east coast, lies on a sheltered bay and is an important ferry terminal for boats to Sumbawa. The landing-stage for the Sumbawa ferries is located on a spit of land outside the vil-

194

lage. In the center of town, there is a market with several *warungs*, as well as two very simple *losmens*. A large number of Buginese seafarers have settled around the bay; in addition to fishing, they are employed in the construction of large wooden cargo boats. A few of their pile houses stand by the water, painted in eye-catching colors. But sadly, very few of these are left.

Labuhan Lombok is connected with the three-town capital, Ampenan-Mataram-Cakranegara, by the broad, well-paved east-west highway. Going west, one passes through a barren, steppe-like, or even desert landscape – Arizona comes to mind – traversed by herds of cattle.

The first settlements of any size are **Pringabaya** and **Aik Mel**. From both villages there are roads leading to **Pegusulan** on Gunung Rinjani. From there you can make a lovely trek up to the plateau of Sembalun. Beyond Pringgabaya, the face of the landscape changes. The road is now bordered by irrigated rice paddies,

and the further you drive towards **Masbagik** along the main road to the west, the more frequent are the tobacco fields and the typical platform-like tables on which the harvested tobacco leaves are dried.

Near Masbagik, a well-paved road turns off to the southeast and runs through Selong, the regency capital, to **Labuhan Haji**, once an important mercantile port and traditionally the harbor from which Moslem pilgrims from Lombok depart on their journey to the holy city of Mecca.

Back on the main highway, there is a turn-off at **Pomotong** for Tetebatu and the north. One or two of the villages south of Tetebatu are noted for their artisan products, and the two neighboring settlements of **Loyok** and **Kotaraja** specialize in raffia work, which you can buy either at the market in Kotaraja or in a shop in Loyok. The village of **Rungkang**, only about half a mile east of Loyok, is famous for its black earthenware pottery.

195

The village of **Tetebatu** lies at the foot of the Rinjani massif, at an altitude of nearly 2,000 feet (600 m), between rice paddies and fishponds. On the far side of the village, there are some areas of thinned-out mountain forest, inhabited by the comical black long-tailed monkeys. It is noticeably cooler here, and perhaps a welcome change just for this reason. Visitors seeking accommodation have two choices: a guest-house dating from the 1920s built by the Dutch colonial administration, which has since been expanded with additional bungalows; or, somewhat farther east in **Kembang Kuning**, a group of relatively new cottages in the rice fields.

From Tetebatu, you can walk to a number of waterfalls; the largest is about 7 1/2 miles (12 km) away. One of the smaller waterfalls is also well worth seeing; walking towards it you cross rice-fields,

Above: Foreigners still cause quite a sensation here. Right: Not every village in the south has a pond like this.

tracts of surviving rain-forest, and areas where the forest has been cleared by burning, and pass a number of small villages. Near the waterfall, the dense jungle is populated by gray-brown Javanese monkeys. Make sure to consult the map in the guest-house before setting out, as it is easy to lose your bearings. However, you can always hire one of the little village boys who offer their services as guides.

SOUTHERN LOMBOK

Worthwhile excursions in the southern part of Lombok include trips to the Batugendeng peninsula in the southwest and to Kuta and the surrounding area on the south coast. There you will encounter, as a rule, a simpler form of tourist infrastructure, if there is any at all, although in the last few years most of the main roads have at least been paved. You often have to bring your own food and water. The two following routes both start from Cakranegara.

The Batugendeng Peninsula

If you start from Cakranegara to the Batugendeng peninsula early enough in the moring, it is well worth making a small detour over to the mountain Gunung Pengson. To do this, leave the main road south of Cakranegara and drive toward **Pagutan**. In the village temple here, in 1894, a rare copy of the *Nagarakertagama* was discovered and preserved by a Dutch ethnologist. Written in Old Javanese in 1365 by the court poet and historian Prapanca, this epic describes, in the form of a poetical eulogy to the rulers of the time, life in the kingdom of king Hayam Wuruk (1350 - 1389) as well as the life and deeds of his great-grandfather Kertanagara (1268 - 1292). The epic, the original name of which was *Desa Warnana* ("description of the country"), was composed on the orders of the statesman Gajah Mada and represents the most important local source of information about the Javanese Majapahit empire.

On **Gunung Pengson**, a small mountain less than 6 miles (10 km) south of Cakranegara, there is a **temple** with white shrines and an altar with an egg-shaped stone cemented into its surface. The steps leading up to it are besieged by a horde of monkeys. Most attractive feature here, however, is the view across the rice-paddies to Gunung Rinjani, which is usually free of cloud until around 10 am. In the evening, the peak of Gunung Agung on Bali provides a wonderful backdrop in the west.

A distinct attraction of the **Batugendeng Peninsula** is its offshore reef, wonderful for snorkeling and diving; too, there are many small islands with similar reefs lying off its shores. Here, too, is the last expanse of lowland jungle, Nusa Tenggara Barat, where deer and wild boar still roam in large numbers. There's more life in the peninsula's steep, rocky cliffs, home to many species of sea bird. But in addition to cliffs, there are plenty of bays and sand beaches along the coast; places to sit in the shade, however, are

197

few and far between. Most of the islands are also ringed with sand beaches.

From **Labuhan Lembar**, where the Bali-Lombok ferry docks, a paved road switchbacks steeply up and down over the hills for 6 miles (10 km) southward to the Moslem village of **Sekotong**. From Sekotong, which lies some way from the coast, you can go (preferably by jeep) either to Sepi and Belongas in the south (see below), or along the mediocre road westward to Taun.

On the way to Taun, you pass beaches of black sand and small settlements with large fish-ponds (*tambak*). **Taun** itself boasts a white sand beach. On the little offshore island **Gili Nanggu**, which is reached either by a charter boat from Labuhan Lembar or from the beaches of the peninsula, you can rent bungalows at Losmen Istana Cempaka.

Some half a mile (1 km) to the west

you come to the inviting sands by the bungalows of **Sekotong Indah Beach**. Further on, there's a group of houses on the beach where fishermen and lime-burners live, called **Ketapang**. From here, a boat leaves every morning (except Fridays) for Koranji Bangsal, which lies on the coast south of Gunung Pengson, a trip that takes about three hours. From Ketapang or from its neighbor to the west, **Pelangan**, you can also get a boat to the largest offshore island, **Gili Gede**. The island has a ship-building yard, where Buginese are employed building heavy wooden outriggers of up to 200 tons, made to order. Each ship takes up to two years to complete and the work is done without any drawings – the master shipwright manages to keep the whole plan in his head.

West of Pelangan there is a whole string of small villages. **Labuhan Poh** is said to have the most beautiful beach for miles around. The last place you come to, at the western tip of the peninsula, is **Bangko Bangko**. Good breakers here draw crowds of surfers, who arrive by motorboat from Labuhan Lembar. A little way inland begins the forest, teeming with wild game, and a favorite spot for wealthy city-dwellers to exercise their love of hunting.

If you drive south from Sekotong, some 6 miles (10 km), past small settlements where there are pitiful attempts at cultivation on steep terraces, will bring you to **Sepi**, an unremarkable fishing village. From here you can get an outrigger to take you to the white sand beach of **Belongas**; a brand-new road also leads there. Scuba-divers tell of seeing sea turtles and sharks as much as 7 feet (2 m) long off this beach; its reef is largely intact and the visibility for snorkeling is good.

The village of **Pengantap**, with its two offshore islands, lies 5 miles (8 km) away to the east. This is one of the last few places where a small group of Budas, the

aboriginal inhabitants of Lombok, still live today. Islanders worship at a nearby stone shrine. If you climb the steep hill behind the village, you will get a good view over the whole area.

After Pengantap, the landscape gets more monotonous. Another 11 miles (18 km) brings you to **Silung Blanak**, passing through a few impoverished hamlets on the way. From **Patu Jangke,** a small market town, the road is once more paved. Silung Blanak lies on a broad bay with a white sand beach and a few *warungs*.

Paved roads then lead through Mangkung and Praya and back to the capital, or through Keling and Kapak on to Kuta.

Southwards to Kuta

Another expedition from Lombok's capital leads to Kuta on the south coast of Lombok. If you're looking for miles of white sand beaches, are prepared to be enchanted by the spectrum of different shades of turquoise in the ocean waters,

and can do without shade palms near the beach or the noise and commotion of mass tourist centers, Kuta and the coastal villages around it are the perfect places for you – for the time being. But hurry. This idyll may not last. Certainly the building plots that have been staked out and the growing number of property deals awaken a sense of foreboding about what is to come.

The road from Cakranegara, on the whole in good condition, passes through Kediri towards Praya, the capital of the regency of Central Lombok.

From **Puyung**, famed for its attractive rattan goods and regular stick-fighting contests, take time to detour to **Sukarara**. This is a typical Sasak village known for its beautiful textiles, and thus a favorite stopping point for package-tours. The locals have adapted to this with alacrity: the village women now charge a fee to pose for photographs; the prices are higher than you might expect; and there are increasing numbers of pushy salesmen soliciting customers. But

199

don't let this put you off paying a visit to the place altogether.

The atmosphere in the weaving workshops is friendly though reserved. Almost every household has at least one simple loom at which a woman will work for weeks and months to produce a single large cloth called a *purbasari*, which is worn at festivals like a sarong. You also see woven sashes and belts (*sabuk*); and you can even buy tablecloths.

Returning to the main road, another 4 miles (6 km) or so brings you to **Penujak**. Here you can look at (and buy) red ceramics made in the time-honored method and with traditional patterns; or you can just watch the skilled potters at work. Offerings here range from containers in the shape of animals to simple bulbous vessels up to three feet (1 m) in height.

The village of **Sengkol** is a special attraction on Thursdays, which is marketday; men and women from the surrounding Sasak settlements come in to buy and sell, many wearing their traditional costume. The women wear a black sarong and a short black blouse which leaves their navels exposed. The only adornment is a brightly-colored hand-woven belt. If you've visited any artisan villages, you may recognize many of the handcrafts on offer here from having seen them in their place of origin; and if you've already been to the market in Sweta, Sengkol's may pale somewhat in comparison.

Some 4 miles (6 km) before Kuta, you can't miss the little village of **Sade/Rambitan**, which sits perched on a flat rise of land. This Wetu-Telu community has opened right up to tourism, but not in an unpleasant way. Even before you reach the concrete footpath up to the village, you will be met by children offering to guide

Right: Kuta's beaches offer lots of sun, miles of white sand – and hardly another visitor in sight.

you round. Some of them are really smart and have learned by heart an entire conducted tour in English. Needless to say, an elementary souvenir trade has developed to accommodate visitors; you can also buy textiles, which you can watch women at simple wooden looms producing on the spot. Although the children's continuous presence as guides can get a bit tiresome, they do let you get a little glimpse of the social structure of a Sasak village. The mosque here can be taken as a typical example of Wetu-Telu houses of prayer.

Beaches around Kuta

Kuta itself is nothing more than a collection of houses near the sea. Its main attraction lies in its beaches, which stretch away in both directions; although there's a notable absence of shade palms, and the sands slope only very gradually into the water. Once a year the *Nyale* festival takes place here. There have been frequent rumors that work is about to start on the construction of large hotel complexes, but at present there are just a few places offering basic accommodation, and one or two simple restaurants dotted along the beaches. Even at the height of the season you get the impression that this whole stretch of coast is sunk in a lethargic sleep.

If you enjoy isolated beaches and enchanting scenery, you should go west to the village of **Mawun**. To reach the most beautiful vantage points, you need to follow the 6-mile (10 km) stretch of road along the coast from Kuta, rather than the slightly longer route through Pegambur. You can detour to the coast before you get to Mawun, at **Are Goling**, where there's a beautiful beach and an offshore island to which you can wade out at low tide. Mawun, too, has a beach of beautiful white sand.

If you select Kuta as your base for further journeys of discovery, there's plenty

more to see further to the east. Quite close by is **Tanjung Aan**, with its magnificent bay and a peninsula jutting out into the sea; the heights of the latter command a superb view of the entire surrounding area.

Surfers drive a bit further on to **Grupuk**, where Australians form the majority of the wave-riders at a spot they've christened **Desert Point**.

Further east lies **Awang**, although it can only be reached by a rather poor road which branches off at Aan, before the turn-off for the coast and Tanjung Aan. Cultivated in the Bay of Awang is a kind of sea-weed which is used in the production of gelatine. Outrigger boats can take you over to Ekas.

On the north side of the bay lies **Batu Nampar**, where immigrant Buginese and Maduran settlers now outnumber the native Sasaks. Many of their houses, which are built on stilts, are decorated with brightly-colored geometrical designs. Near the village there are extensive saltpans.

To reach Batu Nampar you must either drive over extremely rough tracks, or else charter a boat from Awang. There is, however, a third possibility, which is to drive in a wide loop through Mujur and Sukaraja. Except in the rainy season, this route takes you through arid, bone-dry tracts of land. Like Sade, **Sukaraja** has become a kind of Sasak showplace for tourists.

A road as far as **Ekas** has opened up the peninsula in the southeast to traffic. There are rumors that the entire peninsula is going to be fitted out with all the amenities to handle tourism on a larger scale. Hitherto, however, the best way to travel round it has been in a charter boat from Tanjung Luar or some other coastal village.

There's a good "surf spot" near Ekas; surfers and other visitors can stay at the Laut Surga Cottages.

The walk from Ekas to the caves of **Tanjung Ringgit**, on the easternmost tip of the island, takes a whole day. Remember to bring water.

AMPENAN / MATARAM CAKRANEGARA
Accommodation

MODERATE: **Hotel Granada**, Jl. Bung Karno, Cakranegara, tel. 32260, fax 36015, with swimming pool and restaurant, from US$ 28-50. **Puri Indah**, Jl. Sriwijaya, tel. 37633, with swimming pool and restaurant, from Rps. 30,000. **Nitour Hotel**, Jl. Yos Sudarso 4, Ampenan, tel. 23780, relatively quiet and close to all main facilities, from US$ 35-40. **Selaparang Hotel**, Jl. Pejanggik 40-42, Cakranegara, tel. 32670, with restaurant, from Rps. 28,000. **Mataram Hotel**, Jl. Pejanggik 105, Cakranegara, tel. 33675, with restaurant, from US$ 16-28. **Ratih**, Jl. Selaparang, Cakranegara, tel. 31096, with restaurant; rents jeeps, motorcycles, from Rps. 35,000.
BUDGET: **Hotel Shanti Puri**, Jl. Maktal 15, Cakranegara, tel. 22649, owned by a Balinese family, rents out jeeps and motorcycles, with restaurant, from Rps. 12,000. **Wisma Chandra**, Jl. Pancawarga 55, Mataram, tel. 23979, from Rps. 12,000. **Hotel Zahir**, Jl. Koperasi 9, Ampenan, tel. 32403, rooms with small verandahs around a courtyard, motorcycles available for hire, from Rps. 10,000. **Losmen Horas**, Jl. Koperasi 62, Ampenan, tel. 31695, clean and well-run, from Rps. 10,000. **Losmen Wisma Triguna**, Jl. Koperasi Pelembak, Ampenan, tel. 21705, with garden, the place to meet backpackers interested in climbing Mount Rinjani; rents out sleeping bags, cooking utensils, and other equipment, and organizes tours to Rinjani; rooms from Rps. 12,500.

Restaurants
AMPENAN: Pabean and **Cirebon**, Jl. Pabean 111 und 113, Indonesian and Chinese cooking, the Cirebon is particularly popular. **Arafat**, Jl. Pabean 64, Indonesian food, cheap and good. **Setia**, Jl. Pabean 129, **Depot Mina**, Jl. Yos Sudarso 102, und **Timur Tengah**, Jl. Koperasi 22, basic and good value.
MATARAM: Garden House Restaurant, on the south side of Jl. Penjanggik by the Pusat Pertokoan (shopping center), tel. 22233, Indonesian, Chinese and international cooking; also specializes in ice cream (try the durian flavor); nice atmosphere. **Al Azhar**, Pusat Pertokoan, serves *Ayam taliwang*, a chicken speciality from West Sumbawa. **Deny Bersaudara**, Jl. Rumah Sakit Islam 6, tel. 23619, fresh Gourami fish and Sasak specialities. Other recommended restaurants in and around the Cilinaya Center include **Pattaya**, fish, Indonesian and Chinese; **Shanti Puri**, Indonesian, Chinese and international; **Dirgahayu**, Jl. Cilinya 10, tel. 37559, mainly Indonesian; **Muksin Taliwang**, Sasak specialities.

CAKRANEGARA: Flamboyan, Jl. Pejanggik 101, delicious fish dishes, Chinese. **Madya**, Jl. Hasanuddin 7, tel. 35709, Sasak cooking and specialities from Sumbawa. **Sekawan Depot Es**, Jl. Selaparang, seafood, and Chinese specialties.

Useful Addresses
The **tourist office,** Dinas Pariwisata, is on the border between Ampenan and Mataram, Jl. Langko 70, tel. 31730.
Opposite is the **telephone office** of *Permuntel* (international calls and fax available).
The **Central Post Office** with a counter for *poste restante* mail is in Mataram, near the intersection of Jl. Srivijaya and Jl. A. Rahman Hakim. Opening hours: Mon–Thu and Sat 8 am-2 pm, Fri 8 am-11 am.
On the continuation of Jl. Langko in Ampenan is the **Merpati Airline office**.
You can get bus and other transportion information from the **Perama office** on Jl. Pejanggik 66, tel. 23368.

Activities
Provincial Museum of Nusa Tenggara Barat: Tue-Thu 8 am-2 pm, Fri 8 am-11 am, Sat, Sun 8 am-12 noon. Admission: 500 Rps.
For **shopping**, the best streets in Ampenan are Jl. Yos Sudarso (Dina, Jaya Bahagia, Rora, Renza) and Jl. Saleh Sungkar (Sudirman, Lombok Today, Heri), with their adjacent side streets, for genuine and reproduction antiques.
In Cakra it is worth visiting Jl. Selaparang and Cilinaya Square and their side-streets, where you will find textiles and many other local handicrafts.
You can visit a number of **textile factories**, including the following: Balimurti; Slamet Riyadi on Jl. Tenun, near the Mayura water palace; Rinjani Hand Woven, Jl. Pejanggik 44/46, where it joins Jl. Selaparang; Sari Kusuma, Jl. Selaparang 45, all in Cakranegara; and Putra Khatina, Jl. Ismail Marzuki 5, in Mataram.

SURANADI
Accommodation / Restaurant
Suranadi Hotel, Jl. Raya Suranadi, P.O. Box 10, Mataram 83000, tel. 23686, fax 23984, very restful, with swimming pool and tennis court, US$ 12 to 30. The restaurant offers a selection of Indonesian, Chinese and international dishes.

SENGGIGI
Accommodation
In Senggigi, there is a wide choice of accommodation in every price category. However, in the high season it is advisable to book in advance.

LUXURY: **Senggigi Hotel**, Jl. Raya Senggigi, tel. 93210, fax 93200; the complex offers every conceivable facility from a pharmacy to a money exchange office, centrally located on the sea, with restaurant and bar done up in South Seas style, from US$ 135. **Puri Bunga Beach Cottages**, P.O. Box 51 Mataram, tel. 91013, fax 93286, on the slope beyond the main road with a view over the bay, many extras, from US$ 79-91. **Pacific Beach Hotel**, P.O. Box 36 Mataram, Kerandangan, tel. 93006, on the beach, a little way from the center of town, with swimming pool and restaurant, from US$ 42-66. **Lombok Intan Laguna**, P.O. Box 50 Mataram, tel. 93090, fax 93185, very luxurious, from US$ 135. **Graha Beach Hotel**, tel. 93331, very central, right on the beach, with restaurant, water-sports facilities, from US$ 55. **Nusa Bunga Hotel**, Mangsit, on the sea a long way from the town center, from US$ 45. **Sheraton Senggigi Beach Hotel**, tel. 93333, fax 93140, right on the beach opposite the Ida Beach Cottages, from US$ 152.

MODERATE: **Mascot Cottages**, tel. 93365, very central, reliable, from US$ 42; **Lina Cottages**, right on the beach, central, with good, popular restaurant, from Rps. 35,000; **Windy Cottages**, Mangsit, away from the center right on the sea, with an airy restaurant, from Rps. 15,000; **Batu Bolong Cottages**, tel. 93065, fax 93198, huts on both sides of the road, as you come into town, from Rps. 35,000.

BUDGET: **Pondok Senggigi**, tel. 22876, on the landward side of the road, central, with a popular restaurant, occasional open-air concerts, a favorite with long-range trekkers, from Rps. 26,000; **Pondok Sederhana**, on the landward side, simple rooms, from Rps. 25,000; **Pondok Shinta Cottages**, a short walk from the center, rooms from Rps. 12,000. **Santai Beach Inn**, Mangsit, a long way out of town, on the beach, is run by an Englishwoman in an informal style, and is very popular with budget travellers. It has a vegetarian restaurant, and rooms from Rps. 20,000.

Restaurants

Apart from the hotel restaurants, there are relatively few restaurants in town. The **Sunshine**, tel. 94922, in the center is very popular. It serves good fish dishes. The **Dynasty**, tel. 94613, at the edge of town has good Chinese food, but is too far out to be popular. Near the turn-off to the Senggigi Beach Hotel there are some very cheap *warungs* serving traditional Indonesian dishes.

Activities

Senggigi's infrastructure is chiefly geared to beach holidays and water-sports activities. The luxury hotels also offer tennis, badminton, ping-pong and fitness equipment. There are popular day excursions by prahu boat to the three Gili islands to the northwest. In the evenings, dance performances take place occasionally in the Senggigi Beach Hotel, or there is live music in the Pondok Senggigi.

Useful Addresses

Next to the Sunshine you can find a **tourist office**, a *Permuntel*-**telephone office** and a mailbox. You can rent **jeeps** and **motorcycles** either from Surga Rent Car & Motorbike between Ampenan and Senggigi, north of the Asri Beach Cottages, or on the main street in Senggigi near the turn-off to the Senggigi Beach Hotel.

GILI AIR / MENO / TRAWANGAN
Accommodation

LUXURY: **Gazebo Meno Resort Cottages**, Gili Meno, Tel/fax 35795, with its own water-purification plant, rooms from US$ 55.

All the other accommodations on the islands are simple *losmens*. These, however, often turn out to be charming places to stay. On Gili Air, the **Gili Air Cottages** (northern end) and **Gili Indah** (southern end) are very popular. On Gili Meno, the **Kontiki** (in the southeast) and the **Blue Coral Losmen** (in the northeast) are recommended, and on Gili Trawangan, the **Nusa Tiga Bungalows** (northern end) and the **Rainbow Cottages** (southeast).

If you are looking for some action, stay on Trawangan near the jetty. Prices for a double room begin at around Rps. 10,000. The restaurants are mostly quite basic, relatively cheap and serve the usual range of delicious local dishes.

TETEBATU
Accomodation / Restaurants

MODERATE: **Wisma Soedjono**, with restaurant and swimming pool.

BUDGET: **Wisma Dewi Enjani**, very much simpler, but with a restaurant and a lovely view. **Cendrawasih**, Kembang Kuning, bungalows in the middle of the rice fields.

KUTA
Accommodation

To date, there is only a choice of simple and inexpensive accommodation here, always with a small restaurant attached. In the village, there's **Mata Hari Inn**, from Rps. 10,000; then, from west to east: **Rambutan**, from Rps. 7,500; **Segara Anak**, from Rps. 8,000; **Wisma Segar Kuning**, rooms on the upper floor, with a beautiful view, from Rps. 10,000; **Anda**, places to sit in the shade and a good restaurant, from Rps. 15,000; **Cockatoo Cottages**, from Rps. 15,000; **Lamancha**, from Rps. 10,000.

BALINESE CUISINE

As you travel around Bali, you'll come across many dishes which are typical of the whole of Indonesia. Balinese specialities, on the other hand, are unfortunately much more difficult to obtain, since they are often only served at major festivals and require hours of work to prepare. Nevertheless, there are a number of restaurants which will make these dishes to order. In the tourist centers, international cuisine has firmly established itself, and you can find everything from Italian pasta through American steak to German apple strudel.

The most important dietary staple on Bali, as almost everywhere else in Asia, is rice. There's a different word for every stage of its growth or method of prepara-

Previous pages: Parasols protect the throne of the gods. Performances of a Kecak dance. Above: A wayside warung in Asak. Right: Vegetables and spices are at the heart of Indonesian cooking.

tion, and the Balinese name often differs from the Indonesian one. *Padi* is the general name for rice when it is still on the stalk. Once it has been threshed, it has the same name in High Balinese as in Indonesian, *beras*; in everyday Balinese, however, this word is shortened to *baas*. When it is boiled, rice becomes *nasi*. In addition to regular white rice – of which the better-tasting variety *beras Bali* (Bali rice) is becoming increasingly hard to find – there are many other types, including *ketan*, a sticky rice, *ketan injin* (black rice) which is often eaten as a dessert, and *beras barak* (red rice). For the festival of *Kuningan* (*kuning* = yellow) white rice is dyed yellow with turmeric. Rice is eaten in a variety of ways: as *nasi jakau* (boiled rice), or, preferably, as *nasi kukus* (*kukus* = steamed) or as *nasi goreng* (*goreng* = fried). In Balinese homes, rice is freshly prepared every day and kept in a pot in the kitchen. Whenever someone gets hungry, he just goes and take some. Consequently, rice is mostly eaten cold. Rice that has been cooked slowly in little parcels made of banana leaves, called *keti-pat*, makes a good midday meal for the men to take with them to the fields, or the children to school.

A common breakfast is *nasi goreng* or *mie goreng* (*mie/bakmie* = noodles), prepared with egg, meat or seafood, as well as tomatoes, cucumbers, and of course spices and chili. Whatever the additional elements, the main component of a meal is always rice or noodles.

Other typical Indonesian dishes include *nasi campur* (*campur* = mixed), steamed rice with vegetables, meat, pickles and *krupuk*, which are crisps made from fish-flakes or shrimp paste; *cap cai*, a vegetable dish similar to the Chinese chop suey; *soto*, a soup with thickened coconut milk (*santen*); *sop*, a meat and vegetable stew prepared in water; *gado-gado*, a vegetable salad with peanut sauce; and, of course, *sate*, a mini-kebab made from chicken (*ayam*) beef, lamb, pork (only in the non-Moslem regions) or fish. Especially delicious is the *sate Bali*, made from ground pork, spices and coconut. *Tahu* is a soybean pudding, and *tempeh* a kind of cake made from fermented soybeans. Most dishes are automatically served with *nasi putih* (white rice).

Typical Balinese dishes include *babi* or *be guling*, a suckling-pig, and *betutu bebek*, a stuffed duck wrapped in banana-leaves and cooked slowly for several hours. What gives traditional Balinese food its special quality is the way it is cooked over a wood fire in a simple brick fireplace.

When it comes to vegetables, the western visitor will find much that is familiar, such as different kinds of cabbage, eggplant, tomato, and cucumber, but also unfamiliar vegetables such as *kangkung*, a kind of water-spinach, sweet potato, bread-fruit (*timbal*), the flower and stalk of the banana-plant, *nangka* or jackfruit and papaya, both of which can also be eaten uncooked, as fruit.

In general, spices are used generously in the preparation of most dishes. So you will see almost every known kind of spice in the markets of Bali and Lombok. A hot, spicy sauce, used in many dishes, is called *sambal*. The basic mixture is made up of shallots (*bawang*), garlic (*bawang putih/kesuna*) ginger (*jahe*), cumin (*kunyit*), galanga-root (*cekuh/isen*), shrimp-paste (*trasi/ sera*), cardamom (*kepulaga*) and chili (*tabia*). Other ingredients used in flavoring are pepper (*merica/mica*), lemon-grass (*serai/ sereh*), tamarind (*asam/celagi*), salt (*garam/uyah*), nutmeg (*pala*), palm-sugar (*gula merah/gula barak*), coriander (*ketumber/ketumbah*), cinnamon (*kayu manis*), cloves (*cenkeh*), monosodium glutamate (MSG/*pitsin*) and lime (*lemo*).

The Balinese also have some delicious desserts to offer: bananas can be baked, fried or deep-fried in batter. Other sweets are made from rice. *Lontong* is a sticky rice, tasting a little like semolina, boiled in plantain or banana-leaves. Another pudding made from rice is *ketan*, which is cooked in coconut milk and sugar syrup. *Bubur santen* is a sort of rice porridge cooked in palm-sugar and coconut milk. Something you can have either as a dessert or for breakfast is black rice with coconut milk. This delicious dish is even better if served with a fruit salad. Things to nibble between meals include coconut or peanut biscuits, nuts, rice-cakes, banana chips or potato chips, and a lot more. Ice cream, too, comes in many varieties, usually made with fresh fruit, such as durian ice cream. Something very unusual, which is virtually unknown in the western hemisphere, is *rujak*. This is fresh fruit covered in a piquant sauce made from palm-sugar, chili and *sera* (shrimp-paste).

The selection of fruit is enormous. In addition to familiar fruit such as grapes (*anggur*), pineapple (*nenas*), citrus fruit (*jeruk*) and bananas (*pisang/biu*), there are many which are little-known or completely unknown in the west. Even bananas come in a greater variety of shapes and sizes than one would ever guess from the standardized product one sees in supermarkets back home. And each one has a particular name. The *biu batu* is one which always takes Europeans by surprise, because it has a number of kernels or stones; the word *batu* means "stone." The *biu udang* (shrimp-banana) is red; the *biu susu* (milk-banana), only as large as a finger, is especially delicious. The *biu kate* is of normal size but grows on a dwarf plant. The *biu gadang* remains green, even when ripe; the *biu mas* is a deep golden color; and the *biu raja* is the variety which most closely resembles the product exported to Europe from the Americas. A particular favorite are fried bananas (*gogodoh biu*), but the fruit is also processed into chips or flour. The banana plant is so versatile that even the

stalk is eaten (well-spiced, mind you), and the leaves are used as plates or wrapping-paper. Other delicious fruit include the mango-plum, the guava (*jambu biji*), the cape-gooseberry or starfruit (*belimbing*), the pomegranate (*delima*) the custard-apple (*jambu air*), the watermelon (*semangka air*), the papaya, the mangosteen (*manggis*) and the mango (*mangga*). The sapodillo (*sawo*) looks like a small potato but tastes like a ripe pear. The *rambutan* (from *rambut*, meaning "hair") is small and round and covered in long, thick hair. The *sirsak* is a spiny fruit from which a refreshing drink, like lemonade, is made. The *salak* is a pear-shaped fruit with firm flesh, which tastes rather like a mixture of pear and gooseberry. It has a beautiful glowing brown skin which feels like snakeskin; for this reason, it is sometimes also called snakefruit. The jackfruit (*nangka*) is a large spiny fruit weighing several pounds, made up of numerous small segments which are sold separately. The durian is one of the most controversial fruits on the planet. It is similar to the jackfruit but its spines (in Indonesian, *duri*) are sharper, and it does not grow so large. It is the only fruit eaten by tigers. Its flesh has a creamy consistency. It is divided into many segments and has twelve kernels, each about the size of chestnuts, which, like chestnuts, can be roasted and eaten. But it's the durian's overpowering smell which repulses westerners, especially when the fruit has been lying around for a while. The taste is even harder to describe: a mixture of strawberry, gooseberry, pear and camembert cheese. Even if you cannot get used to the taste of the fruit on its own, you should nevertheless sample the durian ice cream in the *Garden House and Ice Creme Palace* in Mataram, on Lombok. Be very careful about combining the durian with alcohol, as this can lead to serious illness.

Right: Coconuts are split open to dry out in the sun.

Then, of course, there is the coconut (*kelapa/nyuh*) which, like rice, has a dif-

ferent name for every stage of its growth. There are something like 300 named species of the family *Cocos nucifera*. Twelve kinds can be found on Bali, differentiated by the color of the nut and the size of the tree.

The young "baby" coconuts are called *bungsil*. When they are a little older, but still not edible they are *bungkak*. The young mature nut is called *kuwud*. This is the best stage to drink the coconut milk (*yeh kuwud*). When coconuts are fully ripe, which is the condition in which they are sold in Europe, their name is *nyuh*. Now you can scrape out the flesh and make coconut-milk, oil or copra. However in Bali, the flesh of the fully ripened nut is considered to be of a lower quality than the *kuwud*, which is softer. The liquid in a young nut is also sweeter and richer. At this stage, the outer skin is still green. When it has become yellow, the Balinese say it is past its best. Coconut palms standing close to houses are harvested regularly, to prevent the falling nuts from constituting a danger to life

and property. For the same reason, Balinese are careful not to park their cars under a coconut palm overnight.

Several different drinks can be obtained from coconut palms. As well as the thirst-quenching *yeh kuwud*, there are two alcoholic drinks: *tuak* and *arak*. *Tuak* is a beer made from the juice of the palm flower. It is frothy and mild. In the morning, immediately after being tapped, it is still very sweet, and is called *manis*, but by the evening and for the next three days, it makes a good strong beer (*tuak wayah*). The British used to call it "toddy," but this name never got established on Bali. *Arak* is distilled from *tuak* and has a powerful, pungent taste. This palm liquor is also used in traditional medicine. Many Balinese avoid it altogether; others add spices to it to make a drink called *mabasa*.

The third of Bali's signature alcoholic drinks is not made from the palm; it's a very sweet rice wine called *brem*. However, a better way to quench your thirst is the local beer, *bir bintang*.

BALINESE DANCES

As well as a virtuoso *gamelan* orchestra, every Balinese village needs to have a good dance group. Like *gamelan* musicians, the dancers are, as a rule, amateurs. They learn to perform a number of specific dances, such as the *legong*, *arja* or *pendet*, rather than dancing in general. A committee of experts determines which dancers have a particular talent for a certain dance; the overall state of their health, the symmetry of their limbs and facial features are as important to the selection as a dancer's potential skill in a given type of dance. Girls are selected for the *legong* dance when they are as young as five, and their career is already over by the time they reach puberty. If there are two village girls who look very much alike, they are both certain to be chosen as *legong* ("woman dancer").

Above: The Barong is the good spirit of the village. Right: In Peliatan, new dances are being created in addition to the old.

The dances are learned purely by imitation, not with the aid of a mirror, as they would be in a ballet school. The teacher stands behind the pupil and positions his wrist properly, corrects the way a hand is held, or moves the knee one way or another. Along the way, the pupil gets a feeling for the movements and after a while can perform them unaided. While they're learning the basic steps, simple sequences and general arm movements, the young dancers also work on developing the flexibility of each individual muscle through regular exercises, so that they become almost "rubber-jointed."

Balinese dancing, like most dancing of Southeast Asia, is somewhat static. Leg-and footwork plays a secondary role compared to gesture and mime. Unlike classical European ballet, the movements of Balinese dance are not designed to free the dancer from the force of gravity. This earthbound quality is epitomized in the *Kebyar Duduk*, a sedentary dance in which the legs are not used at all.

However, it is true that there are some dances, for example the *Baris*, in which it is important, as in classical ballet, to extend the line of the body with bent legs and knees pointed outwards. Whereas in Javanese dancing emotions are expressed through carefully controlled gestures of the arm and hand, while the face remains immobile, in Balinese dance every movement of indiviual parts of the body "speaks" to the audience. The eyes and eyebrows are continually in motion, from side to side and up and down, and although the face remains impersonal, the entire body is alive, expressing a whole gamut of emotions. Sudden changes of direction and precise, jerky steps create a tension which is lacking in Javanese dance. The Javanese, on the other hand, would claim that the Balinese are too exuberant and lack refinement.

Dances are intended to be entertaining for performers and spectators alike, as well as for the gods, while at the same time frightening off evil spirits. The dancer appears literally to glide into another world, and into a state of consciousness which knows no fatigue and which sometimes leads to a trance.

It is possible to divide Balinese dances into three broad categories: 1. dances of animistic and ancient Indonesian origin, chiefly group dances and sacred cult dances, often of an exorcising nature (*tari wali*); 2. dances of Hindu origin, which are also called sacrificial dances (*tari bebali*) and usually tell stories from the Hindu epics, and 3. performance dances (*tari balih-balihan*), which are not only performed in temple precincts and royal courts, but also on stage in front of a paying audience.

Arja (Balih-Balihan)

In this comic folk-opera the performers speak as well as sing. As in the *wayang kulit* shadow-puppet plays, clowns translate the exalted speeches of the lead-ing figures into a more down-to-earth *lingua franca*. The plots are drawn from Chinese love-stories as well as from the *Mahabharata* (see p. 224) and the *Panji* cycle. The latter is a series of stories about the adventures of Panji Raden of Koriban, an extensive collection of tales from the heyday of the Javanese Majapahit dynasty. Panji had rejected the hand of the beautiful Rangkesari without even seeing her, but when they did finally meet, he was consumed with love for her. But the wind carried her off to a distant kingdom. Setting out in search of her, Panji encounters many adventures, until they are finally reunited.

Baris (Wali)

The *Baris* is a war-dance from the pre-Hindu period, when the rulers of Bali were continually feuding with each other. It used to be danced as a way of asking the gods for their help and their blessing in the forthcoming battle. The word *baris* literally means "line" or "row;" it originally meant the battle-line of the warriors, and later came to refer to the warriors themselves. This very masculine dance takes many different forms, whose names derive from the weapons that are carried. Only the *Baris Kekupa*, or Butterfly *Baris*, is danced by young girls. The stage represents the scene of warlike deeds. At first the dancer's movements are hesitant, cautious, as if entering unknown territory. Then he straightens up to his full height, and stands motionless, only his arms trembling with pent-up strength. Then without warning he spins round on one leg, with audacity and arrogance glinting in his eyes.

The *Baris* dancer must have the ability to project a tremendous range of facial expressions: a look of wonderment when faced by an invisible world of magic, astonishment and rage at his enemies, as well as pleasure, tenderness and love. The *Baris* lies at the foundation of all other male dances, and every prince once had to know how to dance it. The dance can be performed either by a group or by a solo dancer. The stylized imitations of the warrior in battle are followed by the gamelan orchestra, and not the other way around.

Barong (Wali)

The *Barong* or *Kris* dance portrays the eternal struggle between Good and Evil; whose forces must in the end be balanced. The power of Good resides in the Barong, a fabled creature with shaggy fur, an elaborately carved mask, and a red beard in which all his strength is concentrated. This protector of mankind is danced by two men hidden under a fur pelt. His opponent is the witch Rangda, who embodies the destructive principle of the death-goddess Durga. She draws

Right: The magic power of the Barong protects the kris-dancers from injury in their trance-state.

her might from black magic and rules over the powers of darkness.

Her entrance through the gates of the temple is first announced by the ghostly appearance of her hands with their excessively long fingernails. The next things to become visible are her long tongue of flame, hanging out of her mouth, and the entrails hanging round her neck. The two figures encounter one another and fight. When it seems the Barong is in danger of being defeated, the *kris* dancers, who have already put themselves into a trance, come to his assistance.

By means of a magic spell, Rangda manages to make them turn their swords on themselves. The Barong is unable to lift the curse, and only becomes weaker. The men dancing in a trance really do thrust their *krisses* against their chests, but without actually wounding themselves. In order to awaken them from their trance, the priest sprinkles them with holy water, in which the Barong has previously dipped his beard. The drama ends with a sacrifice to the evil spirits.

Gambuh (Bebali)

The *Gambuh* is one of Bali's oldest dances, and is known as "the mother of all Balinese dances." The movements are slow and stylized. The performers sing in Kawi, the language of medieval Java. The clowns who, in other types of dance-drama, act as interpreters, scarcely appear here, which means that the choreography must be watched carefully. Mysterious-sounding melodies are played on three-foot-long flutes and two-stringed violins. Except in Batuan, Gambuh groups are hadly to be found anywhere.

Jauk (Bebali)

The *Jauk* is a masked dance, whose theme once again is the conflict of good and evil demons. The good *jauks* wear

white masks, the evil ones, brown; they all have goggle-eyes and long, shaggy hair. Out of the confrontation of the two groups of demons has developed a solo dance, very similar to the *Baris* solo. The musicians have to take their lead from the dancer's movements, which are not linked to any particular story line, but are, for the most part, freely improvised.

Joged (Balih-Balihan)

The *Joged* has many variants, but the common factor in all of them is the participation of the audience. A female dancer, or several of them in turn, begin to perform steps from the Legong. After a short while they start making eyes at a particular young man in the audience and lure him out to dance with them. Since many Balinese have mastered the basic dance-steps, this usually produces an artistically creditable ensemble performance. If the chosen male happens to be a tourist, the locals are hugely amused by his grotesque movements.

Kebyar (Balih-Balihan)

The Kebyar Legong is a relatively modern invention, having been first danced in 1914. It is always performed by two girls. In this case the emphasis is more on the music than on their interpretation. This new approach to dance spread across the island like lightning; indeed the word *kebyar* means "lightning." The dance combines the tender, delicate movement of *Legong* with the heroic posing of the *Baris*.

In the 1920s, one name came to the fore which today is inseparably linked with the *Kebyar*: I Ketut Marya (Mario). He developed the *Kebyar Duduk* (*duduk* means "sitting"), in which the dancer squats on the floor for most of the time, with his legs crossed and a fan in his hand, moving his arms, hands and backside in imitation of the music. To achieve perfection in this dance, the performer learns to play all the instruments in order to absorb the special tonal qualities of each one. He can express their different

215

sounds and moods with the supple movements of his body and the expressiveness of his mime and the movements of his eyes. It is almost as if he himself becomes a sensitive musical instrument. In the *Kebyar Trompong* or *Trompong Duduk*, the dance is supplemented by the playing of a *trompong*, an instrument with a long row of horizontal gongs. Mario was an exceptionally fine exponent of this form of the dance, coaxing sounds from the instrument with theatrical, expressive movements. His balletic gestures with the sticks reinforced the musicality of the performance.

Sanghyang (Wali)

Sanghyang means something like "worthy of adoration," and relates to the divine spirit which for a while comes down to earth and expresses itself through the medium of trance. The *Sanghyang Dedari* is always danced by virginal young girls; the *Sanghyang Jaran*, by a young man or a priest. In the latter version the dancer "rides" on a hobbyhorse around and though a bed of burning coconut shells. All *Sanghyang* dances are intended to protect a village from the forces of darkness and are performed in times of general peril and hardship in order to ward off disaster.

Kecak (Balih-Balihan)

The origins of the *Kecak* lie in the *Sanghyang* trance-dances, in which the young girls or boys are put into a trance by a choir repeating a syncopated chant that sounds like "chackachacka." This form of the dance, which has remained virtually unchanged to the present day, was first developed by Walter Spies for the film *Island of Demons*. At least 50 men, wearing only a *poleng*, or black-and-white checked sarong, sit in several rows around an oil lamp. With their "chackachacka" chant they create a car-

Above: The dances of Bali are far more static than classical European ballet.

pet of sound which is meant to resemble that of a *gamelan* orchestra; in doing so they weave together as many as seven different rhythms. Moving only the upper half of their bodies, they rock back and forth, stretching up their arms and hands and letting them drop again. Because there are so many of them, the men's movements give the effect of a heaving sea with spray from a wave suddenly breaking. Against this background a story from the *Ramayana* (see p. 223) is enacted, culminating in the freeing of Sita from the clutches of the wicked Ravana with the help of the beloved Hanuman and his troop of monkeys. Half the circle of male singers represents the army of monkeys and the other half Ravana's army, or sometimes the serpent into which an arrow shot at Rama is transformed in mid-flight. Earlier, Ravana's flight as he carries Sita off to his kingdom in Sri Lanka is accompanied by a sharp hissing from the choir.

Legong (Bebali)

It is said that the *Legong* is the most charming of all Bali's dances. At all events the best-known is the *Legong Kraton*, which originally only princesses were allowed to dance. Today it is performed by three girls: two *legong* represent members of a royal house, while the third, the *condong*, plays the part of a servant-girl. It is she who begins the piece with a ten-minute introductory dance. At the end of her solo, her eyes light on two fans and she picks them up. Then she turns to the two *Legong* who have appeared on the stage and hands each of them a fan.

The most frequently-performed story concerns Princess Rangkesari, who wanders into the forest, where she is found and carried off by King Lasem. Rangkesari rejects the king's advances by hitting him with her fan. When her brother, the Prince of Daha, learns of her imprison-

ment, he threatens war if she is not released. Lasem opts for war. On his way to the battle he is warned of his impending defeat by a crow, played by the *condong* in gold wings. The king nonetheless continues on to the battlefield, and the dance ends with his death.

The *legong* present the story in pantomime, slipping from role into another. Sometimes they act as a double image of one person, which you can recognize by the absolute synchronization of their movements. Then they separate again and play the parts of different people. Swathed in golden cloaks and wearing crowns of chased gold and frangipani flowers, the young dancing-girls make an extremely attractive picture.

Pendet (Bebali)

This dance originally accompanied the offering of sacrificial gifts to the gods, and could be danced by anyone, without special training. Today the *Pendet* is performed by trained girl dancers as a dance of welcome at the beginning of a *Legong* performance, after which they scatter handfuls of flowers into the audience.

Topeng (Bebali)

Topeng, whose name means "pressed against the face," is a masked dance. All the characters wear masks, but the servants and clowns leave the lower halves of their face uncovered, so that they are able to speak. There are usually three or four dancers, who, with the aid of different masks, each play a number of roles: the comic or the serious man, the young man or the old. There are even long-nosed tourists and Dutch colonial types. The *Topeng Tua* is particularly popular; this is a solo performance which shows the typical behavior and appearance of an old man. A variant of this represents an old soldier in retirement, touchingly trying to recapture his lost youth.

THE MUSIC AND DANCE OF LOMBOK

On Lombok, music and the performing arts – which are still deeply rooted in religious ceremony, unlike those of Western countries – are in the throes of a process of development which can best be described as a clash of cultures. Three different forces are at work on the long-established and overlapping traditions of music and dance: Islamic orthodoxy, modern popular music and the Indonesian government.

Even in its music, Lombok's cultural heritage is a mixed bag, incorporating indigenous Sasak ritual, Javanese and Balinese cultural influences, and religious ideals drawn from Islam. Within this multi-faceted mixture, the more orthodox Islamic religious teachers do not like anything which is reminiscent of the

Above: During a comic dance interlude, a sarong is presented to the winner of a stick-fight.

"heathen" tendencies of the Wetu-Telu devotees and other Sasak traditionalists. Thus the Imams strongly disapprove, for instance, of unambiguous flirtation-dances such as the *Gandrung*, because they present a threat to the decorous separation of men and women.

Foreign observers may be surprised at the apparently trivial details which come in for criticism by the religious establishment. Orthodox Moslems disapprove of the instrumentation of traditional *gamelan* music, because it uses bronze instruments, often called "the voices of the ancestors," which date back to animistic times. This has already led to many *gamelan* orchestras in east Lombok either breaking up or changing over to iron metallophones, or even going back to "Islamic" *rebana* drums. But Balinese music has remained untouched by these influences.

The most recent and probably the most successful opposition to the old customs and dances is the music that blares out from the modern-day audio-visual media.

As everywhere else in the world, young people are captivated by the technical perfection of pop music hits and lose interest in traditional music. The only force which resists this trend, and works to preserve the old traditions – often using the same media to do so – is the Indonesian government. In the cultural sphere at least, it holds firm to its motto of "Unity through Diversity," and recognizes the attraction which these ancient and exotic cultural forms hold for foreign visitors, and their importance in the tourist economy. However, the battle is not yet won.

Quite a number of dances have been preserved, and these differ considerably from those of Bali. As you travel across the island, you are most likely to come across procession-dances. In the region round Lingsar the rather martial-looking *Batek Baris* is still performed. Dancers dressed in old Dutch uniforms and armed with wooden rifles drill in rank and file to the harsh commands of an angry or at any rate very serious-looking commanding officer. They lead a procession, which includes *Telek* dancing girls and the rest of the village, from the village to a sacred spring. In the context of village festivals, female Telek dancers often play male roles. In the *gamelan* orchestra that accompanies them, you will notice an instrument that is unique to Lombok: called a *preret,* it is a woodwind instrument that rather resembles an oboe.

In central Lombok, the festivals marking the significant stages of life are accompanied by a *Gamelan Tawa-Tawa.* A striking element of this music is the sound of cymbals affixed to lances; it provides the perfect accompaniment for processions and parades. Also attached to the lances are tassels which dance in time to the music. In the same region it is common to see a procession with a Barong monster. In the monster's "body" kettle-gongs are beaten. This type of orchestra, called a *Gamelan Barong Tengkok,* usually accompanies a wedding pro-

cession, in which the happy couple are carried around on wooden horses.

From an earlier age a whole series of war-dances can be traced. In one of these, called *Tari Oncer*, and which can be seen in eastern and central Lombok, two dancers approach each other with drum-like instruments and dance around each other in dramatic poses. This symbolic contest is not based on any particular story. The *Paresean*, or stick-fight, though thinly disguised as a dance, can get pretty violent, and blood quite often flows.

For romance one turns to the *Gandrung.* Here a girl dances in the middle of a circle and sings a song full of longing and melancholy. After she has danced alone for a while, she gives one of the men a little slap with her fan and challenges him to dance with her. He then gives her a small sum of money and follows her movements in an improvised dance which covers a whole range of expression from the eccentric through clumsy comedy to suggestive eroticism. This delightful performance nearly always gets a storm of applause from the audience.

There are also dance performances in a theater which last a whole evening. Like the *Arja* opera in Bali, they tend to be based on the *Panji* cycle of stories. A specifically Moslem achievement in this field is the *Kemidi Rudat* – the word *kemidi* is derived from the English "comedy" – which is based on the *Arabian Nights.*

In Bayan, in northern Lombok, you will be struck by the unusual, old Turkish costumes worn by the actors. It appears that this custom was started by an islander returning from a pilgrimage to Mecca at the beginning of this century. There he was so impressed by the uniforms of the Ottoman *Kaaba* guards that he brought some back with him, complete with the fez- and turban-like headgear, and introduced them to Lombok.

BALINESE GAMELAN

In the days of the Majapahit empire, Bali was entirely dedicated to the courtly art of the Javanese gamelan. This music was slow, restrained and melancholy. *Gamelan* is an ancient Javanese word for an orchestra, and is used all over Indonesia today. However, the Balinese call their orchestras *Gongs*, as for instance in *Gong Gede*, the "Great Orchestra" of the rajas which dominated the Balinese musical scene until well into the 20th century. In the colonial period, the art of the courts changed. The splendor of the princely houses faded in the 1930s, and with it the great gamelans disappeared.

The instruments were either placed in mothballs or sold to village communities and their music clubs. The latter often had the bronze instruments melted down to make new ones which had greater ap-

Above: The big gong signals the end of the piece. Right: Every village worthy of the name has its own gamelan orchestra.

peal to the popular audience. Thus the change to popular *gamelan* music was complete: the style became louder, faster and more cheerful, and was played with greater passion. Since then, there has been continuous experimentation, encouraged by state support of festivals. In 1938, a competition between five regions was won by a *gamelan* from Peliatan, led by A. A. Gede Mandera, and playing music which "tenderly caressed the skin like the rays of the sun," as Colin McPhee described it in his book *A House in Bali.*

Often a *gamelan* will consist of two sets of instruments, one tuned to the 5-note scale (*slendro*) and the other to the 7-note scale (*pelog*). But even with the 7-note scale, the five notes of the *slendro* system are especially important and are played more frequently. They correspond roughly to the notes C, D, F, G and A in the Western diatonic scale. The individual instruments of a *gamelan* are tuned to each other at the time they are made. The one exception is the *rebab*, a stringed instrument which is thought to be the forerunner of our violin. Different *gamelans* are tuned to their own particular pitch and therefore cannot play together. In an orchestra most of the instruments perform in pairs. Each pair is tuned in such a way as to produce a slight dissonance. And even single instruments which have a range of more than one octave are tuned so that the high notes are slightly sharper than the corresponding low notes. This produces a multi-layered and more appropriate sound. Fleshing this out is the great range and depth of sounds provided by drums, gongs and cymbals; instruments with a high-pitched sound are used more frequently than lower-pitched ones.

Balinese music is characterized by sudden changes, syncopations, unexpected bursts of rapid virtuoso playing, crescendos and diminuendos from tempestuous fortissimos to a barely audible murmur, and an elaborate system of

counterpoint based on simple melodies. The standard 4/4 beat can quickly be split into a multiple rhythm. The mode of playing follows the principle of *kotekan*, two complementary and interweaving parts: *sangsih* and *polos*. Two musicians play simultaneously as fast as possible to produce a single melodic line at a speed twice as fast as either musician would be capable of playing on his own.

Basically, the instruments can be divided into four groups: one plays the melody, a second embellishes this melody, a third accentuates the composition, and the fourth acts as leader of the orchestra, controlling tempo and dynamics.

The instruments consist mainly of metallophones, xylophones and drums. The metallophone's special timbre results not only from metal, but also from the fact that its keys are placed over bamboo pipes which act as resonators. The whole thing is then encased in wood, which is elaborately carved and painted. These instruments are specially repainted for big

occasions; red and gold are considered particularly festive colors.

The larger instruments, with just five notes, are the *jublag* and the *jegog*, which are both played rather slowly. The smaller *jublag* plays the basic melody, while the larger *jegog* amplifies the important notes of the *pokok*, and punctuates longer phrases.

The smaller instruments of the second group are the *gangsas*, which embellish the basic melody. They have two 5-tone scales, and exist in various different sizes; the smaller they are, the faster they are played. The player wields the mallet with his right hand, and the left hand mutes the sound a fraction of a second later, while the right hand is already striking the next note.

The *riyong* is a long wooden frame, holding a a row of horizontal gongs. Four people sit behind it to play it. The gongs have a protruding knob in the center, which is where the players most often strike them; they can obtain other effects by touching the edges of the gongs.

The *trompong* is similar to the *riyong*, and, like the riyong, paraphrases the melody, but it is played by only one instrumentalist. It is, furthermore, the only instrument which is sometimes used for solos or improvisations.

In the third group there are a series of hanging gongs, none smaller than 2 feet (75 cm) in diameter. The fullest tone comes from the largest gong, which is struck at the beginning and end of each piece of music. The other gongs mark accents and divisions in the composition as a whole. Individual smaller, horizontal gongs (*kempli*) are used to hold the whole piece together and maintain a steady tempo.

However, the most important instrument is the drum. Again, there are two of these, one of which plays the lead part. The *kendang* is a two-headed drum which can be played from either end. It

can produce different sounds depending on whether the player strikes it with the palm of his hand, his knuckles, or his fingertips; whether or not he mutes the sound; and whether he hits the middle or the edge of the drum. Sometimes the drummer also uses a drumstick. A player does not graduate to the drum until he has mastered all the other instruments. He holds the whole performance together and introduces changes of tempo or pauses. Like a conductor, he uses his head and movements of his hands to communicate with the other musicians and the dancers, who rehearse the basic elements of the melody and its accentuations alone with the drummer beforehand. If the ensemble works well, a whole elaborate polyphony can be built up, without confusing the dancers.

Musicians start very young, and are almost exclusively male, though Ubud boasts a fine all-woman *gamelan*. The complexity of this music has fascinated many Western composers. Balinese, by contrast, find our music much too simple.

Above: The kendang sets the rhythm and gives the cue for changes of tempo.

WAYANG KULIT

Wayang kulit is the term for plays performed by colorful leather shadow-puppets, which are decoratively cut and perforated so as to create memorable silhouettes when held up against the light. The puppet-master is the *dalang*, whose voice and agile fingers endow the figures with souls and personalities. He needs a white linen screen (*kelir*), a coconut-oil lamp (*damar*) which gives off a flickering light, musicians and assistants. The bulk of the audience sits in front of the screen, but a few people go round the other side to admire the colors of the puppets and to follow the activities of the *dalang* and the musicians with rapt attention. The orchestra consists of two large and two small *gender*, or metallophones, whose keys, like those of the *gangsa*, are suspended over bamboo resonators, but which are played with two mallets and are muted almost instantaneously. The musicians pay very close attention to the movements of the *dalang* with his puppets, so that they can illustrate the action musically, underline certain points and, when there is a fight, give an acoustic counterpart to every blow.

At the beginning of the performance the *dalang* knocks on a big wooden chest (*kropak*) with a wooden or horn clapper held between the toes of his right foot, to bring the puppets, who are in the chest, to life. He then selects from his large supply anything from 30 to 60 puppets, which, with the help of his assistants, he places in the soft banana-stem (*gedebong*) along the bottom edge of the screen. The figures are of two principal types, easily distinguishable from each other: *alus* and *kasar*. The first group are sensitive and even-tempered, the second vulgar and irascible; the first are considered good, the second, bad. The good protagonists come in from the right side of the screen, the bad from the left. The more important a character's role is in the play, the closer he stands to the *kayonan*, or Tree of Life, which looks like a large, finely etched leaf. The *kayonan* is brought on at the beginning and end of every performance, and in every important scene. Sometimes it also serves to represent the forces of nature, such as fire, wind and water. On these occasions the *kayonan* is flapped about violently, and moved closer to or further from the screen, so that its sharply defined contours alternate with blurred shadows. An excited vibrating of the figures creates a mysterious, restless mood. In addition there are the courtiers (*panasar*), two loyal servants and two ne'er-do-wells with fat stomachs and jaws which move, so that you can actually see them speaking. They have the task of translating the speeches of the king's sons and the gods into ordinary Balinese, for these characters only express themselves in Kawi, the ancient, Sanskrit-based language of the theater, of poetry and religion. They use 47 different couplets from the *Ramayana* and the *Mahabharata*. Those two Hindu epics form the basis for the plays' moral framework, ensuring that in the struggle between Good and Evil, the latter does not prevail.

Probably the best-loved theme, and one which is presented in many different dramatic forms, is the *Ramayana* epic. It is set in the kingdom of Kosala, near the Himalayas, which is ruled by King Dasarata. When he expresses his intention of abdicating in favor of his son Rama, his second wife Kekayai, who is the mother of Barata, insists that Dasarata keep his promise of granting her two wishes. She demands that her son Barata be crowned king, and that Rama be exiled for 14 years. Rama respects his father's promise and, with his wife Sita and favorite brother Laksmana, he withdraws to the solitude of the forest. After a time, the demon-king Ravana notices the beautiful Sita and vows to have her. He sends his minister, disguised as a golden hind, to lure Rama and Laksmana deeper into

the forest, leaving Sita alone. Rawana then comes to her, and carries her off. As they fly high through the air towards Ravana's kingdom in Sri Lanka, the brave bird Jatayu attempts to rescue Sita, but in the ensuing struggle he is mortally wounded, and only just succeeds in getting back to tell Rama of the encounter.

On their journey to Ravana's domain, the brothers meet the monkey-king Sugriva. He promises to help them liberate Sita if they in turn agree to support him in winning back his rightful position as monarch in the Realm of the Apes. After this is accomplished, Sugriva sends his general Hanuman with his troops of monkeys to help Rama. Hanuman personally informs Sita of her impending rescue, then orders his troops to build a causeway from the southern tip of India across to Sri Lanka, so that Rama and his allies can reach the island. After a terrible battle

Above: The dalang at work. Right: The skill of the dalang breathes life and personality into the shadow-puppets.

in which Ravana is fatally wounded by one of Rama's arrows, Rama and Sita are finally united again. Upon their return to Kosala with Laksmana, Barata gladly hands over the reins of monarchy to Rama, since in spite of his mother's ambitious plans for him, Barata had only been exercising power provisionally in Rama's absence.

The second epic, the *Mahabharata,* which also comes from India, concerns a feud between two families of the Bharata people, who both claim the right to rule the kingdom of Hastinapura. The occupant of the throne, Dhritarashtra, fathers a hundred sons, the Kauravas. His brother Pandu is granted five sons of divine descent, the Pandavas: Yudhistira, the eldest, is the son of Yama, the god of death; Bhima is the son of the wind-god Vayu; Arjuna is descended from Indra, king of the gods, and then there are the twin brothers Sahdeva and Nakula. Pandu acts as regent, ruling the kingdom on behalf of his brother Dhritarashtra, who is blind. Upon his death, Pandu's

eldest son, Yudhistira, is to rule in his place, but the Kaurava brothers are not at all happy about this arrangement. They plot against the five Pandavas and force them to flee with their mother, Kunti, and to wander through the country living as beggars. On their way they learn from a Brahman that the princess Draupadi is to be allowed to take a husband of her own choosing. The rival suitors hold an archery contest and Arjuna, who is an incomparable bowman, is the winner, thus gaining the hand of Draupadi in marriage. Returning home, he tells his mother of his good fortune. However, she commands all of her sons to seek Draupadi's favors; in this way, the princess becomes the consort of all five Pandava brothers.

After a temporary truce in their quarrel, the Kauravas enlist the help of Prince Sukani, who is an accomplished cheat, and lure Yudhistira into gambling away not only his whole kingdom, but also himself, his brothers and Princess Draupadi, in a game played with loaded dice.

Thus were the Pandavas sent into exile for twelve years and were then obliged to live another year unrecognized among their own people. At the end of this time, the Pandavas return with the intention of reclaiming their rights to the kingdom. However, this claim is rejected by the Kauravas. Thereupon the battle of Kurukshetra breaks out, and for eighteen whole days the sky is darkened by the enemies' arrows.

During their exile, the Pandavas had gained the friendship of Krishna, whose sister Subhadra had married Arjuna. Krishna does not wish to take an active part in the battle, but acts as Arjuna's charioteer. When Arjuna refuses to wield his weapons in this murderous fraternal war, Krishna reminds him of his duty as a warrior, and at the same time extols the immortality of the soul. This passage of the epic, called the *Bhagavadgita*, is held to be India's most important didactic poem. The Pandavas are victorious, but their triumph is overshadowed by grief, since Arjuna and Bhima lose their sons.

225

ART AND ARTISAN WORK

Until the 1930s all creative activity in Bali which could in any way be described as art was of a sacred character. Virtually every artistic or handcraft skill was put to the service of decorating or beautifying the temples or adorning religious festivals. And the fact of being an artist did not release an individual from his normal social and economic obligations. Indeed, no distinction was made between ordinary manual work and the most elevated form of art. The decorative construction of a tower of offerings to the gods, the delicate weaving of a rice-goddess from palm-leaves or the ornate painting of a cremation-coffin – each had to be done with the same degree of care and imagination. Accordingly, there was no word in the Balinese language corresponding to our concept of "art."

Whenever a temple festival was coming up, everyone in the village would contribute to its success to the best of their ability. Anyone who displayed a particular talent was naturally held in high esteem, and would be invited on the next occasion to put their skill to the service of the gods. After a day's work in the rice fields, people would gather to produce cult objects and sacrificial offerings in the traditional manner. It is therefore not surprising that no individual artists from the period prior to 1930 are known to us by name; in any case it was not the contribution of the individual which was at the heart of the creative process, but rather the ritual value of the object in question. Even today, though circumstances have changed, in many places people prefer to work in groups, rather than as individual artists set apart from the community. Thus, for a long time, the point was not to produce original, subjective creations, but to make successful imitations of favorite tried and tested motifs.

Another factor that distinguishes the creative activity of Bali is that much of what is produced is not intended for posterity, but rather for one brief religious occasion. The woven palm-leaf is the very next day crushed and dried up, the flamboyantly decorated coffin goes up in flames in a few spectacular moments, and even the temple demons, carved in sandstone or tufa, are usually eroded by wind and rain within a decade, reduced to toothless and faceless lumps. This creates a continuous need for temple decorations of all kinds, which demands the permanent involvement of everyone; thus a large number of talents are kept active in whatever manual skills are required. This ensures that artistic traditions are kept alive and handed down uninterrupted from generation to generation. With time, even the simplest object becomes refined. This is what has given rise to the impression has been gained that every Balinese is an artist.

However, this picture of a democratic, egalitarian art needs to be corrected, inasmuch as, along with village culture, there existed recognized centers of artistic activity: the courts of the feudal rajas. Here, there was definitely a concentration of particularly gifted painters, sculptors or wood-carvers, most of whom belonged to the higher castes. Their work can be distinguished from village art in that it often drew its inspiration directly from the ancient scriptures, and was therefore more academic than the primitive fantasies of the villagers. Their technique was also often much finer, though this does not mean that their content was any more sensitive or refined (think of the graphic depictions of torture and sex in the ceiling paintings of the Kerta Gosa in Klungkung).

It was this courtly art which suffered the most after the Dutch conquest of 1908. Having been deprived of their

Right: The "Bumble-Bee Dance" by Anak Agung Gede Sobrat.

power, the rajas also lost their financial resources, so that their ability to promote the fine arts was severely limited or disappeared altogether.

The Boom in Painting

The renaissance in the 1930s was the product of a variety of sources. First, the Dutch colonial administration made a great effort to preserve Balinese culture, on the one hand by funding the restoration of important cultural buildings, and on the other by trying, with considerable success, to shield the island from Western tourists and Christian missionaries. Secondly, some of the influential aristocratic families of Bali, like the Sukawatis in Ubud, began once again to support artistic activity. From a European point of view, it is particularly interesting to note the impact of the wealthy, international, art-loving dropouts from the west, who introduced their ideas and techniques to the Balinese artists. Among the first of these were the German painter and musi-

cian Walter Spies and the Dutch painter Rudolf Bonnet. Spies settled in Bali in 1927 and soon moved to Ubud, where, in a very short time, he became a much-visited and much-consulted interpreter of Balinese culture to the western world. It is to a great extent his image of Bali which has determined Western perceptions of the island. Bonnet, who was equally fascinated by Bali, was concerned about the possible damage which might be done by outside influences. These two men, together with Cokorda Gede Agung Sukawati, were responsible for the founding of the *Pita Maha* school of painting, in which about 125 Balinese artists have worked. Among them was a personality who in many respects stands out from other native artists: Gusti Nyoman Lempad. Even before the arrival of Spies, he had already made a name for himself as a designer, as a builder and sculptor of temple gates, as a carver of *barong* masks, and as a constructor and decorator of burial-towers. He now became famous the world over for his portrayals of the physical and spiritual world of his native island. He produced his last work shortly before his hundredth birthday, and died, laden with honors, in 1978 at the veritably Biblical age of 122.

A second influential art school can be attributed to Arie Smit, another Dutchman, who stayed on in Bali after World War II. In the then rather impoverished town of Penestanan, Smit gathered around him a group of young people and let them paint according to their own inclinations and ideas. These *Young Artists* differ from the painters of the *Pita Maha* school principally in their choice of subjects. The peasant children painted from their solid experience of everyday life in the country, things that affected their own lives, whereas the *Pita Maha* painters for the most part remained wedded to the the traditional techniques and subjects – myths, epics etc.

With the rapid growth of tourism after 1965, the output of Bali's painters increased to unprecedented levels. As well as traditional styles of painting, such as were still practised in Kamasan, near Klungkung, you will now see every conceivable form of artistic expression. There also seems to be no limit to craftsmen's ability to reproduce, on a mass-market scale, legion virtually identical objects in every conceivable style. Ubud has always been the center of this almost industrialized art production. But it is also possible here to get a very good general idea of Balinese art as a whole. Before touring round the innumerable artists' studios, it is a good idea to visit two museums: the Puri Lukisan Museum in the center of Ubud, and the Neka Museum in Campuan. Both of these give a good overview of Balinese art and Bali's interpretation of western painting. Once you know what to look for, your studio ramble will be more valuable.

Right: Rough hands can often shape delicate objects.

The Wood-Carvers with the Art Deco Touch

Just as in the field of painting, the year 1930 marked a turning-point in the art of wood-carving. Up to that time, wood-carvers mainly produced tableau-like reliefs and religious figures, which were destined either for temples or the palaces of the rajas. In these princely residences, you can still admire finely chiseled door-panels and ceiling rafters.

The story goes that the contemporary Balinese style of wood-sculpture can be traced back to a work which Walter Spies commissioned from a local carver. He asked the man to carve two figures from one fairly long piece of wood. But instead of two, he only carved one figure, with an exaggeratedly long body and thin limbs. The artist made the excuse that the soul of the piece of wood did not permit any other design. The figure appealed to Walter Spies straight away, not least because it reminded him of the Art Deco style, which at the time was much in vogue. It became the prototype of a new style of Balinese art. In Mas, Kemenuh and Sumampan near Batuan, good but expensive figures can be found.

Thanks to the thriving tourist economy, wood-carving began to blossom again. It started with carvings of banana-plants in light wood; then came anthropomorphic frogs and other kitschy creatures. No doubt these will be replaced by other big sellers in due course. Whole villages in the area between Ubud and Sebatu are kept busy mass-producing cutesy items of this kind.

An object which was once shrouded in a certain shy secrecy has long since found its way onto the mass market: the almost grotesque carved dance masks. It used to be believed that anyone putting one of these over his face would lose himself a little, if not entirely, in the figure which the mask represented. It is still the case that only the *topeng* masks made

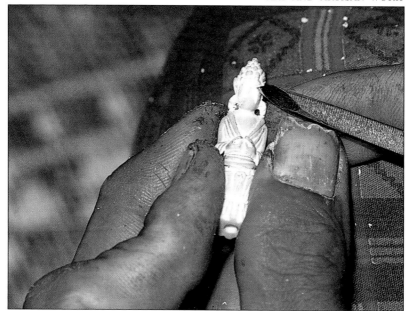

by the best carvers, from Mas or Singa-padu, are used in certain very special dances or dramas.

Gold- and Silversmiths

Today, the traditional center of the gold- and silversmiths' art is still found in Kamasan, south of Klungkung. It is from here that the priests order valuable ritual objects in precious metals for their temples. There has been no decline in the number of religious ceremonies, and it is for that reason that this branch of crafts-manship is still very much alive. Their main products are sacrificial bowls, betel-nut containers and adornments.

In the town of Celuk, silver jewelry, in particular, is produced for the tourist market. If you want something made es-pecially for you, head for the side streets and take a drawing with you. For a small down-payment, these masters of the jeweler's art will accept your com-mission and execute it promptly accord-ing to your wishes.

Shopping

Anyone wishing to get an overall im-pression of what other types of handi-crafts are on the market should visit the tourist centers of Kuta and Sanur, or make inquiries at the art centers in and around Denpasar. The market in Suka-wati is a good place to make comparisons on quality and price.

Apart from textiles, the best buys are *wayang kulit* puppets (either cut from leather, or in the form of dolls), waxed parasols, bags and baskets woven from rattan or palm-leaves (often imported from Lombok), wind-clappers (useful as scarecrows in the garden), pottery jars from Ubung (near Denpasar), and terra-cotta figurines from Pejatan (Tabanan). You may also be interested in antiques, such as *krises* or furniture. If you are thinking of buying anything made from bamboo, you should bear in mind that this material cannot tolerate the dryness you get in central-heated homes, and is very liable to split.

229

IKAT AND DOUBLE-IKAT

Looking at Balinese clothes and fabrics, the eye is delighted by their variety of color and the often sumptuous materials – you would never suppose that the Balinese consider them "impure." But they do hold this view – so strongly, indeed, that they even avoid walking under washing that is hanging out to dry. Indeed, the more conservative Balinese won't enter a two-storey house, because you never know what might be upstairs.

In spite of this ritual impurity associated with clothes, the Balinese devote much time and imagination to the task of making them and adorning them, using a variety of traditional techniques. Three types of fabric are produced on the island. Each one has a particular significance in the social hierarchy.

Above: Threads are dyed by hand in the Nyantri technique. Right: Threads are untied and stretched on a frame before being steeped in the dye.

First, there is the *songket*. It is a brocade material which is never woven to a greater width than 30 inches (75 cm) and is shot through with gold or silver threads. These threads are introduced in such a way as to make a contrasting pattern on the cloth. The motifs are usually flowers, birds or animals.

At one time, *songket* was only worn by Brahmans or the nobility. Nowadays it is worn by anyone who has a fairly high position in society, or for special ceremonies. One piece of the cloth can cost as much as several hundred thousand rupiahs.

Next comes the *kain prada*, a cotton fabric on which a pattern is applied after weaving with gold-leaf or gold paint. This is mainly worn for family ceremonies such as tooth-filing or weddings, as well as at dance performances.

If *batik* is considered the "national textile" of Indonesia as a whole, then the equivalent for Bali is *ikat*, or *endek*, as it is more commonly known on the island. The word *ikat* comes from the Malay lan-

guage and means something like "knotting" or "tying". In this process, the threads are dyed in bunches before weaving, so that a blurred pattern emerges. This can be done in one of three styles: a) the warp-*ikat,* in which only the warp-threads are dyed, while the weft remains uncolored; b) the weft-*ikat,* in which the process is reversed; and c) the double-*ikat,* in which both the warp and the weft are dyed before weaving. For those who need clarification, the warp is the lengthways thread, and the weft is woven across, over and under the warp.

In Bali, it is chiefly the weft-*ikat* that is produced. The weft-threads are stretched horizontally over a frame in precisely counted hanks and tied with strips of plastic in such a way that a pattern emerges. The hanks are dyed, washed and dried. If the material is to be multicolored – some factories use as many as six dyes, others only one – plastic strips of various colors are used for tying, and are gradually cut away during the dyeing process. In Bali, and also in Lombok,

where the Balinese have introduced this technique, an additonal process is employed, called *nyantri* or *coletan* – a kind of crowning glory of *ikat*. It consists of applying additional colors by hand, using a brush-like instrument. The dried threads are wound on to specially marked spools, and used as weft-threads so that during the weaving a slightly fuzzy pattern once again emerges. The finer a pattern has to be, the more labor-intensive and expensive is the *ikat,* because fewer threads can be bunched together. On the other hand, the process can be simplified by using a frame of half the usual width. The threads are turned in the middle and stretched back double on themselves. In this way a mirror-image of the pattern is created.

Far more complicated and time-consuming, however, is the making of the double *ikat,* also called *geringsing,* "cloth of flame." There are only a few places in Bali where it is still manufactured, generally Bali-Aga villages. Probably the most famous of these is Tenganan, also known

as *Tenganan Pegeringsingan*, after the fabrics that are woven there.

The complexity lies in the fact that that the previously dyed warp- and weft-threads must be woven together in such a way that a recognizable pattern emerges. For this reason the weavers will often restrict themselves to geometrical designs, which are easier to produce.

All over Bali, the *geringsing* has a ritual significance. It is used at ceremonies or to heal sickness. In Tenganan itself, fragments of Indian double-*ikat* are used for this purpose, since they are supposed to have the same magical powers as *geringsing*. But it is also worn as part of everyday clothing. The men wear it as a sarong, while the woman wrap it round their torso and bosom, when it is called an *anteng*.

In Bali, *kamben sarung* is the name of the garment traditionally worn by men around their hips. The two ends are sewn

together to make a sort of tube. What the women wear is not really a sarong at all but a *kamben lembaran,* called *kamben* for short. Its ends are left open. *Kamben* is the Balinese word for a piece of material which in the rest of Indonesia is called a *kain.* This *kamben* is also worn by men, who let the longer end hang in folds at the front. In order to allow more freedom of movement for the legs, when dancing or playing sport of some kind, this "tail" can be pulled back between the legs and tucked into the waist of the sarong. The women always tie their *kamben* in a simple way, slung around the hips without any additional embellishment.

Men usually wear a shirt over their sarong, except on ceremonial occasions, when, like the women, they wear a cloth over their chest, or a kind of sarong which reaches from the chest to the legs. For everyday purposes the women wear a *kebaya*, which is a tight-fitting, long-sleeved jacket, closed over the chest with a broad ribbon.

Above: Examples of modern batiks. Right: Master craftsman Soerono at work.

ENCOUNTER WITH A BATIK ARTIST

We had thought that Mr Soerono would be one of those "typical" Balinese painters, who sit in their open-sided studio-pavilions, surrounded by their pupils, composing delightful pictures in the traditional style: pictures with scenes from mythology and everyday life, in which the magical world of demons, ghosts and witches is often drawn into the reality of the modern world with its towns and traffic; pictures filled to the very edges with careful portrayals of plants, animals and people in pastel shades, and which, in their detailed, stylized representation, are reminiscent of the narrative illustrations of medieval Europe.

We found Mr Soerono's studio a few hundred yards outside Kuta, a little way off the busy road to Denpasar. A large wooden sign points the way for us: a grassy front garden, a little ocher-colored house, and next to it an open workshop, smothered in red flowering bougainvillea. Inside, on a rough wooden table against the back wall, pictures and batiks are piled higgledy-piggledy. We are in for a surprise. This is no traditional Balinese painter's studio: the style is western, the colors strong; the pictures are full of energy, even drama, at once passionate and sensitive. And yet it is clearly not European painting.

We do not notice the artist until he is right beside us, a small, wiry, boyish figure, barefoot, wearing a tattered T-shirt and a silk sarong. He welcomes us with a smile, the courteous but inscrutable smile of an oriental sage. We strike up a conversation, and when he sees that we are genuinely interested in his work and have time to spare, he willingly tells us about himself.

He is a Javanese by birth, 64 years old, who came to Bali as a child, and later, as a schoolboy, studied for two years with

the Dutch painter Velthuysen. His subjects are many and various: arresting, realistic impressions of rice-growers at harvest-time, river scenes, portraits of women, young and old. Among his tender, sensitively drawn batiks are a classic head of a girl in profile which makes one think of Picasso; a powerful and dramatic vision of demons from the legends of his people; and, again and again, self-portraits imbued with a passionate grief – he lost his family in World War II – or of the artist at his easel, refusing with a violent gesture an offer of money from Death. He interprets this for us: "If I were to sell myself for money, it would mean my death as an artist." Yet he knows exactly what his pictures are worth. For one of his Batik pictures costs US$ 75, a sum which a teacher in Bali would have to work three weeks to earn.

"Would you like to see how a batik is made?" Soerono asks suddenly. "Have you got time?" And he takes us into the house to fetch the material. Here, too, there is a table laden with pictures, which are suffering from damp, a figure of a Buddha and all manner of junk. On the left-hand wall hang two pictures: Christ on the cross and a large head of Buddha, both in brownish-black tones, with bright highlights, in the style of a woodcut. Underneath them, hanging horizontally, is an electric guitar. The versatile Mr Soerono sits down with the instrument and plays the German Christmas carol *Silent Night*, followed by a Balinese dance. His earring glints, and the wide bronze band around his right ankle glows like gold. The time is passing, but what do we care?

However, Soerono has not forgotten the batik. He leads us into a shady back yard behind his studio, surrounded by a hedge and bordering on a field of ripening rice. Here, he draws up two bamboo chairs for us, under the projecting tin roof. With a practised hand he stretches a piece of cotton cloth over a frame. Then with rapid, sure strokes he draws on it with a piece of chalk. Soon a Balinese temple appears under a setting sun, whose last rays fall through the crown of a palm tree and onto a young girl carrying offerings to the temple on her proudly erect head. At her feet, a pot-bellied pig trots out from the lush, tropical undergrowth. Soerono pauses briefly, pulls a small gas stove towards him, then with hot, melted wax, goes over the drawing, in brisk, unhesitating sweeps, and spreads wax with a broad brush over the areas which are not to receive the dye. While his buxom assistant stirs the dye, he explains the next steps in the process. Then he seems to forget us. In a kind of ecstasy, he dances like a boxer back and forth between the bowls of dye, dips a corner of the cloth into the red, another into the green, a third into the yellow, leaps up, holds the fabric up to the light and dips it in again, first into a dye, then

into water, examines it once more, hangs it over a washing-line, squeezes it between his fingers, squirts some dye on a particular spot, takes it down from the line, dips it again...

His feet dance on the soft earth floor, his bare, wiry torso glistens, his expression is remote, full of concentration, while his hands work away for a good hour with a wondrous sureness which bespeaks a lifetime of practice.

From time to time, at the end of one of the stages in the work, he stops, emerges from his rapt concentration, and, as a way of calming himself, he strokes the little gray monkey that is chained up there. He tells us that he occasionally takes on pupils for a few weeks, tourists from Japan, Australia and America, and some Germans and Dutch. He regrets never having met Picasso – and the fact that he has ten children, all dependent on him. Two of his daughters are Catholic, and two Protestant, but that doesn't worry him, he is all for liberty and tolerance; he himself is devoted to Buddha – and here he kisses the bronze pendant that he wears round his neck. He lives here alone, he tells us, because he too needs his freedom, in order to work. Sometimes he gets up in the night to paint, if an idea comes to him; and sometimes he makes ten batiks one after another, and then sleeps for two whole days. In the afternoon he often goes to the beach and throws javelins.

Soerono's hands are black with dye and acid. The batik is now ready and his assistant washes out the wax with hot soda-water. While drinking a cup of coffee, we wait for the cloth to dry in the sun. The master's creation is an impression of Bali that has a thrilling intensity: in the blood-red glow of the setting sun, the young girl carries her sacrificial offerings with unwavering steps through the ghostly, threatening shadows of evening, towards the dark silhouette of the temple.

Right: This fighting-cock is his owner's pride and joy.

COCK-FIGHTING

In the mind of the devout Hindus of Bali, the world is full of demons. They are responsible for disaster, grief and sickness. In order to keep them at a distance, innumerable small gift-offerings are laid out every day at all key points of the threatened area. Sometimes, however, the demons seem to require a sacrifice of blood. On these occasions, even today, animals are sacrificed at important temple festivals and purification ceremonies. When, for example, at one of these festivals, the quarrel between Barong and Rangda is ended, a member of the congregation, in a trance-like state, bites the head off a live chick. The blood of the creature moistens the ground and thus is meant to mollify the malevolent forces of the spirit-world.

It is in this context of a religious sacrifice that cock-fighting has its origins. It was and is a fixed element in temple festivals, but certainly goes back to pre-Hindu times. Long before the Dutch arrived on the scene, cock-fighting in its secular form had emerged from religious ritual. It is true that even in its worldly version, the cock-fight did not begin without a short religious ceremony, but the important thing, both for the owners of the cocks, and the spectators, was to see their "own" roosters in an exciting fight. Although the Dutch colonial rulers were to a great extent prepared to see Balinese cultural individuality preserved, they nevertheless found cock-fighting so barbaric that they banned it – as they did the notorious burning of widows on the pyres of their deceased husbands. However, cock-fighting continued to thrive undercover, and after Indonesia's independence it was once again legalised. But in 1981, the government in Jakarta made the decision that henceforth cock-fighting should only be permitted in its religiously inspired form. The reasons for this were principally social, and had less to do with the bloodthirsty nature of the fighting than with the dire economic effects of the passion for betting which is enflamed

by the sport. One only has to observe the hectic activity surrounding these fights to understand clearly what was upsetting the government.

Before a fight is held, the owners of the cocks, or their ringside agents, inspect the fighting birds and come to the mutually exclusive conclusions that each of their birds is going to win. Only then do they agree to a fight. Since experts are at work here, they are each unshakeably convinced of a favorable outcome for their contender, and bet correspondingly large sums on their victory. This is the first phase of the betting negotiations. The two owners also offer an equally large sum for the other's rooster. This sum has a lower limit and is announced publicly as a point of reference for subsequent bets. The organizers of the contest receive a 10 to 25 percent share of the

Above: A fighting-cock spends a large part of his life in a basket-cage. Right: The quality of the cocks is always the object of speculation.

turnover; whatever happens, they can't lose.

In the second round of betting, the spectators take part. First come the professional punters and tipsters, according to whose judgement one or other of the cockerels emerges as favorite. Then everyone starts in with shouts and gestures, haggling with their betting-partners over acceptable odds. When two punters have reached agreement over odds, they briefly touch heads, then turn to another betting-partner. The owners of the competing birds often place further bets with the public, using front-men, because these bets are not subject to any deduction payable to the organizers. The wagers mount ever higher, the more so since the professionals make their living from this activity. The simple farmer who wants to keep up runs a high risk. It is reported that at many contests the starting bet for one fight is as high as 100,000 rupiahs. The owner of a fighting-cock often has to borrow a sum of that magnitude from members of his family or clan. It is not unheard-of for a peasant farmer to gamble away more than a whole year's income on a single fight, or even for an entire village to be plunged into penury because their favorite rooster let them down at the moment of truth.

In view of the fact that this sport has become a matter of life and death, it is no surprise to learn that the cock-fighting business has been invaded by all sorts of skullduggery. Cases have been discovered where owners of birds have deliberately had their metal spurs fitted too loosely, then been seen to place moderately high bets on them, while using front-men to put very high bets on the opposing cock, in the absolute certainty of cleaning up. At one time, the outcome of a fight would determine whether whole families went into slavery or could afford to buy another field. The passion for betting was so universal that it was said even to have turned rajas into paupers.

It must have been examples like these that the Indonesian government had in mind when they issued their prohibition. Even so, you cannot walk through any town or village in Bali today, without seeing a row of cages at the roadside, from which fighting-cocks observe the passers-by. Every male Balinese worth his salt is the proud owner of at least one of these feathered troublemakers. And just so the bird doesn't get bored, he is allowed to watch the activity of the village. But chasing hens is another matter altogether. The job of the cock is to fight, not to flirt! To this end he is pampered, massaged and fed a special diet.

Whenever the men of the village gather for drink and a chat, they swap experiences, make predictions for future fights, and allow their prized possesions to test their strength against each other. After about a year and a half, they get down to serious business. The natural instinct of the creature to assert itself against any male member of the same species is enhanced with the deadly weapon of a metal spur attached to the foot. It is from this spur that cock-fighting gets its Balinese name: the razor-sharp piece of metal, up to 6 inches (15 cm) long, is called a *taji*, hence the word *tajen* for the fight itself. Each contest lasts a maximum of five rounds. However, as a rule, two or three direct hits with the spur are enough; the wounded cock sinks into the dust of the arena, which is called a *wantilan*. Only if both birds can still stay on their feet after five hard-fought rounds is the match declared a draw. A cock which has survived unbeaten in four contests earns himself retirement as a superannuated champion. He is given permission to strut around the village with as much dignity as his injuries will allow, and only has to take care not to get tangled up in the spokes of someone's motorcycle. And what about the ban on cock-fighting? It is still in force, and for this reason fights of more than three rounds may only be held on temple festival days – with no betting. At other times, the 11th commandment applies: Thou shalt not get caught!

237

STICK-FIGHTING ON LOMBOK

Narmada is one of the centers of the sport of stick-fighting called *perisean,* or sometimes *peresehan.* On frequent days demonstration fights are held in the open sports-hall, just on the right as you go in. Two youthful fighters advance on each other, dressed in the traditional sarong, with a head-cloth, a roll of padded material around their hips, a stick and a shield. Their elegant, balletic duel is accompanied by a small *gamelan* orchestra. Although the blows are extremely violent, the spectators are relieved to see that they are always aimed at the shield. It looks most spectacular, and the clatter of stick on shield makes a hellish din, but no one gets hurt.

If you want to see a "genuine" stick-fight, you have to ask around, and Narmada is the best place to start. In the grounds of the palace (on the street side) fights are sometimes held on Sundays. It is still a fairly well-kept secret that in Puyung stick-fighting goes on nearly all the time, even during the week. The fighting arena is on a football field, tucked away at the end of the village. The fights begin at 4 pm, and gates open half-an-hour earlier. The spectators squat on the ground around a roped-off arena, about 10 to 15 yards square (100 -200 sq. m). On one side sits a *gamelan* orchestra under an awning, playing the audience in as they arrive. Later, during the fight, the crescendo and diminuendo of the music accompanies the action like a well-written film score, underlining the dramatic moments. In addition, a vocalist comments on what is happening, in a mixture of recitative and song, and often in a very bawdy manner, which always provokes the large crowd to gales of helpless laughter.

Right: In the final phase of a fight the action grows increasingly frantic and violent.

By around 4 o'clock the arena is full. Under the supervision of the organizers, the two seconds, called *pekembar*, start selecting the first pair of contestants. In the two corners facing the *gamelan* orchestra they look for likely contenders. They do this while performing a provocative and almost feminine kind of dance, in which they shimmy with their hips and make their eyes roll and glint. When a second sees a likely-looking contender, he prods him out with his stick. Meanwhile, the other second points to his chosen champion. The two men who have been selected now consider, with advice from the spectators, whether they will accept the other as an opponent. The *pekembar* themselves also check to see that the two fighters are of roughly equal strength. If an opponent is accepted, the seconds strike each other's shields. The contestants are now equipped with weapons and prepared for the fight.

The shield is woven from bamboo and rattan and covered with buffalo-hide. The stick is also made of rattan. Thin string is wound round each end, so that one end can be held firmly in the hand, while the other can cause no stab-wounds with its sharp point. Injuries are also prevented by the headgear and the padded material wound round the kidneys. But to make sure the protective padding really does its job, a lucky-charm amulet is often woven into it, or some reassuring motto printed on it.

At last the referee gives the signal for the fight to begin. With considerable elegance the two contenders skip and dance towards each other. This is their way of getting into a fighting mood and shaking off their nervousness. Each man wants to let his opponent see he is not impressed by him. The first blows are usually fended off. Then they start hitting their mark. The moment the human fighting-cocks get wedged close together, the referee separates them. The first trickles of blood appear on their naked torsos.

Whichever of the two is so inclined, will endeavour to save face by transforming the winces of pain into a little capering dance. Sometimes his second will playfully join in with prancing steps. For some moments all the tension and danger seem to have gone out of the fight, and the universe is in harmony. Then comes the next round. Now that the gloves are off, so to speak, the fight takes a more violent turn. Three to five rounds is the usual duration. The chief and assistant referees keep a score of the hits. Blows to the head rate the highest. The man who receives three head-blows suffers not only pain but a premature defeat. If the fight lasts for the agreed number of rounds, the result is decided by the referees on the basis of the number of blows, the loss of a stick, and the number of times the contestants are thrown to the ground.

If both fighters are equally strong, it is possible to declare the match a draw. But more often the fight is stopped before the end, because one of the contestants is bleeding from a gaping wound. A medical auxiliary looks after him. When the result is announced, a prize is awarded to the victor either by a dancer or by one of the seconds, after a little dance interlude. In Puyung, the prize is usually a sarong. Then other fights follow.

When darkness falls over the arena, at about six o'clock, the best fighters of the day make a final appearance. The atmosphere among the spectators reaches a peak of excitement.

Today, this rough, tough contact sport is, as it appears to be, played by amateurs for fun; but in the past it was intended to get warriors battle-fit. It was also customary to hold *perisean* contests after the harvest, on the rice-field during the dry season, because they believed that the sacrifice of blood would provoke the heavens into dropping their much-needed rains.

In many villages it is still said today that no man who refuses to take part in a stick-fight has any chance of taking a bride home with him.

TRAVEL PREPARATIONS

Climate

Being close to the equator, Bali and Lombok enjoy a warm climate all year round. Daytime temperatures vary little from season to season, remaining in the range of 80°-85°F (27°-30°C) near the coast. At nights there is only a slight drop in temperature. Even in the "coldest" month, July, it only goes down to 60°-70°F (16°- 21°C). But at higher altitudes it can feel distinctly cool.

There are two seasons: the rainy season, which runs from November to April, and the dry season for the rest of the year. In the mountain regions of Bali it can rain on 160 to 210 days of the year, with a total precipitation of 118 inches (3,000 mm). In the south it rains on 100 to 140 days, giving 79 inches (2,000 mm), while in the dryer north there are only 50 to 80 rainy days a year, with a precipitation of less than 40 inches (1,000 mm). Thus the rainfall is anything from 3 times to 5 times heavier than in Europe.

But even in the rainy season the rain tends to fall in short, heavy showers, rather than continuously over a longer period of time. Nevertheless, rainfall of 24 inches (600 mm) in a single day is not uncommon. Even in the dry season there can sometimes be short, heavy showers, usually in the late afternoon. Very occasionally there are tornadoes. Lombok is, on the whole, rather warmer and dryer than Bali.

When to Go

As it is particularly hot and humid in the rainy season, the best time to visit Bali is in the dry season, from May to October – especially if you plan to go walking in the mountains. Even if you are not comfortable in the heat, you need not worry: by the sea there is a gentle but steady breeze which gets stronger towards evening, and takes the edge off the heat.

Clothing

If you plan to stay on the coast, all you need are light, airy summer clothes. If you have to meet officials, or when you are visiting temples, it is important to wear a long-sleeved shirt or blouse and long trousers. If you are heading for the mountains, you will need strong footwear, warm clothing and ventilated raingear. If you plan to go motorcycling, you should bring your own helmet and something to protect your kidneys; the helmets issued by the rental companies may meet legal requirements but are pretty useless. Motorcyclists and their passengers should wear strong jeans, unless you want to get your calves burnt by the hot exhaust pipe.

On the subject of light clothing, unless you are a very large size, there is no need to bring a lot with you. There is no shortage of such things in Bali. Quite the reverse: there is a wider range of fashionable leisure clothes for sale at lower prices than back home.

Entering the Country

To enter Indonesia, citizens of the following 30 countries only require a passport valid for 6 months, with one unstamped page and a return or onward air ticket: Australia, Austria, Belgium, Brunei, Canada, Denmark, Finland, France, Germany, Great Britain, Greece, Iceland, Ireland, Italy, Japan, Liechtenstein, Luxemburg, Malaysia, Malta, Netherlands, New Zealand, Norway, Philippines, Sweden, Switzerland, Singapore, South Korea, Spain, Thailand and the U.S.A.

On arrival, you are given a tourist visa which entitles you to stay for 60 days and no more. The visa can only be extended in case of illness or if you are involved in legal proceedings. In all other cases you must leave the country and re-enter. This is usually achieved by flying to Singapore or Thailand. Citizens of countries not listed above must apply for a visa at the Indonesian embassy or consulate in their own country.

Currency

The Indonesian unit of currency is the rupiah, which circulates in the following denominations: bills of 100, 500, 1,000, 5,000, 10,000, 20,000 and 50,000 rupiahs; coins of 25, 50, 100, 500 and 1000 rupiahs. Its value is linked to the US$ and fluctuates in relation to other currencies in step with the dollar. Prices in hotels and tourist centers are often quoted in US$, though paid in rupiahs.

It is forbidden to bring more than Rps 50,000 in or out of the country. However, there is no limit to the amount of foreign currency you can bring in. The safest way to carry money is in travelers' checks denominated in U.S. dollars, Australian dollars, pounds sterling or Deutschmarks. These can be exchanged for rupiahs at banks and officially approved money-changers.

Eurocheques are pretty useless in these parts. Outside the tourist centers and large towns, only cash is accepted and there is usually no way of changing money. Anyway, you get the best exchange rates in the tourist centers, although the rates in hotels are the least good. Money-changers give the quickest service and offer rates comparable with the banks.

Banks are open on Mon to Thu from 8 am until 2 pm and closed on Sat and Sun, while exchange offices are often open in the afternoon. Recently, credit cards have started to be accepted in most hotels, larger souvenir shops, the better restaurants and by art dealers. Sometimes this is the only way of getting hold of some cash in a hurry.

When changing money, make sure you always get a selection of bills in smaller denominations, because *bemo-* and taxi-drivers and *warungs* are not usually able to give you change for a 10,000 rupiah note. Sometimes you may encounter problems out in the countryside if you try to pay with worn-out banknotes.

Health Precautions

Long before leaving for Bali, you should consult a doctor, or better still an institute of tropical medicine or a quarantine authority. They will be able to tell you what precautions are necessary. You should particularly ask about inoculations against typhus, cholera and hepatitis A and B, as well as anti-malaria tablets. You should definitely be injected against tetanus and polio. As regards malaria, enquire about any new, resistant bacilli that have been discovered. Since all anti-malaria medications have side effects, you should pay particular attention to minimizing the risk of getting bitten by a mosquito. This is done by always sleeping under a mosquito-net, wearing a garment that covers most of your body, and treating any uncovered parts such as wrists and ankles with mosquito repellant. Oil of cloves seems to be pretty effective.

You should always wear shoes, or at least sandals, as a protection against hookworms and other parasites that live in the ground.

Get your doctor to put together a little traveling pharmacy for you. It should include an antiseptic for all sorts of small wounds, since even a scratched mosquito bite can become seriously inflamed in the tropics. You should also take with you some medication for diarrhoea and for various degrees of infection.

The best safeguard is simply to exercise common sense in extreme heat or when eating and drinking. Give your body time to get acclimatized to the new conditions; find some shade in the midday heat; take plenty of fluids in the form of non-alcoholic drinks; to start with, eat in moderation, and at all times only eat things that have been well-cooked; peel your own fruit; avoid any drinks containing ice cubes of dubious origin. (There is state-produced ice which is perfectly usable.) Avoid restaurants and accommodation whose standards of hygiene do not impress you. Water that you use to clean your teeth should always be sterilized first with a product like Micropur, to get rid of any bacteria.

It is advisable to take out travel health insurance which covers the cost of getting you home in an emergency. It is true that both in Lombok and Bali there are hospitals in the capitals, but they are not up to the standard that westerners have come to expect.

Therefore in emergencies you should – if possible – get yourself to Singapore. This is where you will find the nearest first-class hospitals in the region, with western-trained specialists, such as at the **American Hospital**, tel. 3451516. Also recommended is the **Pertamina Hospital** in Jakarta, Jl. Kyai Maja, Kebayoran Baru, tel. 021/707214. Hospital costs have to be paid in cash, but these are much lower than in the west, and will be reimbursed by a private travel insurance company.

TRAVELING TO AND WITHIN BALI AND LOMBOK

Arrival

Most travelers arrive in Bali by air. Many airlines land at Denpasar's Ngurah Rai airport, which is south of the capital and of Kuta. These include Air France, Alitalia, American Airlines, British Airways, Cathay Pacific, Delta Airlines, Garuda, Gulf Air, Iberia, KLM, Lauda Air, Lufthansa, Quantas, SAS, Singapore Airlines, Swiss Air, Thai Airways and TWA.

If you are flying with the Indonesian airline, Garuda, you should enquire about current reduced fare offers on internal flights (e.g. to Mataram on Lombok). Many airlines offer reduced-price packages which include stopovers in Singapore. Independent travelers who are visit-ing Java before going on to Bali, can fly to Bali in a small plane operated by Merpati Airlines. Or you can take the ferry from Ketapang to Gilimanuk (q.v.). The overland buses which connect all the major towns in Java with Bali also use this ferry to cross to the island.

Traveling from Bali to Lombok

Merpati, a subsidiary of Garuda, operates up to seven flights a day both ways, between Denpasar and the capital of Lombok, Mataram. The half-hour flight costs about Rps. 60,000.

In addition, it is possible to go there by ferry from Padangbai (q.v.) or with the faster hydrofoil from Benoa Port to Labuhan Lembar. In Kuta (q.v.) you can book bus trips to Senggigi or to the boat-pier where you leave for the three islands to the northwest of Lombok.

Traveling around Bali

A very practical and inexpensive way of getting around the island is by minibus or *bemo*. These public transport vehicles connect almost all the villages with each other. There are also bus routes along the main highways. In the tourist centers and in the capital there are plenty of taxis on the streets.These are also affordable, but it is as well to negotiate the fare in advance.

In all the tourist centers you can rent small jeeps and motorcycles. You have to show an international driver's license. If you do not possess a license to ride a motorcycle, you can obtain one valid for six weeks on Bali only. They are issued in Denpasar in the space of a morning. There is a brief oral examination. It is basically impossible to fail, because there are eager touts who look after the necessary. Every motorbike hire company knows what is required.

Every year there are a number of serious accidents in Bali, usually involving inexperienced motorcyclists. So, if you have to use a motorcycle, exercise extreme caution. And remember that traffic drives on the left.

Traveling on Lombok

In addition to the means of transportation mentioned above, Lombok also offers a large number of small horse-drawn carriages called *dokars*. A trip in one of these does not cost much and is a unique experience. Sometimes you have to get out when you reach a small hill, because the load is too much for the delicate little horses.

Leaving the Islands

On departure you have to present the tourist visa which you were issued when you arrived. Remember to confirm your return flight in good time, and at the same time ask what the current level of airport tax is, as you will have to pay this when you leave.

PRACTICAL TIPS

Accommodation

In Bali and Lombok you will find accommodation in all price categories, and in the tourist centers there is abundant choice. Away from the main centers, there is generally only simple accommodation or rooms in private houses which the village headman (*kepala desa*) will organize for you in return for a small fee. The simple lodgings are called *losmens,* and are often run as family businesses. Many are idyllically located amidst tropical vegetation. Washing facilities are restricted to a *mandi,* which is what the locals use: this is a basin of water with a ladle to scoop it out and splash it over yourself. You should never wash directly in the basin, still less step into it. That way it is kept clean and hygienic. The toilets are usually the standing or squatting kind, sometimes with no paper, and with only a small water-tap.

You may not always find an intact mosquito-net, which is why you should always carry your own with you. You should also bring your own light bulb of a decent wattage, since you are quite likely to find nothing stronger than a 15-watt bulb in the room.

Although the Balinese are generally very careful about cleanliness, you nevertheless come across cockroaches and other insects from time to time. Also, most houses have their complement of geckos, which do a useful job by eating insects but do leave little messages around, so it is advisable to keep delicate clothing in covered shelves or in protective bags.

Alcohol

Alcoholic drinks are obtainable in all tourist centers. But imported brands are very expensive in comparison with the west. On Lombok it is difficult to buy alcoholic drinks during the fasting month of Ramadan, and in remote districts at any time.

Bookshops

In the capitals and the tourist centers there are a number of bookshops where you can usually find an extensive range of new titles and standard works on Bali and Lombok. Very often these bookshops also do a lively second-hand trade, and you can pick up a useful range of holiday reading in English, German, Japanese, Dutch, French, and sometimes, Spanish and Italian.

Business Hours

In the tourist centers the shops often remain open right through from 9 am to 9 pm or even 10 pm. However, if trade is a bit slow they may decide on a long lunch break, in which case you will not find them open again until 4 pm. Official institutions may say they are open until 3 pm or even 5 pm, but to be on the safe side you should always visit them in the morning. Don't expect to find the required official at his desk on a Friday.

Crime and Drugs

Crimes of violence are very rare on the islands compared to any western country. Nevertheless, the real or imagined wealth of tourists does lead to crime against property. Therefore, particularly in the tourist strongholds, you must always keep a close eye on your valuables, especially in rooms which cannot easily be watched or locked.

Muggings are rare, so you can have adequate security by wearing a money belt or a bag across your chest. From time to time you will be warned of thieves, who may get out of a *bemo*, taking your camera case or other items of luggage with them. They often do this with the help of a partner who is there to distract you.

On Lombok, *bemo*-drivers sometimes try to increase the fare retrospectively, lending emphasis to their proposal by pointing out that you have no idea where you are. In this situation it is helpful to mention the police, in order to get back on the "right road."

Keep well away from any kind of illegal drugs, because the penalties, even for foreigners, are extremely severe.

Customs Regulations

It is forbidden to import into Indonesia weapons, drugs, any media with pornographic content, any material in the Indonesian language that has been printed in China or any other foreign country, and Chinese medicinal products. You should leave your video cassettes at home, as these will be subjected to a wearisome examination for pornographic content.

You are allowed to bring in up to 2 liters of alcoholic drink, plus 200 cigarettes, 50 cigars or 100 grams of tobacco. In order to protect the islands' endangered animal species, these may not be exported. This also means you may not take out a sea turtle shell or any product made from this material. National antiquities are also protected by law, and so you may not export any genuine antique articles.

Eating and Drinking

Indonesian food is in general easily digestible, though certain dishes are heavily spiced. You very quickly get used to the hot, spicy flavors and later on, back home, you will find the food seems very bland in comparison. The spices also serve the purpose of preventing food from going bad in the heat.

In order that your eating enjoyment is not followed by remorse, you should avoid certain dishes, especially at the beginning of your holiday. These include: salads, fruit that is unwashed or not washed in sterilized water, freshly squeezed fruit juice, home-made ice cream, meat that has gone cold, raw seafood, cold sauces etc. Where drinking is concerned, you should always go for industrially bottled soft drinks and other such drinks. Drinks with fresh fruit added may taste delicious but should only be drunk in moderation.

Electricity

In the outlying districts of Bali and all over Lombok the mains power is 110 volt or 50 Hz. In the towns and tourist centers they have now switched over to 220 volt/50Hz.

Festivals and Holidays

Since the calendar of local festivals is not only filled with events, but their dates are different every year, you should, at the beginning of your stay, go to the tourist office in Denpasar or Mataram and obtain a list of festivals. In the better hotels you can also get a list of upcoming events. If you have good contacts among the local hotel or restaurant staff, it is possible to find out about purely local festivals, which are not announced officially and which are well worth visiting.

As in the west, Sunday is the day of

rest. But on Friday, which is the Moslems' principal day of prayer, and also on Saturday, different business hours apply. National holidays, such as Independence Day on August 17, are on fixed days on the Western calendar.

The cycle of festivals in Bali is determined both by constant and variable factors: the calendar and the vicissitudes of life. To make things easier, there is not just one calendar, but at least four. For the whole of Indonesia two calendars apply: the Gregorian or western calendar, which governs national holidays as well as the weekly rest-day for offices (Sunday), and the Islamic lunar calendar, which determines the Moslem festivals, the fast of Ramadan and the date of the pilgrimage to Mecca. These dates vary from year to year in the Gregorian calendar.

In Bali two further calendars are added to these: the South Indian Saka calendar and the pre-Islamic Javanese Wuku calendar. The Saka calendar is a lunar calendar with 12 months, each having 29 or 30 days. A month runs from new moon to new moon. Every three or four years, unlike the Moslem lunar calendar, an extra month is put in, to bring it approximately back into step with the Gregorian calendar and also with the sequence of seasons in the northern hemisphere (since it was originally intended for use in India). Thus it happens that in this calendar the New Year festival of *Nyepi* almost always falls in a period shortly after or before March 20. Many of the temple festivals which are held regularly, like the *Odalan*, are fixed in accordance with the Saka calendar, in mid-month at the time of the full moon. However, in temples of the underworld, the *Odalan* festival is usually held at the time of the new moon. (There are also *Odalan* festivals which follow the Wuku calendar.)

The much more complicated Wuku calendar is referred to when a favorable date is sought for island-wide temple fes-

tivals and all sorts of other celebrations and ceremonies, including those which govern the course of one's life, like birth, marriage and death. This calendar covers a period of 210 days. Each period is independent of the seasons and of the phases of the moon, and is repeated continuously without alteration. It comprises a series of concurrently running ten-day weeks, nine-day weeks etc. right down to 210 "one-day weeks." The most important are the 30 seven-day weeks, the 42 five-day weeks and the 70 three-day weeks. From the latter, the market days are determined – one every three days.

The occasions when the last day of a seven-day week coincides with the last day of a five-day week, are considered to be especially propitious for festivals. These are the so-called *Tumpek* days. Since the average Balinese can easily get lost in all this, when it come to fixing the date of a family festival he will turn to a priest, to whom the fixing of the dates of major festivals is also entrusted.

Language

In the tourist centers one can get by perfectly well with English. However, if you are making expeditions into the hinterland, it is recommended that you learn a few important phrases of Bahasia Indonesia (See "Language Guide," p.250).

Pharmacies

Pharmacies selling western medical preparations can be found in all the tourist centers (and even in the shopping arcades of the luxury hotels) as well as in the big towns. It is always useful to have with you the packaging of any medication you take regularly, so that you can identify an equivalent preparation that may be sold here under a different name.

Photography

Taking photographs of bridges and military installations is strictly forbidden. Even when taking a souvenir photo at the airport, you must be careful that there are no military aircraft to be seen. Apart from this, you should show a great deal of discretion when photographing temples or Balinese people. Children and men are generally quite happy to be snapped; but with older people and women you should always ask their permission first.

In the tourist centers you can buy perfectly good film at prices only a little higher than you would pay at home. And you can have adequate prints made very quickly.

Post, Telephone and Fax

In Bali there are four post offices, *Kantor Pos*, which are suitable addresses to give as *poste restante* (mail to be collected), in Kuta, Denpasar, Ubud and Singaraja. The post office in Denpasar is in the Renon district and is difficult to get to by public transport. In Lombok, the post office at Mataram is the only *poste restante* address. On the envelope your surname must always be underlined or written in capitals. Important letters should always be sent by registered mail.

Air-mail letters take at least a week to reach Europe or the U.S.A. Coming the other way they take even longer, because of local delivery. Parcels are accepted up to a weight of 44 lbs (20 kg).

The state telephone company is called **Telkom**. Through their offices in the tourist centers you get astonishingly clear connections overseas, after waiting about half an hour. To make a call to Bali from abroad, first dial the international code for Indonesia, 0062, then 361 for Bali, for Singaraja 362, Amlapura 363, Negara 365, Klungkung and Bangli 366, Lombok 364. Within Indonesia the code starts with a zero, for example: code of Bali is 0361.

Most Telkom offices are also equipped with fax machines. To send one page to Europe costs about US$ 6. You can also have faxes sent to you for which there is only a small charge.

Time Zones

Bali belongs to the mean time-zone of Indonesia and is 8 hours ahead of GMT and 7 hours ahead of Central European Time. However, Lombok is in the central time-zone of Indonesia and is one hour ahead of Bali. This information does not take account of the introduction of Daylight Savings (Summer) Time in many countries.

Weights and Measures

The metric system is used on Bali and Lombok.

ADDRESSES
Consulates on Bali

Australia: Jl. Raya Sanur 146, P.O.Box 243, Denpasar, tel. 235092/3, fax 231990. (Also for NZ and Canada).

Denmark and Norway: Jl. Serma Gede 5, Sanglah, Denpasar, tel. 235098.

Finland and Sweden: Jl. Segara Ayu, Sanur, tel. 280228/288407.

France: Jl. Sekar Waru 3, Blanjiong, Sanur Kauh, tel. 287152/288090.

Germany: Jl. Pantai Karang 17, Sanur, tel. 288535, fax 288826.

Italy: Jalan Padanggalak, Sanur, tel. 288372/288777.

Japan: Jl. Mohammad Yamin 9, Renon, Denpasar, tel. 234808, fax 231308.

Netherlands: Jalan Imam Bonjol 599, Denpasar, tel. 751094/751497, fax 752777.

Switzerland: Jl. Pura Bagus Taruna, Legian, tel. 751735, fax 754457.

U.S.A.: Jl. Segara Ayu 5, Sanur, tel. 280228/288478, fax 287760.

(At present there is no British Consulate in Bali, but British citizens' affairs are handled by the Australian Consulate).

Tourist Offices outside Indonesia

Australia: Garuda Indonesia office, 4 Bligh St., P.O. Box 3836, Sydney 2000.

Germany: Wiesenhüttenstr. 17, 60329 Frankfurt, tel. 069-233677/8.

Japan: Asia Transport Co., 2nd Floor, Sankaido Building, 1-9-13 Akasaka, Minato-Ku, Tokio, tel. 5853588 /5821331.

Singapore: 15-07 Ocean Building, 10 Collyer Quay, Singapore, tel. 5342837/ 534 1795.

U.S.A.: 3457 Wilshire Blvd., Los Angeles, CA 90010, tel. 0231-387-2078.

(At the time of going to press, Indonesia has no official tourist office in London, but a number of tour operators organize packages to Bali, as does the state airline, Garuda).

STATISTICS AND OTHER USEFUL INFORMATION

Population and Government

Indonesia has around 195 million inhabitants, which makes it the fifth most populous nation in the world. More than 85 percent of Indonesians follow the Islamic faith. As well as Islam, other monotheistic religions are recognized as state religions. These include Christianity and the Balinese form of Hinduism.

The official language of the country is Bahasa Indonesia, which has evolved from the language of commerce spoken by the Malay traders all over Southeast Asia. However, only about 12 per cent of the population speak Bahasa Indonesia as their mother tongue. The rest are obliged to learn it from their first year at school.

The population of Bali is about 3 million, with a density of 200 inhabitants per square mile (540 per sq. km). This means that of all the thousands of islands in the archipelago, it has the second-highest population-density, exceeded only by Java. Lombok is in third place.

About 10 per cent of Bali's population live in the provincial capital of Denpasar, in the more populous south. In the larger towns, traders from Arab countries, India and China have established communities. The Chinese minority, in particular, have in the past been the victims of frequent bloody pogroms.

You come across European business-people, artists and drop-outs in the tourist centers. On the coast, Bugi people from Sulawesi have settled in isolated fishing-villages since the 16th century. In contrast to the rest of Indonesia, the overwhelming majority of Balinese are Hindu.

Lombok has 2.5 million inhabitants and so is almost as densely populated as Bali. The great majority of the population belongs to the Sasak race. In the west of the island there is a large Balinese minority, representing about 5 percent of the island's population. In Lombok, too, there are Arab, Indian and Chinese communities in the towns, and Buginese minorities on the coast. The majority of the population is Moslem.

The Republic of Indonesia was formerly a leading member of the group of non-aligned nations, and today the military stills plays a decisive role in government. The republic is made up of 24 provinces, two special autonomous districts and the capital district, around Jakarta.

The province of Bali is divided into eight *Kabupaten* (regencies) plus the capital district of Denpasar. The *Kabupaten* correspond approximately to the historic principalities or rajadoms which grew up in the pre-colonial era, namely: Badung, Bangli, Buleleng, Gianyar, Jembrana, Karangasem, Klungkung and Tabanan.

Below the level of regencies are administrative units called *Kecamatan* (which might be translated as counties or boroughs). Below these again are the *Desa,* either villages or districts in towns. Finally, the villages and districts are divided into the smallest administrative units of all, the *Banjar.*

Lombok is part of the province of Nusa Tenggara Barat. It is divided into three *Kabupaten:* Lombok Barat (west), Lombok Tengah (central) and Lombok Timur (east), plus the capital, Mataram.

LANGUAGE GUIDE

Good morning . . . . . . *selamat pagi*
Good afternoon . . . . . *selamat siang*
Good evening . . . . . . *selamat sore*
See you later . . . *sampai bertemu lagi*
What's your name?(m) *apa nama tuan?*
What's your name? (fem.) :

. . . . *apa nama nyonya*?
My name is . . . . . . *nama saya...*
I am staying at . . . . *saya tinggal di..*
Where is the...? . . . . . *(di) mana...*?
How far is the...?

. . . . *berapa jauhnya?*
How do I get to...?

. . . . *bagaimana saya ke...?*
How much is that? . . . *berapa harga?*
Can I see the menu, please?

. . . . . *saya mau lihat daftar makana.*
I'd like something to drink

. . . . *saya mau mimim*
The bill, please! . . . *saya mau bayar.*
I'm staying here...days

. . . . *saya tinggal disini...hari*
What is that? . . . . . *apa ini / apa itu?*
What time is it? . . . . . *jam berapa?*
I . . . . *saya*
you . . . . *kamu*
we . . . . *kita*
we (excluding person addressed)

. . . . *kami*
O.K . . . . *baik*
yes . . . . *ya*
no . . . . *tidak*
big . . . . *besar*
small . . . . *kecil*
now . . . . *sekarang*
today . . . . *hari ini*
afternoon . . . . *siang*
night . . . . *malam*
week . . . . *minggu*
month . . . . *bulan*
year . . . . *tahun*
clean . . . . *bersih*
dirty . . . . *kotor*
hot . . . . *panas*
cold . . . . *dingin*
please . . . . *tolong*
thank you . . . . *terima kasih*

less . . . . *kurang*
more . . . . *lebih banyak*
come . . . . *datang*
go . . . . *pergi*
price . . . . *harga*
shop . . . . *toko*
medicine . . . . *obat*
market . . . . *pasar*
room . . . . *kamar*
vegetables . . . . *sayuran*
water . . . . *air*
tea . . . . *teh*
milk . . . . *susu*
sugar . . . . *gula*
salt . . . . *garam*
butter . . . . *mentega*
food . . . . *makanan*
breakfast . . . . *makanan pagi*
1 . . . . *satu*
2 . . . . *dua*
3 . . . . *tiga*
4 . . . . *empat*
5 . . . . *lima*
6 . . . . *enam*
7 . . . . *tujuh*
8 . . . . *delapan*
9 . . . . *sembilan*
10 . . . . *sepuluh*
11 . . . . *sebelas*
12 . . . . *duabelas*
20 . . . . *duapuluh*
30 . . . . *tigapuluh*
40 . . . . *empatpuluh*
50 . . . . *limapuluh*
60 . . . . *enampuluh*
70 . . . . *tujuhpuluh*
80 . . . . *delapanpuluh*
90 . . . . *sembilanpuluh*
100 . . . . *seratus*
1,000 . . . . *seribu*
10,000 . . . . *sepuluhribu*

Pronunciation

ai . . . . like "eye"
au . . . . like "ow" in "cow"
c . . . . like "ch" in "chin"
j . . . . as in English "jet"etc.
h . . . . at end of word is a soft,
. . . . hissing sound.

AUTHORS

Bernd F. Gruschwitz, editor and one of the principal authors of *Nelles Bali/Lombok Guide*, is a historian and student of English literature based in Bremen, Germany. His earliest travels took him round Europe, the Mediterranean and North America, but some years ago he discovered his love for southern and southeast Asia. In Bali and Lombok he has explored the remotest corners on foot and by motorcycle, documented proof exists in the form of numerous photographs taken for this book. He wrote the chapters on "The History and Culture of Bali," "The History and Culture of Lombok," "Lombok – Austere Beauty," and the features on "Music and Dance of Lombok," "Art and Artisan Work," "Cock-fighting" and "Stick-fighting on Lombok."

Dorothee Krause is studying textiles and textile production, a field which awakened her interest particularly in Indian and Indonesian techniques of textile weaving and dyeing. This took her to Tenganan, Mataram, Cakranegara and Sukarara to find out more. As a dancer of ballet and jazz, she was immediately fascinated by the unfamilar Balinese dances; she became equally enchanted by the *gamelan* music and has since tried to play it herself. She wrote the features: "Balinese Cuisine," "Balinese Dances," "Balinese Gamelan Music," "Wayang Kulit," "Ikat and Double-Ikat."

Barbara Müller studied romance languages and is a freelance journalist, writing chiefly on social and religious topics. In the course of her work she has made several visits to Africa, Latin-America and Asia, including Bali. For this book she wrote the feature "Encounter with a Batik Artist."

Berthold Schwarz, editor-in-chief, studied geography and ethnology. Since 1975 he has been travelling professionally and privately in Africa, Asia and the Far East, and has regularly led, since 1984, treks and study-trips through these areas. Bali is one of his favorite destinations. The fact that he is equally at home in other countries is proven by his *Nelles Guide Morocco*. For this book he wrote the chapters "Southern Bali," "Central Bali," "Western Bali," "Northern Bali" and "Eastern Bali."

PHOTOGRAPHERS

Fischer, Peter 66
Gruschwitz, Bernd F. 16, 17, 18, 19, 30, 33, 34, 41, 42, 43, 44, 45, 48, 49, 68, 87, 88, 89, 90, 95, 97, 104, 105, 112, 115, 122/123, 131, 132, 134, 135, 137, 142, 147, 151, 154, 155, 156, 160/161, 162/163, 166, 167, 168, 170, 172, 174/175, 176, 181, 186, 188, 191, 192, 195, 196, 197, 199, 208, 209, 213, 216, 218, 222, 224, 235, 239
Hellige, Wolfgang 38, 46, 82, 94, 204/205, 221, 229, cover
Höbel, Robert 206/207
Kohl, Günther 96, 98, 102, 120
Koninklijk Instituut voor de Tropen, Amsterdam 22, 26, 28L, 28R
Koninklijk Instituut voor Taal-, Land-en Volkenkunde, Leiden 24, 25, 27
Krause, Dorothee 10/11, 32, 36, 37, 76, 86, 102, 140/141, 150, 164, 173, 182,190, 193, 198, 201, 230, 231
Maeritz, Kay 52/53
Müller, Barbara 232R, 233
Pansegrau, Erhard 14, 51, 56, 61, 73, 107, 116, 117, 124, 212
Rex, Peter 12/13, 20, 35, 39, 54/55, 80/81, 101, 110/111, 130, 153, 169, 211, 215, 220, 227, 237
Schaefer, Albrecht G. 91, 103, 148, 157, 236
Scheibner, Johann 99, 146
Schmerheim, Sigrid 185, 225
Schwarz, Berthold 8/9
Schwarz, Heiner 183
Steinhardt, Jochen 67, 71, 118, 232L
Tetzner, Marina 60

Explore the World

Explore the World

AVAILABLE TITLES

Australia
Bali / Lombok
Berlin and Potsdam
Brittany
California
  Las Vegas, Reno,
  Baja California
Cambodia / Laos
Canada
  Ontario, Québec,
  Atlantic Provinces
Caribbean
  The Greater Antilles,
  Bermuda, Bahamas
Caribbean
  The Lesser Antilles
China
Corsica
Crete
Cyprus
Egypt
Florida
Greece - *The Mainland*
Hawaii
Hungary
India
  Northern, Northeastern
  and Central India

India - *Southern India*
Indonesia
  Sumatra, Java, Bali,
  Lombok, Sulawesi
Ireland
Israel - *with Excursions*
  to Jordan
Kenya
London, England and Wales
Malaysia
Mexico
Morocco
Moscow / St Petersburg
Munich
  Excursions to Castels,
  Lakes & Mountains
Nepal
New York - *City and State*
New Zealand
Paris
Philippines
Portugal
Prague / Czech Republic
Provence
Rome
South Africa
Spain - *Pyrenees, Atlantic*
  Coast, Central Spain

Spain
  Mediterranean Coast,
  Southern Spain,
  Balearic Islands
Sri Lanka
Thailand
Turkey
Tuscany
U.S.A.
  The East, Midwest and
  South
U.S.A.
  The West, Rockies and
  Texas
Vietnam

IN PREPARATION

Scotland

Nelles Guides – authorative, informed and informative.
Always up-to-date, extensivley illustrated, and with first-rate relief maps.
256 pages, appr. 150 color photos, appr. 25 maps